Questers...

Dare to Change Your Job

...and
your life

Carole Kanchier

KEY PORTER·BOOKS

Canadian Cataloguing in Publication Data
Kanchier, Carole Joyce
  Questers: dare to change your job and your life

ISBN 1-55013-134-6

1. Career changes.   2. Executives—Interviews.
I. Title.

HF5384.K36   1988   658.4′09   C88-094281-9

Key Porter Books Limited
70 The Esplanade
Toronto, Ontario
Canada M5E 1R2

Cover Design: David Montle

Printed and Bound in Canada

88 89 90 91 92 6 5 4 3 2 1

To my Father

*Whose love, support and encouragement
helped me to be myself.*

Contents

Acknowledgements

I would like to express my deepest appreciation to the following individuals:

The Questers, who willingly gave their time and candidly shared their experiences. Although their names and, in a few cases some particulars, have been disguised to maintain their confidentiality, their stories have a factual basis.

The numerous students, clients and research participants who taught me a great deal about adult and career development and offered valuable feedback with respect to the questionnaires.

Kathy Teillet, whose creative editorial assistance helped put the book in its final form.

My friends and colleagues who took the time to read the entire manuscript and offered constructive suggestions and needed encouragement: Drs. Marnie Finstad, David Tiedeman, Norman Feingold and Kathleen Samphire, Sonja Eisler, Jean Yarwood and Sandra Mallett. Many other colleagues also shared information: Drs. Wally Unruh, Lorne Seaman and Roman Odwazny, and Elsie Wingeno and Murray Axsmith Western Ltd.

Vicki Ross, who cheerfully and competently typed various revisions of the manuscript.

Preface: Planning for change

This book is for anyone who has ever made a career change or anyone contemplating a career change. A major shift in the direction of your career can create important gains and losses. It forces you to step out of the well-worn groove of your life and confront yourself in very basic ways. It offers you the chance for either an expanded or a diminished sense of self, for growth or stagnation, hope or despair. *QUESTERS* was written so that I could share with you my research and experience on the career quest.

A career really is a quest. When I look back over my life, I think my quest started when I was a teenager. As the physical and emotional tumults of adolescence raged on, I tried to make sense of who I was and what I wanted to do with my life. As the options floated in and out of my consciousness, I realized that what I wanted most was to enjoy every day to the utmost. Since a great part of my day would be devoted to work, I wanted to find a satisfying and rewarding career. I wanted to be involved, to find challenge, variety, autonomy and a sense of meaning and purpose in my work. I wanted to be excited about my work and life. I graduated from university and with high hopes struck out into the work world. There, I made a discovery: When I no longer felt enthusiastic about a job, I felt lifeless and dull. My satisfaction and productivity nose-dived. I left job after job, never lasting more than seven years before my restless spirit landed me in another. Why did I, unlike my colleagues and friends, quit positions that I had initially loved and, according to society's yardstick, had been successful at? Was it because my life lacked balance? No matter how caught up I became in hobbies and relationships, the old ache returned – and the jobs changed.

Then I began my doctoral research. Slowly the answers came. As I hunted through volume after volume of theory and research into adult development, personality, vocational and industrial psychology, I began to find myself. Journeying across the country, I sought out the life stories of 464 male and female executives to see how and why they made career changes. I was beginning to understand my own feelings and motivations better. Since then I have conducted research on many other aspects of adult development and, as teacher, counselor and psychologist, have worked with adults from many different occupations and educational backgrounds. The conclusions have been the same. They are presented in this book.

The life stories will give you a clearer picture of the contemporary career from the viewpoints of adult development, personality, vocational and industrial psychology. You will discover the complex psychological dynamics that come into play when you dislike your work and are considering taking a risk by changing jobs.

The questionnaires will allow you to examine your own personality and life situations. They will help you determine how satisfied you are with your career and life, how well you are coping with both and whether you are a Quester, the new breed of creative risk taker. You'll get a better understanding of the complex psychological factors that influence job changes.

The Questers will teach you all about the process of making risky decisions so you can sidestep the ruts and potholes they encountered when you are ready to make important changes in your life. Most importantly, *QUESTERS* doesn't encourage you to take risks you are not ready for or really don't need.

Trying to stop change is one of the riskiest steps you can take today. Your life – your growth and career development – is fueled by the dynamics of change. The energy you spend fighting to keep the status quo is energy that can be better used understanding the causes and nature of the changes occurring around you. The ability to take planned risks is just what's needed to cope with today's dynamic world. Without risk, there is no vitality or joy.

The ideas you will encounter in *QUESTERS* are not new. Many popular and informative books on career and adult development are only as far as your nearest library or bookstore. But few provide a holistic picture of the contemporary career. Most describe career planning and job searches. They look at how to put together the right resume, dress for success or survive an interview. Little is said about emotions. None describe career growth and development throughout the life cycle. They can't give a thorough understanding of the contemporary career. They don't describe what makes you like or dislike your job or show how these feelings are related to your personality development and the many transition periods in your life. Nor do they tell you about the intricate dynamics of making risky decisions that come into play when you change jobs.

As you journey through the book — and through your life — do not hold yourself back because of concerns about the state of the economy or comments you might read or hear about the availability of jobs in your field. Whether the country is in an economic explosion or recession, whether you are looking in a broad or narrow field, attractive jobs are available. They are created by the mobility of the work force, the deaths, retirements and promotions of current job holders and the growth of companies throughout the economy. Regardless of prevailing economic conditions, good positions are out there. Somewhere, there is a company that can use your talents and experience and will pay well for them. You can find that job or become self-employed more easily than you think. Keep your options open. Focus on the opportunities available. By following the examples of the Questers who thrive on challenge and growth, you will gain the strength to take an active stance in your own career development. You will learn to become the manager of your own life, in charge of your own destiny. You will have the knowledge and the courage to improve the quality of your life and work, and make your innermost dreams come true. You will have the power to achieve a more meaningful, satisfying and productive life in a changing, challenging and exciting world.

1: *Questers and the contemporary career*

THE QUESTERS

Would you know a Quester if you met one? Are you one? Could you become one? Who are Questers, anyway?

The answer comes first through jobs. Questers think of their work differently from most people. Like many of us, Questers will probably spend half a million hours at work during their lives. But, unlike most, at crucial points throughout their careers, they set off on a quest to find the missing links in their lives. Their life stories start out a lot like everyone's — until one day when they begin a personal journey of discovery to find a better life and a better career. You, too can take this journey.

Questers are the new breed. They prevail during uncertain times by keeping their options open. Questers are not perfect. But, in varying degrees, they develop qualities most non-Questers would envy.

Questers tend to be complex, individualistic, flexible, autonomous and open to risk. They may have the best of male and female strengths. They tend to possess a high level of self-confidence and have a sense of purpose and meaning in their lives. Many hunger for more responsibility and more vital work, for tasks worthy of their talents and skills. They question authority and often desire socially responsible work. They tend to have a high need for job involvement and for other vital work rewards: challenge, self-fulfillment, a sense of achievement and opportunity for growth. They take criticism and failure well, viewing defeat as a useful experience from which to grow. Their coping devices can include hard work, prayer, support from friends or spouses — and a sense of humor. When they experience life crises, such as divorce, the death of a relative or close friend, job loss or dissatisfaction, marriage or birth, they undergo intense critical self-analysis. Transition periods, like the age-30 or the mid-life transition, are times for taking another look into the mirror to find if they like what they see.

Questers can be found in a wide range of occupations, from law, management, education, the civil service, accounting and engineering, to construction, medicine and health. They may change their occupations or status several times throughout their careers, sacrificing financial rewards and status for self-expression.

For many Questers, economic security and status come second to intrinsic satisfactions and the desire to have alternatives. They value flexibility and reshape their identities through self-determined career choices. They have a playful, task-centered approach to problem-solving. They measure success by internal standards and value self-respect more than peer respect. Questers tend to be free from conventional restraints. They are independent and innovative spirits with a rich supply of inner resources. They strive to maintain some balance between work, love and leisure. They love a challenge.

Questers tend to have a cheerful, positive outlook. Cheated or disappointed in life? Never! Going to work is usually a joy. Few are ever bored (unless they stay at one job too long). Questers generally arise with a smile, ready to meet the challenges before them.

Surely, Questers must be extraordinary, glamorous people. Not so. They are just ordinary people who faced career problems common to all. But they have learned to do something about their problems — to take control.

You probably know some Questers. They have been around in every age but nobody recognized them. Organizational behaviorist, Douglas Hall, called Questers "protean" persons. Searching for self-fulfillment through self-determined career choices, they tend to continuously reformulate their identities. Motivated by freedom, growth, achievement, job involvement and job satisfaction, they measure success internally. They are unlike the Traditionalists who tend to be passively committed to an organizational career and who value advancement, power, position, salary, job satisfaction, and respect and esteem from others. The mobility of Traditionalists is low and their adaptability tied to organization-related flexibility and survival.

Questers can be distinguished from Traditionalists by their willingness to take control of their careers. Many Traditionalists are concerned about how their careers measure up with the approved timetables for their professions. Failure to stay on track may leave a number of Traditionalists feeling panicky. Conforming rigidly to a single, narrow career track, they feel that they must travel systematically from section head to supervisor, to manager, to executive, from law clerk to junior, then senior partner. Recognition, they hope, comes to those who are faithful, attentive and loyal.

Although security is temporarily achieved, their future options are severely limited. The desire for security has its cost. Traditionalists worry too much about doing the right thing. They choose career paths that conform to what is expected of them.

Self-Seekers tend to be the opposite. Motivated by desire for personal fulfillment, Self-Seekers refuse to work as hard as their parents and contemporaries. They want the perfectly-balanced life with time for love, leisure, family and personal expression. Their happiness formula is giving and getting love. Ambition and leadership are shunned in their search for the comfortable life. They want gratification now and responsibility later. These are the Self-Seekers' rights: to work less and be self-fulfilled while enjoying life's genteel comforts.

Self-Seekers have selected a lifestyle that suits them. They willingly pass up promotions or difficult business challenges that might threaten their comfortable lives. While satisfying work is important, Self-Seekers aren't prepared to sacrifice for their careers or to have their jobs dominate their lives. Their greatest fears are not having enough money or being trapped by the constant pursuit of money. This is their dilemma. To pursue freedom at the sacrifice of a comfortable life is almost unthinkable.

Which are you? Traditionalist, Self-Seeker or Quester?

You can be whichever you desire. Your personality is far from frozen. You can create and recreate it every day. You can become more purposeful, confident, loving, independent and willing to risk. Yes, researchers such as James Cattell, Hans Eysenck, Arnold Buss and Robert Plomin have shown that certain aspects of personality, like sociability and energy levels, are genetically based. But those, too, can be changed.

To achieve the transformations you want, look to the Questers.

Carl is an achiever, a winner, the kind of guy who thought life was a warm sea breeze. He is husky and handsome with clear blue eyes. Carl grew up in an orphanage, but through hard work, won a scholarship to an Ivy League college. He taught for a while, then went on to graduate school for a master's degree in educational psychology. Eventually he found himself in a government department where he rose with relative ease through several offices. But something was wrong.

"On paper I had it all," he explains. "Maybe more than I thought I should have had — a prestigious, secure and well-paying job, a pretty wife and two kids, a house in the suburbs, club memberships and a respectable backhand. But I had a persistent and nagging feeling that life wasn't working. It wasn't adding up. Something was missing. I should have talked to someone about it but the last thing I wanted to show was my vulnerability. Search as I might, I seemed able to deal only with the symptoms. I got myself a raise, cut down on my drinking. I never looked at the big tapestry — what I really wanted — because that was too scary and besides, didn't I already have the American dream?"

Then Carl started thinking of changing jobs. No single event started the process (that's rarely the case). Instead, a series of small jolts forced him out of his velvet-lined rut. First, he learned his wife was having an affair. What shocked him most was that he wasn't angry. He just didn't care. Soon they were on the road to divorce and Carl was looking at life from a new angle. If his marriage had been a mistake, maybe his career was too. In fact, marriage and career had something in common. He had gone into both because people expected him to. But now he began to question whether he should be devoting his energy to living up to other people's expectations? He had traded off self-fulfillment and meaning for security. Not long after that, Carl quit his job. He stepped into the void. He had no idea what he was going to do.

Carl was a little frightened when he took that first step. He needed someone to talk to.

He found that person in the wife of a friend. "The first woman other than my wife I'd ever really confided in." His "overdone macho" had prevented him from revealing his vulnerability to any woman, Carl says now.

Carl began his search for a new job with a painful but necessary transition. He moved from his comfortable home to a bare room in a flat borrowed from a friend. He had a bed, a lightbulb and a stereo system. He missed his house and his children and felt especially guilty because, as an orphan himself, he'd vowed never to leave his kids. For the first time in his adult life, he allowed himself to cry. Yet, despite his loneliness and guilt, Carl also felt what he calls "the exhilaration of trusting myself for the first time."

He now feels he was unhappier before he made the break than during the transition itself. "Earlier, I was using up more energy just justifying a life that wasn't working," he says. "But after the break, I was confronting myself for the first time. The fear and loneliness didn't begin to offset the feeling of integrity I had. The best way to describe it is to say that it was wonderfully terrifying."

Carl survived because he made the right decision. After leaving Washington, he started a management consulting firm in an eastern city. Carl and his ex-wife became friends again. These days, his young son lives with him. His daughter lives with her mother. He thinks that switching jobs made his divorce less bitter than it might have been. "I would have been unhappy with myself and have taken it out on others," he admits.

Evelynne understands what Carl went through. An attractive, petite woman with large, expressive brown eyes and dark brown hair, she looks 15 years younger than her 45 years. But Evelynne's early life in a large eastern city was far from happy. She was the second daughter in a family whose social standing never quite compared to their neighbors'. Her school years were tough. Treated shabbily by many of the "snobs", she determined to excel at everything she did. After high school, Evelynne joined a large clothing manufacturer as a secretary and a model. At 21, she married an athlete and continued working for several years until the birth of their first child. She had a second child and, with two babies at home, found time to take a part-time job writing fashion and food articles for a local newspaper. But as time went on, boredom set in. Evelynne turned 30 as her youngest entered kindergarten. Joining the newspaper full-time now, she soon graduated to a daily column. She had been on the job just over three years when a large department store asked her to manage an exclusive women's clothing department. The timing was perfect. Feeling stale and bored with her column, she eagerly accepted the new position. It proved to be challenging and full of variety. She was given enough freedom to develop a department about which she was justifiably proud.

Evelynne's 38th birthday changed all that. Her marriage began to crumble and her freedom at work was drastically reduced by new management policies. With much of the decision-making taken from her, the quality of her department's merchandise declined. After three years of soul searching, at 41, Evelynne decided to separate from her husband, leave the department store and open her own boutique. Her parental responsibilities were decreasing as both her children entered their late teens and became increasingly independent.

Evelynne's first step was to thoroughly investigate the banks in her city. Then, preparing a well-researched proposal, she presented it to one of the city's more liberal bank managers. Her boutique took off. And Evelynne, then 45, began divorce proceedings as she contemplated marriage to a man she had known for the last five years. She feels her 50th birthday will bring new business projects. She looks to the future with excitement.

Kathy is looking forward to the future now, too. While she already had a BA, what she didn't have was a clear career goal. Pretty, a good athlete, and with many interests and abilities, Kathy worked at a series of jobs until, at 22, she went to a state employment agency for career counseling. That led to a one year managerial training program with a large insurance firm. Kathy enjoyed her training. The job seemed challenging enough. But within four years, her feelings had changed. Bored and suffering from extreme mood swings, she realized that she needed, even craved, challenge. Her father's death forced Kathy to take another look at her life. Again, she went for career counseling. This time she decided to leave her job, return to school, and re-train for another occupation — law. Three years passed from the onset of her dissatisfaction before Kathy decided on a new course of action. Then, at 31, after seven years in insurance, she embarked on an entirely new occupation and life-style. Today, she is enjoying articling and is excited about her new law occupation.

Like Kathy, *Tom* is also making a new start. For 30 years, Tom worked his way up from mechanic to middle manager for a trucking firm. Then, at 52, he bought a hardware store in a town 70 miles from the western city where he had lived his whole life. Was the decision spur-of-the-moment? No. "I planned my getaway. I saved my money and explored the communities within 100 miles of my hometown. I liked fixing things and the hardware business will let me expand the store into a repair shop later, if I feel like it."

Tom is talking like a Quester. He feels like one too. This is how he describes his job now: "It provides me with a sense of accomplishment, the opportunity to use my skills and the feeling that I have some control over my life. I now have more energy left over at the end of the day to do other things. I feel rather peaceful and content."

Like these Questers, you, too, can journey along similar paths to take charge of your life and career. Career, family, relationships and leisure will cross and intersect, clash and complement. The paths you choose will depend on your personality, goals and life situation. To understand how you can control the direction of your life and make well-informed choices, you need to understand your place in the modern work world.

CONTEMPORARY LIFE

CAREER AS MOVEMENT

Career development involves a continuing quest for a better fit between who you are and what you do. Your occupation is based upon skills earned through education or training. But while you may have several occupations or several positions within an occupation during the course of your life, you will have only one career because you have only one life. Your career is made up of a series of occupations or positions — yet it is more. Your career is a lifelong process.

Like an obstacle course in which you climb, stretch and swing to develop your muscles, your career spiral continues on — widening, ever-changing, mutable, dynamic, ascending, expansive — throughout your life. So it may be that one occupation satisfies just one facet of your personality. Each step suggests more challenges ahead. Moving on restlessly, using each job as an opportunity to grow, you plot your next move. What matters is not advancement on your job but advancement of the whole person. To be fulfilled, you need a job that satisfies your whole person.

Howard discovered the difference when he reached 32. Throughout high school, Howard dreamed of becoming an executive with a large manufacturing company. He had worked part-time for the firm during high school and was excited about becoming a manager. It seemed prestigious. At 23, he was well on his way to middle management. During the first six years, Howard enjoyed his work. His first two supervisors were "fine people, supportive and helpful." But the next six years brought different supervisors and changing company policies. Howard's position became meaningless. The work was "monotonous" and the atmosphere "oppressive." The money and the prestige no longer seemed to matter.

Whatever his difficulties at work, Howard's marriage was in good shape and he enjoyed playing in a local band. As he became friendly with two of the band members, both policemen, they told him of the pros and cons of police work. He learned more by participating in several volunteer police programs. Then, just after his 31st birthday, his mother became unexpectedly ill and died. For Howard, this was a turning point. He realized that life is too short. If he was going to change, it would have to be now.

So at 32, he decided to enter the police training program. He had discussed his disillusionment with his wife, and now found her willing to take a part-time job to help pay the bills. Today Howard is a police captain. He has found a career that will let him grow one that will provide meaning, variety and an outlet for his desire to help others.

What happened to Howard? Like many, he simply outgrew his job. His needs, values and priorities all shifted. He was no longer so interested in status. Money meant less to him. The decision to change jobs had not come easily; it was agonizing and took time. Moreover, Howard and his family had to give up many comforts. But today, Howard is confident his decision was right. So is his family. His career grew and so did he.

CAREER AS JOB-PERSON FIT

Imagine the growth and development of your career as a spiral. If you could draw it, it would look like a track moving around a continuous curve toward a central point. That central point is you. You are the center of gravity and balance for your career spiral. If you look closely at the central point in your spiral, you will see a subtle, wonderful portrait of yourself. This portrait captures everything about you. . . . It is a portrait of you as a whole person.

From this whole person, your energy radiates — your temperament, needs, values, interests, skills, aptitudes and goals. Like a dynamo that fuels your spiral, your energy feeds into your career track. Building a successful career relies on evaluating the harmony among your portrait, your job satisfaction and your goals.

Like your career, your personal characteristics and goals will change as you grow. As your portrait changes, so will the results of your evaluation.

Let's take a look at *Al's* career to see how it developed and changed over the years. Al was born and raised in a midwestern town. After high school he entered a computer science program at a nearby university because, in his words, "computers was the field to be in. . .the opportunities for employment and making good money was excellent." At 23, Al graduated with a master's in computer science, got married and accepted a position as a systems analyst with a large firm 1,300 miles from his boyhood home.

At first Al enjoyed his work. He felt it gave him challenge and autonomy. As his star continued to rise, he and his wife had their first child. But, seven years later, as he neared his 30th birthday, Al began to feel as if something, some sense of purpose or meaning, was missing. For three years he searched his soul. Then Al left his job and returned with his family to the midwestern town where he was raised. Using some of his savings to realize a lifelong dream, he bought a farm. Now he and his wife are devoted farmers. They enjoy their lifestyle and their work.

Al changed because his needs and values changed. But why and how? As in Howard's case, the changes Al made were caused by many different events. Al's job had lost its challenge. He felt stifled. The birth of his child and the joy of becoming a parent helped him realize that his family really was more important than his career. Al was also beginning to realize that time was passing. He was anxious to try something new — his long-time dream of becoming a farmer. The feelings and thoughts Al experienced were part of his age-30 transition, a time of questioning and evaluating earlier decisions. He had to choose between either deepening or abandoning his earlier commitments.

Al abandoned them. But what if, at the very moment that Al looked into his life — his portrait — he had suddenly received a fabulous offer: a promotion to senior analyst and a fantastic raise? If Al had accepted, what would have happened to his career spiral? Would it have shot forward and upward? Unfortunately, no. It would have remained precisely where it was, in a state of suspended animation. Why? Because Al's development as a human being, as a whole person, would have come to a grinding halt.

Al's glance into the mirror of his dreams at 30 helped him to change. By moving back to a small town and buying a farm, Al created harmony between his portrait and the energy it was radiating for his career track. When he changed occupations, his career track leapt forward because Al, as a whole person, had advanced.

Marion's career also developed and changed over the years. Marion worked as a microbiology researcher for eight years while her husband went to medical school. Finally, she took time off to raise their two children. She filled her spare hours with volunteer work. Then, at 39, Marion made a decision that would radically change her life. "I wanted something to do — not just a job to earn grocery money — something that would excite me. But like most women, I had the feeling that I didn't have the right to please myself. After a great deal of thought I decided what I really wanted to do was go back to the university and get a master's degree in counseling psychology. So I did.

"At first, I was terrified. What if I failed? How could I compete with young people? Who would organize my family?" Today Marion is a counselor at a women's resource center on the west coast. She spends her time counseling women who are asking the same questions she once did. "I understand exactly where these women are because I was there myself. Like most women, they're asking a very important question: 'What should I do with the rest of my life?' "

Like Al, Marion decided what to do with her life by checking her image in the mirror. In her early 20s, she saw a young woman in a white lab coat. In real life, she worked hard for eight years to fit that image. When Marion looked at her portrait again, in her late 20s, she saw a young mother. She had changed and so had her life situation. After eight years as a lab researcher, she was getting bored. Her husband was now practicing medicine and could support them both. The biological clock was ticking. If Marion wanted children, the time was now. So Marion fused her portrait and her career by taking time out to have and raise two children.

The youngsters kept her busy for many years. But nine years later, when she looked into her portrait again, the image was blurred. Marion was confused. The children were in school and her husband was busily engaged in his career. Marion knew she wanted to go back to work, but could she and should she? All her upbringing told her that a good wife and mother should stay home to cater to her family's needs. Marion didn't want to go back to research. That job no longer suited her. Nor did being a full-time homemaker. Marion's interests, needs and values had changed. She wanted a job that suited her new personality. But what? Marion was perplexed. It took long deliberation, talks with her family and career counseling before Marion concluded that what she really wanted to do was to become a counselor.

Now when Marion looks into her portrait, she sees a career woman. The picture is clear. Marion created harmony between her portrait and herself by moving forward when she became dissatisfied with her life. Making changes wasn't easy. But she did it.

Just as the course of your life is in constant movement, so, too, is your career. For both your career and your life to be truly satisfying, you must keep exploring the state of all your life components — occupation, family, relationships and leisure — and then make the necessary changes to bring your inner and outer worlds into harmony.

Al, Howard, Kathy, Evelynne, Tom, Marion and Carl are all Questers — people who dared to change. Their work gives them a livelihood, pleasure and a sense of purpose.

Today, career development has become a continuing quest to create greater and greater harmony between your occupations and your personal characteristics. Surprisingly, studies show many people would continue to work even if they inherited a vast fortune or won a lottery. And amazing numbers of people nearing retirement fantasize about dying very soon after they stop working. But why is work so important?

WORK THROUGH THE AGES

Most people will spend nearly half their waking hours at work. How ironic that work, once considered by the early Greeks and Romans to be punishment and drudgery, is now so important. Earlier societies considered manual labor tiring, vulgar and degrading.

Leisure, on the other hand, was exalted. Once, man's loftiest occupation was the exercise of the mind and spirit.

Early Christianity slowly changed the meaning of work. As the centuries passed, the now powerful Church came to recognize agriculture, then handicrafts and commerce, as valuable professions. Work acquired "spiritual dignity". But not until the Renaissance was work recognized as a source of joy and creative fulfillment. The Reformation followed on its heels, shaping modern ideas about work and stimulating the development of capitalism.

The Protestant Reformation elevated work to a new status. The search for excellence had begun. Yet another twist was added with the emergence of Calvinism. Work and wealth were okay, as long as they weren't enjoyed. To select a calling and follow it industriously was considered a religious duty. Hard work, worldly achievements, high profits and individualism were already entrenched in the work ethic when developments in scientific technology gave birth to the Industrial Revolution. The world was transformed. Entrepreneurs employing specialized labor and costly equipment needed workers for efficient production lines. Since work was considered mindless and repetitive, workers could be subordinated to machines. Independent thinking, creativity and personal ability were thrown to the wind.

Adam Smith believed money was the driving force behind capitalism and that if capitalism was to succeed, specialization and the division of labor were vital. Few people really enjoyed work, Smith pronounced. Most were lazy and only motivated by selfishness and lust for money.

The late 19th century brought a radical change to Smith's theory. Now Taylorism was grafted onto Smith's philosophy. Taylor's theory of "scientific management" was based on his belief that most workers were stupid. Inventing time and motion studies and a wide range of authoritarian procedures to increase productivity, he chained employees into systems that controlled their every movement. Money was the reward for getting the job done on time.

Even in today's workplace, that attitude persists. Some employers still believe that all employees need to be told exactly what to do and how, that independent thinking is dangerous, and that the only motivation for work is money. Industrial capitalism brought even more restrictions. The modern corporate bureaucracy was born. The evolution of the bureaucratic pyramid strengthened the idea that only those at the top had the intelligence to make decisions. Once again, employees were considered simply a mindless accessory.

In the 1920s, management began to question some of its own beliefs. How valuable was authoritarianism? Were people only interested in money? Should all decisions rest with the managerial talent at the top of the pyramid? In the late 1940s, the answers emerged. Mayo discovered a clear connection between productivity and work satisfaction. It had little to do with money or even physical conditions. What people really wanted was a satisfying social milieu that offered involvement, attention and recognition. The human relations school of management had been born. Job satisfaction and career development had become important issues.

THE COMPUTER AGE

Technological, social and economic change also accelerated in the 1960s. Today knowledge is power. The worldwide communications explosion means that if you don't or won't learn about computers, word processors and telecommunications, a large number of doors will be closed to you. Many believe automation — the development of machines controlled by computers — may represent the greatest change in the history of mankind. As automation increases, so the jobs of millions of employees are drastically altered. Machines will soon relieve humans of almost all dirty, dangerous, strenuous, menial and repetitive tasks. In factories of the future, the only humans employed will be those who install, program, monitor and repair the robots which do the work. In offices of the future, word processors, intelligent copiers and automated information systems will eliminate some of the drudgery in filing and stenography and will probably do away with much of the rote work of the typing pool.

To survive, you will need generalist skills such as the ability to manage information, design and plan, research, think critically, solve problems and make decisions. The need to retrain large segments of industry and business to deal with the new technology has made managers even more valuable. Those who succeed will be those who are adaptable.

The implications are enormous:

1. **How we define success is changing.** Some people are now using their own definitions of success to derive more meaning from work and leisure activities. They are not prepared to sacrifice their personal and family lives for the sake of their careers. The movement toward a more wholesome life, where career and other life components are balanced, is beginning. A growing number are becoming less willing to pay the high personal cost of health and family problems caused by excessive ambition.

2. **Dissatisfaction with authoritarian and impersonal work environments is leading to decreased loyalty.** Corporate control is

breaking down as employees strive for freedom and decision-making power.

3. **New social attitudes toward personal liberation and occupational change are developing.** Changing jobs is beginning to be seen as a desire for personal and professional growth rather than as a sign of personal instability. Some adults are learning that it's okay to continually explore and change their values and goals. As middle-aged people realize they will continue to develop and grow throughout life, some are developing new attitudes about themselves. The lifelong occupation is beginning to disappear. Some people are retiring early, then embarking on new occupations. Other factors are contributing to change:

● Surviving — to say nothing of thriving — is much more likely in this era of rapid and sweeping changes for those who keep their options open.

● Well-educated adults with high expectations are insisting upon opportunities to express themselves and to make a meaningful contribution to society.

● The changing face of family life — divorce, death and the empty nest — is forcing people to re-examine their relationships, to discover shifts in their goals and values and to switch occupations more frequently.

● Spouses are helping each other through the change cycle by shouldering financial and family obligations while their partners study or search for more rewarding jobs. Couples are reversing roles and obligations.

● People are living longer. Many different personal and environmental experiences will affect their occupations and how they feel about themselves throughout their lives.

THE NEW ATTITUDE UNFOLDS

As these changes take place, traditional career paths are being altered. Most people face tremendous pressures to readjust to the new demands of career development. To adapt, you will have to learn new attitudes and patterns of coping, new values and new skills. You will also need to find new ways of achieving a sense of belonging, personal identity and self-fulfillment. In other words, there is a whole new set of attitudes toward careers that you will have to stay in tune with to get ahead.

The new attitudes are beginning to change old theories about career development. To your parents and grandparents, the idea of career was a simpler concept. The rewards of work usually centered on moving up the corporate ladder, achievement, security and delayed gratification. Success meant being a good parent and sacrificing for your children, having money to buy the good things in life, as well as saving money, surpassing your parents' goals, and having social standing and respectability. No one agonized over self-fulfillment or even discussed it. No one thought of quitting a job. That was a sure sign of personal instability or irresponsibility. The future was as certain as the day was long.

Today nothing is certain. The career ladder is a dead topic among a growing number. They speak instead about the altruistic and intrinsic — how to satisfy the body, mind and spirit. The value of work is judged more by personal and job satisfaction and less by money and status. Success has no one definition, it has many. Authenticity is making a comeback.

TAPPING INTO CAREER REWARDS

There are a number of rewards you can derive from your career: identity, self-confidence, status, stability, material comforts.

But if who you are is what you do, what happens when you don't find your work meaningful or satisfying? Like a steam cooker, life's pressures can build up until they explode. To resolve this pressure positively, you must discover what you need and value, then find a job setting that satisfies those rewards. By neglecting your needs and values, by "biting the bullet" and hanging in there (however great your excuses), you permit the malaise and lack of purpose to grow until it gnaws at every thread of your fibre.

Family life is tied into your work identity. No matter how hard you try, your family life and work life simply cannot be separated. You are a whole person. Your actions, feelings and thoughts, your physical, psychological and spiritual well-being, are one. Expressing yourself fully requires the careful meshing of all ingredients that go into making you who you are. Every experience in your life, not just those you wish, has an impact. As an adult, you must live with the experiences of childhood. As an employee, you must live with your role as husband or wife, as parent or child. How you feel about one is interwoven with how you feel about all the others.

Related to this is a growing reluctance to sacrifice personal and family gratifications for the sake of a job. Many are less willing to accept frequent transfers, even when promotions and raises accompany them. Desirable lifestyle and locale and personal fulfillment are heavily weighed before a job is selected or accepted. Expectations about work hours, advancement opportunities, status, salaries and involvement are now judged as rewarding, demanding or unreasonable. Always, there is the bottom line assumption that your occupation, or series of occupations, should fit your developing personality.

Your career may also function as a way to gain varied experiences. Frequent job changes no longer signal instability or indecision. A variety of work roles can be a hedge against obsolescence and can indicate personal drive, flexibility and good generalist skills. Acquiring many different skills can also be good protection against unemployment. High unemployment, new technologies, even the move to overseas locations, have thrust the threat of job loss into our reluctant consciousness. Now, changing jobs is often a necessity. People who carefully attend to their careers allow their career paths to unfold in many new directions. Along the way, they increase their skills and sharpen their intellects, becoming better prepared for the future. Some monitor their careers and direct their energies to new opportunities to prepare for unemployment. They are careful not to stay too long in repetitive jobs which may rob them of their flexibility and their opportunities to grow. They know they can be easily replaced by younger and cheaper talent.

Abe understands that. From attorney to retail executive to administrator in the state college system, Abe has changed occupations several times. Currently he is director of the human development department at a state unversity that offers career counseling and development programs. The key to an ever-evolving career is to monitor your own development and to be open to new opportunities. As Abe says, "You have to attend to what is happening to you personally, as well as to your economic value. Are you growing or are you just hanging on? Ask yourself: If you had to move, could you move? And where to?"

Issues related to career are being debated in the public forum. Today, career is viewed as an area for achieving social equality and humane working conditions. The movement toward civil rights in the workplace promises fair hiring and promotion practices. Organizations face increased pressure to eliminate unsafe working conditions that threaten the physical or emotional well-being of their employees. As people become increasingly aware of their rights and responsibilities in the contemporary work world, job quality and employment practices have become issues for political drum beating. Studies in vocational, industrial and social psychology are showing how career satisfaction and adjustment, including job involvement, organizational commitment and burnout, affect your life.

And all these many reasons, causes and effects, influence a number of Questers to change the direction of their careers in midstream. They are the people who view their jobs as vehicles for self-expression and growth. They value movement — the right to grow and to maintain their usefulness. Their career goals are often open-ended. They find challenge in a wide variety of occupations and environments. They take the initiative in changing jobs, leaving when they no longer derive desired growth rewards. So they proceed through several occupational cycles of entry, mastery and disengagement throughout their careers.

At the same time, many Questers are not simply job hoppers. Questers tend to make appropriate choices. They usually initially like their work and are committed to and involved in it. But after four or more years, when they can no longer grow, they leave. They are willing to take a prepared risk. They are not irresponsible. They don't forget the family, say "to hell" with their obligations or decide they couldn't care less about money, status or respectability. They usually do want some degree of financial, interpersonal, family and material well-being. But they also struggle to make room for greater personal choice against what they consider to be institutional encroachments.

You may suspect by now that many Questers are either highly successful in their careers or complete failures. The truth is that success is measured differently by Questers than by Traditionalists as we have already seen. Yet many famous successes are indeed among the ranks of the Questers. Most of them also found purpose in their work. *Pablo Picasso* had this to say about his work: "What is always there is your work. It is the extension of you — not your child, but you. You are your work. The passions that motivate you may change, but it is your work in life that is the ultimate seduction." Picasso was one of many creative people who learned to express hidden emotions through work. "Painting and making love were very much the same for me. At the greatest moment for each, painting and sex were the same. But painting you can do alone."

Eminent French designer *Coco Chanel* was masterful at work, but in private she was totally vulnerable. Everything worried her. "I believe that every little girl should be taught as early as possible something she can do to take her through her whole life. I shall always be grateful to my work because it taught me independence. Even more important, it saved me from boredom. Boredom is a terrible thing."

Lee Iacocca suffered a devastating emotional blow before masterminding Chrysler's remarkable financial turnaround. Iacocca had spent 34 years working his way up to president of Ford Motor Company when he was fired in 1978. A generous separation agreement guaranteed him $1 million a year until 1980 if he remained unemployed. By joining Chrysler, he would trade $2 million for the helm of a faltering auto giant teetering on the brink of bankruptcy. To fail would add hundreds of thousands of Chrysler employees to Detroit's unemployment rolls. The future of Detroit was on the line. To take the job would be to jeopardize his reputation. He did. By December 1984, Iacocca's marketing genius had turned a dying company into a $2.3 billion financial giant. All for the love of a challenge and through concern for humankind.

The Questers you have already met have found both the courage and the means to take command of their lives. Why did they do it? What personality trait or traits gave them the courage to risk and to persevere? Could you do the same? Are there characteristics you already possess or could develop that would turn you into a Quester?

2: *Questers are made — not born*

There is nothing wrong with being a Traditionalist or a Self-Seeker. Questers, however, are the people who will maintain career flexibility and survival in a changing world.

You could say no two Questers are like. Yet they share many of the same personality traits. A very few have them all. The willingness to take control of their careers is what distinguishes Questers from Traditionalists and Self-Seekers. In order to make the changes you want, let's take a closer look at the Questers. Some started taking charge of their careers quite early. Others were near retirement. By reading about the courage and imagination Questers relied on to find career happiness and growth, you may discover ways you can take better control of your career and life. Maybe you share some of the major personality characteristics Questers tend to have: a sense of purpose, a desire for autonomy, the capacity for intimacy, confidence, the ability to combine the best of male and female strengths, the desire to achieve and the need to grow. Where do you fit in?

PURPOSEFUL

Questers give their lives purpose by pursuing activities they enjoy. Work, an idea, other people, a social goal — it can be anything. For many, much of that purpose comes from their career. It satisfies their need to believe in something or someone. Making a commitment to a project (or another person) helps them move outside themselves. They feel good because they are achieving something or helping someone.

Some jobs, such as those in educaton, health or social services, naturally have social benefits. A dedicated principal who saves a dying school, a nurse or physician who helps the sick, the therapist who aids a troubled family. All these professionals derive a sense of purpose from their work. But Questers go beyond the ordinary. Debra, Gerald and Brenda are Questers.

Debra is petite, attractive and fragile-looking. Who would guess she is 50? She began her career as a physical education teacher who wanted to make gym fun for all her students, not just the few truly gifted. So Debra did what she could to change the system. She made sure more time, space and effort were devoted to programs just for girls. She started a keep-trim club to teach her students how to eat a balanced diet and keep their bodies healthy. She offered classes in dance, badminton and golf, activities her girls could use in later life. Debra's students went on to become top competitors in the city and state competitions. But more than that, Debra let her ideas be known to her peers and superiors. She pioneered a program girls of every level of ability could enjoy.

The challenge was over. Debra needed a new cause now. She took a job as vice-principal and was quickly promoted to principal. Debra believed she could have more influence as an administrator. She picked a hotbed of deprived kids and underprivileged minorities. And, as the years went on, Debra did it — building up teacher morale, reducing dropouts, improving the behavior of her often-difficult charges.

Debra's next project was setting up a school for unwed mothers. It was a radical idea for the midwest of the late 1950s. But Debra's persistence won out. The project is now part of the midwest school division's services. Her next achievement was starting a training program in a nearby penitentiary.

In her late 40s, Debra went back to school to pick up some courses in geriatrics. Helping seniors has become her new goal. Debra's mission was, and still is, to provide educational services for the deprived. Like most Questers, Debra had to keep changing to keep the challenge alive. The sense of purpose she gets from her work gives her life more meaning and fulfillment than "just a job" ever could.

Gerald feels the same way. An eye specialist in his late 40s, he started off as a general practitioner, but soon became interested in the eye problems of his patients. So in his early 30s, he returned to school to specialize. On first impression, Gerald seems nondescript, a colorless man. But when he talks about his work, he shines. His eyes light up and the sympathetic, warm, caring doctor emerges.

Gerald likes finding new and better ways to help his patients. Research is a big part of his life. Gerald has pioneered many projects, like the use of laser eye surgery and radio keratotomy, which help the severely short-sighted to see better (sometimes without glasses). Many of the operations are performed in his office because Gerald believes the trauma of a hospital stay prolongs recovery. Those who can't pay, don't. His holidays are spent in Third World countries performing eye surgery for free. Gerald's life really is his work, though he also enjoys his family, friends and peers, plus regular workouts in the pool and on the racquetball court.

Even Questers whose work doesn't seem to have social benefits find a sense of purpose in what they do. They know their accomplishments are good and worthwhile.

Brenda finds meaning in writing. She has yet to create the great novel, but she loves to write short stories and poetry. It started when she was a young mother with four kids. A few night courses led to short stories in magazines. Brenda squeezed in a BA and then MA in English while the children were growing up, graduating from university with her eldest son. Now in her late 50s, Brenda does public relations and writes in her spare time. Both her work and leisure time involve writing. Brenda has even won some writing competitions. She is truly content with her life.

AUTONOMOUS

Questers tend to motivate themselves. They make their own decisions, do and say what they want. They're not afraid to swim against the tide. Questers avoid situations where they have to conform. They resent the binding ties of custom and habit. They move forward at their own speed, doing what they know is right for them.

Questers are free. But their freedom is not bought by rebellion or by using someone. Nor are they unconventional in everything they do. They usually behave in socially acceptable ways and within legal and ethical structures. Questers know how to transcend their environment.

Being inner-directed is part of being autonomous. Questers know they control their destinies. They take responsibility for their successes and failures. They say: "I was successful because I worked hard." Or: "I succeeded because I'm bright." Or: "I failed because I didn't try." Because Questers know they can control their lives, they don't depend on others to reach their goals. People who take charge of their own lives have higher expectations of getting what they want. Moreover, they have the marvelous, exuberant feeling of personal power that comes with believing anything is possible and what happens depends on you.

Jay understands the importance of taking charge of his own career. A stocky man with a square, honest face, Jay quit school in the Depression to support his family. He was lucky to find a job as a construction worker. A go-getter, Jay worked hard to learn his trade. By 30, he was a successful contractor. At 36, Jay decided to satisfy a long-time dream. He entered municipal politics. For the next seven years, he ran unsuccessfully for city council. Some laughed at this simple working man. Friends and advisers told him to change his home and his lifestyle. Jay and his wife lived in a modest two-bedroom bungalow in a lower-middle class part of the city, dressed plainly and refused to "show off" their new-found wealth. Although a prosperous businessman, Jay didn't forget the people who were kind to him in his hungry days. He remained loyal to his basic principles and values.

Jay was an optimist. He persevered. He knew he would win. And he did! At 43, Jay became mayor and continued to be re-elected for 20 years. He was a kind, honest and caring administrator, who increased tourist trade, renovated the core, restored historical buildings and expanded the city's parkland. Social climbers who earlier laughed at Jay now begged him to join their circle. A perceptive and forgiving man, Jay did. But he also remained loyal to his friends and supporters.

Jay had the courage to be himself and the conviction to follow his goals. He also learned from his mistakes. Jay is individualistic, self-directed, self-reliant and independent. This persistent man didn't complain about being "unlucky". He listened carefully to what others said, but made his own decisions. Jay isn't afraid of social disapproval and won't give in to societal pressures.

Many other Quester qualities fortify and are fortified by their sense of autonomy. Let's look at a few.

WINNERS SEE THEMSELVES AS WINNERS

Many Questers know they can make things happen. So they do. Questers accept bad luck. They understand some rotten breaks are an unavoidable part of the game. But they don't let them rule their lives.

Erika didn't let bad experiences hamper her career. Her first venture into the work world was a disaster. Fired from her first job for chronic lateness and laziness, Erika didn't realize a rare, easily-treatable blood disease was causing her lassitude. "I wasn't able to get a second job because of the unfavorable reference from my first employer," Erika remembers, "and it was a whole year before I was diagnosed. After I found out what was wrong, I went back to my former boss and explained. I got my old job back and within six months I was promoted. I don't deny that I had an awful piece of bad luck, but I think you have to expect some undeserved blows sooner or later. You just have to cope with them as best as you can."

Vanessa is a beautiful, vibrant woman who lived through a disastrous marriage to a man who beat her. Hounded by an obsessive, frightening man, she came through both a divorce and the failure of her career as a professional dancer. Her unfailing aura of hope and good cheer managed to attract and keep a faithful circle of friends. "I've got nowhere to go but up," she would say, undaunted by yet another unsuccessful audition or a midnight phone call from her unbalanced ex-husband. Vanessa critically evaluated each audition and set herself a time-frame to make it on Broadway. Then she gave up on elusive stardom and opened a dance school. "I just admitted I didn't have what it takes to be a star. But I did have the makings of a good teacher. I faced the realities of my own talents and limitations." And, at about the same time, Vanessa's ex remarried and dropped out of her life.

But most Questers also know when to quit. They have no hesitation about abandoning unrealistic goals or ill-conceived projects.

Knowing your own limitations is important. You don't have to settle for second best. You just have to find out what your best really is. Vanessa, the aspiring Broadway star who finally opened a dance school, could have ended up a loser if she had single-mindedly pursued her goal without reassessing her true talents. Instead, Vanessa is now a real winner. She makes a good living from the art she loves because she shook off the chains of an unattainable dream. Questers tend to win because they know their own limitations. They don't beat their heads against a brick wall or blame others for their failures.

LEARNING HOW TO BE AUTONOMOUS

Positive thinking goes a long way toward improving your sense of control. Getting new and better coping skills is the first step. You can become more autonomous just by learning how to set and achieve goals.

Setting goals puts you in control. You feel better when you are in charge and so you do better. Adults who are in control are better able to cope with the few problems they do have. Biological researchers have discovered people who are taught coping strategies have lower levels of cortisol. They are healthier, develop fewer illnesses and are less likely to suffer setbacks in chronic conditions. Your mind and body interact. Stress-related illnesses and behavioral disorders are really created by your body's chemistry interacting with psychological and sociocultural stressors. Because most Questers have learned to be in control of their environment, they are happier and healthier. You can be, too.

INTIMATE

Real Questers tend to understand the importance of intimacy. They can tell their deepest dreams and fears to others. They can also accept others' needs for intimacy.

Developing the capacity for intimacy is the first step to developing supportive relationships. Neither marriage nor sexual relationships can buy intimacy. Even the most active sexual partners can feel isolated if they lack mature, caring attitudes.

Real intimacy demands that you commit yourself to relationships that require sacrifice and compromise. It's the ability to share empathy, to give and receive pleasure without exploitation, to regulate your own needs to another's. It's the ability to say: "I don't want to use you. I want to love you. I want to experience you. I want to know you. I want to smell you. I want to feel you. I want to grow with you." Those who share real intimacy know it takes energy, risk and adjustment. The only way you can ever grow is to experience intimacy.

THE INTIMATE MARRIAGE

Tom and *Elva* share real intimacy. They married when both were 26. Tom is tall, blond, athletic. Elva is a bookkeeper, tall, willowy and blonde. "We are good friends as well as lovers," they both said at the same time. They have an open, supportive, tender relationship. As they grow closer, neither fears losing his or her own identity. They can make independent judgments. But they also achieved intimacy because both saw themselves as valuable, competent, meaningful individuals, with needs of their own, before they married.

As Tom approached 30, his management position became restricting and frustrating. Elva knew he was disturbed and encouraged him to talk. Tom didn't really know what he wanted to do, besides drop out of the bureaucratic treadmill. He needed time out — an extended trip, somewhere, anywhere — to rethink his goals. And he wanted Elva to go with him. She was hesitant. Elva liked her job. Leaving it for the unknown was scary, risky. But she also saw Tom's apathy and depression. Tom, on the other hand, saw what his request was doing to Elva. So he didn't push. After a year of talking over their feelings and hopes for the future, they decided on a moratorium — time from responsibilities and future commitments. They sold most of their belongings and bought a van. "But you're giving up everything — good jobs, losing money on your belongings. What will you do when you come back?" their baffled and concerned friends and relatives cried.

For a year and a half, they drove up and down North America, from Alaska to Central America, up the east coast and into Labrador, through northern Quebec and Ontario and down into the central states. They had no plans, no schedules to meet, no phones to answer. They had no one to answer to except each other. They stopped in little agricultural towns, big cities, fishing villages, mountain parks and mobile parks. Finally, they settled in a scenic Oregon town. Tom wanted to work with his hands, to do carpentry, an old hobby, and odd jobs. He set himself up as a jack-of-all-trades. Elva got a bookkeeping job in a local motel.

Two years later, both are healthy and happy. Each has made new friends and found activities they enjoy alone. They also have plenty of time for one another. Tom and Elva are thinking of starting a family. This combination of autonomy and shared interests not only strengthens their marriage, but reinforces their independent strengths. Still young, they have achieved the empathy and commitment that makes a good marriage a sanctuary. "Your relationship becomes much more precious and intimate when you commit yourself to doing something like this together," Tom said.

Not all Questers have been happily married all their adult lives. About a third (as with the general population) have been divorced. But by the time most reach their 40s and 50s, they are happily involved with another mate.

FINDING INTIMACY WITH OTHERS

Intimacy is the ability to commit yourself to genuine love. But it's more. Intimacy is the ability to communicate at a sharing level with friends of both sexes. It means having close friends to share your dreams, sorrows and experiences. Close friends can be just as intimate as married lovers. Many Questers are more intimate with their friends than a great many married couples are with each other.

To Questers, intimacy also means nurturing humankind. It

means helping people in trouble, assisting the less fortunate, treating others with kindness and sympathy, doing small favors, being generous, listening to confidences with empathy and understanding.

You need intimacy to grow and be healthy. When you are cared about, that person (your "care-taker") helps you grow and develop by giving you positive feedback and constructive criticism about your strengths and weaknesses. This honest and caring feedback helps you see yourself more objectively. It helps you understand yourself better so you can learn to capitalize on your strengths and minimize your weaknesses.

ACHIEVING INTIMACY

Having successful relationships requires several qualities. You can develop them. Many Questers have them. As you become more confident and independent, your capacity for loving will expand, too. Rather than fearing that an independent spouse might leave, Questers understand that it is their individuality and belief in themselves that allows men and women to accept the emotional risks of intimacy. A popular quotation from John Donne sums up how Questers feel about those they love: "If you love something, set it free. If it comes back, it is yours. If not, it never was." So it is with Questers. They can accept the need for intimacy without losing their individuality.

Questers know the secret of maintaining balance between love and work. Even though many are achievers and work hard, they don't let work take precedence over the people they care about. Many try to spend some time each day with their partners. They have freed themselves from the tyranny of trying to please. Rather than looking to one man to confirm their worth, most female Questers develop multiple sources of identity. Questers tend to be comfortable revealing their innermost thoughts and feelings to their mates as well as their closest friends.

Questers remember they have needs, too. They can be loving and, at the same time, love themselves. Many of us forget to look after our own needs. We take care of our physical needs, like food, shelter and health. But we forget to look after our psychological needs to achieve, to be accepted, recognized, creative and autonomous, to enjoy the world and to grow. Unless we love and respect ourselves, we cannot love and respect others. Questers have learned this. Liking ourselves and doing things to please ourselves is not being selfish and does not stop us from achieving successful intimacy.

EVERYONE NEEDS INTIMACY

The overwhelming desire for intimacy is reflected in the

high percentage of divorced people who remarry. The happiest men in the world are married, the unhappiest single and childless. By their own account, young, unmarried men are lost. They have little motivation, no emotional nourishment and suffer from loneliness and dissatisfaction. In contrast, survey after survey shows the happiest men are married men with young children who were planned. Looking back, many successful men in their 50s and 60s regret not giving more energy to "this human thing". For many women, too, the happiest years are the married years.

SELF CONFIDENT

How Questers feel about themselves colors their dealings with the world. Self-confidence gives them the courage to set higher and higher expectations, to change jobs, to risk, to dare to grow. Self-confidence is a vital component of their personalities. Earl and June possess self-confidence.

Earl is self-confident and self-accepting. In his mid-60s, Earl is rather short, five foot four and average-looking. Earl is kind, caring, warm, friendly and has a sense of inner calm. Currently, he heads a research and development department at a university on the west coast and teaches a few courses to undergraduates. Because his field is research methods and statistics, he has taught at several universities and worked on a variety of research projects in many disciplines.

Earl began his career at an Ivy League college where he was a full professor at 34. He then spent six years on the west coast doing research for industry. In the late 1960s, he moved back east to teach and set up a computer services program at a large university. Then it was the mid-west to head a university research department.

Earl is a brilliant man, very much in demand. He has many books and articles to his credit. But he doesn't flaunt his intelligence. Earl works hard to accomplish things. This gives him a humility that is neither self-deprecation nor diffidence, but one that promotes self-acceptance and self-respect. Earl isn't embarrassed to say he doesn't know the answer to a student's question. He has learned how to be wrong. In fact, he rather enjoys having students challenge his views. Earl says this about criticism: "You need constructive criticism and feedback from other people. That's how you learn. I know I'm not infallible. I often get good advice from the criticism of others. I decided early that I would learn how to take criticism in a positive way. I had to, to grow as a professional and a person."

Unlike Earl, many people fear criticism. They avoid experiences where they might be criticized. They take jobs that are too easy or lovers who won't ask for too much. What they don't realize is that they are losing out on opportunities for growth.

Earl wasn't a self-confident young boy. He acquired his self-confidence through friendships with other people. Success in his work also enhanced his level of self-confidence. Earl said: "As a child, I lacked for nothing but confidence. I was a small, skinny boy and I had few friends. I spent most of my time in the library. Most of the boys my age were into sports and I wasn't. But gradually, as I became successful at work, it came. I was a success and suddenly I had more confidence in me."

WHAT ARE YOUR LIMITATIONS?

June has the look of self-confidence. Forty-six, a youthful woman with auburn hair and aqua eyes, June operates her own gift shop. She married right out of high school and had four children. Because money was tight, June went to work as a telephone operator, then as a sales clerk and finally, a restaurant hostess. When the children were in school, June signed up for a real estate course and sold houses. Her husband was transferred to the west coast when she was in her late 30s. By then, June was ready for something different. She wanted to open a gift shop. Her husband didn't mind her working and, by now, the children were independent.

June loves her work. She feels good about her accomplishments. Because she believes she will do well, she does. Like Earl, June can take criticism and learns from her mistakes.

Looking at June, you would never guess she once lacked self-confidence. Her carriage, her well-modulated voice, her private smile, all exude confidence. Surprisingly, June says: "For a long time, I thought of myself as an ugly duckling. . . .My nose was too long, my eyes were too close together, I was fat. So I played up to it. . .making jokes about my looks and putting myself down. I know now that was a mistake. If you look at yourself in a negative way, everybody's going to look at you that way. I finally realized I could improve the looks I had. I became involved in an exercise program, styled my hair so it emphasized my good points. But more important, I placed more emphasis on internal qualities. I learned to be more accepting and tolerant of others, to see the good in them, to see what each person had to give. I learned not to dwell on mistakes I made, but to use these as learning experiences. I learned how to stop feeling sorry for myself, how to take advantage of growing older, and how to accept myself and to become more independent."

June has learned to accept herself for who she is, independent of other people's standards. Instead of being indecisive and afraid of criticism and change, she's learned to accept that some people will like her and some won't. She's no longer in the business of pleasing everybody. June knows you have to love yourself first.

Trying too hard to make others like you makes you dependent. June tried so hard to be all things to all people that she made herself feel wishy washy and insignificant. June has learned to cultivate qualities she likes in herself, and now others like her, too. The qualities she developed had nothing to do with good looks, status or contacts. She learned how to enjoy her own company, to have fun with her family and friends. And they, in turn, enjoy being with her.

Liking yourself and doing things to please yourself does not mean you are selfish. June is not selfish. She explains: "I'm not self-centered. . . .I'm happiest when I'm not absorbed in my problems. When I'm nice to others, I get that back. And that makes me feel good about myself. Much of what we do in life is motivated by selfishness. When you give money to charity, it makes you feel good. Givers get!"

Even though June is content, she keeps working on herself. "I'm trying to get rid of my silly inhibitions. . . .I want to be more spontaneous. Spontaneity is freeing the child in you. Not being childish, but childlike."

ENERGIZING YOURSELF

June and Earl have a lot of energy because self-confidence is energizing. They don't waste time and effort trying to impress other people or worrying what others will think. They search for and accept situations that relate to their own self-image rather than those which are socially desirable. They don't waste time and effort deciding what's right. They do it!

Self-confidence and self-acceptance are qualities June and Earl acquired and developed as they grew older and more experienced. Many things contributed to their newfound self-confidence. Past experiences — triumphs, the way they handled humiliations, the way parents, teachers, friends and other people have reacted to them — all contributed to their self-confidence. Much of their self-confidence is also the result of their successes at work. The positive feedback they receive from performing a difficult job well enhances their self-confidence. Their self-confidence gives them courage to contact new employers. to tackle difficult assignments and to solicit the support of others when they need help .

Similarly, the way Earl and June behave with their spouses and other people affects their self-confidence. Because they give and receive love, June and Earl feel good. They get positive feelings and acts that tell them they are worthy, too.

June and Earl carry with them positive pictures of themselves and then proceed to act upon these. In short, they behave like the sort of people they believe they are.

You can learn from people like Earl and June. You are never too young or too old to start developing self-confidence and accepting yourself. Appreciating your own worth is not egotistical. Nor are you ruined or worthless because you are too short or too fat, or have a long nose or made a mistake, any more than a violin that sounds a sour note is worthless. Don't hate yourself because you are not perfect. You are not alone!

Accept yourself. Be yourself. You cannot possibly realize your potential if you keep turning your back on yourself. Just as it is important for you to recognize and accept your limitations, it's important, if you can, to change those shortcomings. Suggestions for enhancing your self-confidence are found in Chapter Three.

ANDROGYNOUS

Few Questers play gender roles by the book. They possess the best of male and female strengths. In other words, they are androgynous. Androgyny is used to describe people who blend traditional feminine and masculine characteristics. Depending on the situation, Questers are both feminine and masculine, both introverted and extroverted, nurturant and assertive, confident and tender. Female Questers are loving and empathetic, but they also have ambition and courage and are open to new experiences. The most satisfied men are assertive, brave and able to lead others effectively. But they are also comfortable with intimacy and nurturance. Simply speaking, Questers have incorporated the characteristics of their gender opposites. For men, comfort with intimacy and cooperation. For women, ambition and courage.

Androgynous behavior is healthy. It allows you to adapt to a greater variety of situations. It is also more functional. Both men and women should be able to cry, to be assertive, to hug — whatever the situation calls for. Men become manicurists, dental hygienists or househusbands. Women become crane operators, bank presidents or breadwinners.

Rigid gender roles can cause conflict that robs you of vital energy. Highly masculine males tend to suffer from high anxiety and low self-acceptance. The picture is not much prettier for women. Highly feminine women also tend to be very anxious and suffer from low self-confidence. In contrast, androgynous people have much higher levels of self-confidence, are well-adjusted, more creative and have happier marriages.

Because androgynous persons have no gender-typed image to maintain, they can remain sensitive to changing situations and engage in whatever behavior seems most appropriate. For them, "masculine" and "feminine" traits simply don't exist.

Almost all people experience some form of cross-over as they age. Men and women in their 40s and 50s begin to adopt qualities typically thought exclusively male or female. Women may become more independent and strong-minded. Men may become more emotionally responsive and interested in attachment. Older men are often more interested in giving and receiving love than in conquests or power trips. Women may develop exactly opposite.

Questers tend to start the process of becoming androgynous early. Some in their 20s and 30s are already androgynous. By the time most are in their 40s and 50s, they have acquired many of the emotional characteristics of the opposite gender.

BECOMING ANDROGYNOUS

Kathy, whom you met in Chapter One, was androgynous all her life. She was brought up in a mid-sized, mid-western city. Her father was a lawyer, her mother a homemaker who enjoyed volunteer projects. She had one sister, two years older. Kathy's father encouraged her to be open to new experiences, regardless of whether they were typically "male" or "female". Her mother agreed. As a young child, Kathy had the opportunity to play with dolls and chemistry sets, to play doctor or nurse. She could take dancing lessons or play football, try out for cheerleader or for the basketball team. Since she had no brothers, her chores were both masculine and feminine. Kathy took out the garbage, mowed the lawn and shoveled the walk. She also washed the dishes, made the beds, baked cookies and sewed. To Kathy, there was no such thing as masculine or feminine behavior. She did what was appropriate to the situation. As a teenager, Kathy had both male and female friends and she related to both as equals. She considered becoming a lawyer, policewoman, manager, geologist, physical education teacher, interior designer or dietitian. Because she was a good student with numerous interests and abilities, Kathy had her choice of any occupation. But because she had many options, she had a difficult time deciding. Her parents would have supported her in whatever occupation she chose. As it turned out, Kathy's first occupation was manager with an insurance company. She will soon be a full-fledged lawyer.

Adrian's childhood and adolescence weren't as ideal as Kathy's. Adrian also grew up in a mid-western city. A middle child, he had an older brother and a younger sister. His parents divorced when he was 10. Adrian's mother worked as a nurse to support the family. Adrian recalls doing a variety of chores around the house. "We all helped at home. I learned that it was okay to do male and female activities."

Like Kathy, Adrian came from a home where a parent modeled, encouraged and supported androgynous behavior. Parents who are warm and supportive facilitate the development of androgyny, autonomy and achievement.

A number of Questers, however, were pushed by circumstance to take on the strengths of the opposite gender when they were in their 30s, 40s or older. They show what goes into the making of a Quester. They remind us that Questers are made, not born.

Women forced by divorce or abandonment to fend for themselves and their children are often marveled at for their pluck, calm and logic. Wilma started a lucrative typing business in a one-room apartment while her three children learned to become independent by helping out and taking part-time jobs. Elaine completed her social work degree in the evening while she worked during the day to support her two children. Gretchen established her own drugstore while caring for an invalid husband. Yet all three, well-indoctrinated in gender stereotypes they never thought to question, had set off into adulthood expecting to find a man who would take care of them. Here's Gretchen's story:

Gretchen was brought up in a small town on the west coast. She was the only daughter of a merchant and a pampered mother. Gretchen never finished college because she met Matt. Together, they decided she wouldn't need her degree. She would never have to use it. Gretchen worked as a cashier in a bank until they had their first child. Three more came along. Gretchen enjoyed domestic life. When the youngest was in school, she worked as a volunteer two half-days a week at her children's school, watched the soaps, gossiped with the neighborhood caffee klatch and kept a clean house. Paradise didn't last long. Gretchen was forced to become the breadwinner when Matt was crippled in a car accident. She went back to the bank, but didn't like it. By going for broke and cashing in the family's savings, Gretchen returned to school to earn a pharmacy degree. When she completed her education, she got a job as a pharmacist in a hospital. Within five years, she was promoted to director of research, a job she held for six years. The political hassles, coupled with the children's increasing independence and the mid-life transition, led to Gretchen's decision to open her own drugstore. It was hard at first. Gretchen was at work at 7 a.m. in the morning and didn't get home until 10 p.m. She was open seven days a week. Today, Gretchen can afford to take it easier. She has two pharmacists and two sales clerks working for her.

Gretchen has learned to be more ambitious, assertive, competent and confident — the whole parcel of qualities usually associated with men. But she has not lost any of her female strengths, either. She is still loving and lovable, empathetic, warm and supportive. As a matter of fact, Gretchen, Wilma, Elaine, and other women like them, have assumed male strengths at a remarkable rate. But Gretchen also had other Quester qualities to fortify her. She possessed a willingness to risk, which permitted her to change; she was open to new experiences and she planned for her future. Her need to achieve only surfaced because she had the courage to allow it to, because she had picked up new skills to support it, and because she had the energy to follow through. As director of research, she had learned to think for herself. Among other things, Gretchen also has a strong sense of purpose in her life — her children, husband and a job she enjoys.

Mike's story is similar. Mike was a macho male. As a young man, he nurtured the classic male fantasy. He ate, slept, played and worked football. His little remaining time was spent in weight lifting and body building. As he now admits, he was a louse as husband and father. So at 35, his wife gone, Mike was left to pick up the pieces of a shattered marriage — a son 14 and two daughters, 13 and 11. The simple mechanics of being father and homemaker — working, shopping and cleaning — stymied him at first. But these things were soon learned. It was the idea of intimacy that really threw him. "I didn't understand the language my children were speaking," he said. "I didn't know how to communicate with them. They would come home from school and spill their guts, and I didn't know what to say to them. I knew how to talk to the boys on the team, but this was different. In time, I learned. We learned together. Being a single parent is the most emotionally draining job I've ever had."

In the meantime, football and weight lifting were gradually becoming less important to Mike. The callous views he held as a young athlete had disappeared. He needed another occupation. Sketching and painting caught his interest. Recovering from a broken hip, an athletic injury, he plunged into the paints and "how to" art book his daughter brought him. He loved it. Next came evening art courses. Now, at 42, Mike is teaching art part-time at a high school and taking more courses. He wants to be a full-time art teacher and freelance artist. Mike's only involvement in athletics now, other than jogging, is leading a weekly weight lifting class. He's even marrying a woman he met in art class.

Mike is a good model for younger boys. He has shown that a man is capable of releasing the tender side of his nature without losing his virility. Learning how to care, how to feel and communicate these feelings to his children and being open to new experiences have made Mike's personality and his life more complete. The new androgynous Mike will probably bring newfound joy and liberation into his marriage. Having the best of male and female strengths allows partners to be equal. Adrogyny is an important part of a happy marriage.

ACHIEVING

Do you have a high achievement quotient? Many Questers do. Most are motivated by an inner drive. They strive to overcome obstacles, to achieve excellence, to do well at something difficult. This inner drive gives them feelings of accomplishment. Questers tend to seek settings where independence of thought, creativity and growth are rewarded.

SUCCESS IS DOING YOUR BEST

Because Questers have a high need to achieve, they tend to strive for perfection, to do a good job.

Jason is an achiever. Tall, lean but well-built, with dark hair and blue eyes, Jason is an architect. He began his career in the early 1960s as a junior member of a large architectural firm. In the mid-70s, Jason decided to go it alone and established his own firm. Now in his early 40s, Jason has six younger associates. Because he is a perfectionist, Jason does considerable research before beginning a project. He makes certain that he delivers a quality product. He'll go to great lengths to ensure all details of a home match the personal qualities of the client. Jason particularly enjoys the challenge of doing a big and difficult job well. He feels good about an elementary school he just completed — and so does the school board.

Jason says this about success: "Success is an attitude. It makes you push hard at whatever you're doing. Success means never being satisfied that you've done well, always trying to do better. I work just as hard now as I did in my 20s. If you have passion, it will make you successful. Why else would Michelangelo have lain on his back for three years to paint a ceiling?"

Jason's positive attitude shines through his whole personality.

He is driven by the desire to do his best, the need for challenge and the will to work hard. Jason says: "I love my work. That leads to a strong identification with it and a high degree of motivation. I aim for excellence in whatever I do. Moreover, I have a 'can do' approach. I will try just about anything no matter how difficult it appears — it's a challenge to me!" Jason usually starts work at seven a.m. No work appears too demeaning for him. "The more dirty work you do, the more you learn your job." Jason also manages to find time for fitness. He works out at the health club and plays racquetball as often as possible.

Jason admits to being preoccupied when he's working on a project and to neglecting his wife and family. He can also be incredibly messy. But he's trying to improve.

ENERGY IS LIFE!

How does he do it? Jason has high levels of energy and can stay with a task until it is completed. Having the energy to accomplish tasks and meet deadlines is vital to the achiever. Jason can go for two days without sleep to complete a project. Like many Questers, Jason's passion for work spills over into his playtime, too.

Feeling "energetic" comes from being alive and involved. You feel wide awake and excited when you are doing things you really enjoy. A number of Questers over 30 have high energy levels because they are optimistic. They set out with high expectations, anticipate the obstacles, put criticism in its place and find meaning and direction in everything they do. Disappointments rarely slow them down. Nothing creates energy like living energetically!

Your energy level may partly be determined by genetics. But don't use that as an excuse! You can raise your energy level by having a positive attitude, taking care of yourself (getting enough sleep, eating right and exercising), becoming involved in an exciting job or project and having an intimate relationship.

SETBACKS ARE GOOD EXPERIENCES

Jason wants to succeed. But he's also willing to risk, to be flexible and learn from his mistakes. "Setbacks are important," he said. "Maybe a rejection every few years is essential. It sort of revs up the engine. A number of bids I've made were rejected, so next time, I worked harder. People usually don't mention their rejections and mistakes, which is too bad, because you think you're the only one not making it. But you know what I found out? That some very successful people have lived through many rejections."

Questers have failed just as frequently as and maybe more than most of us. But they don't see themselves as failures or doomed. They've learned not to fall victim to self-fulfilling negative prophecies.

EVERYONE NEEDS CHALLENGE

Where does the need to achieve come from? Some psychologists believe you are born with "competence motivation", or the need for challenge and stimulation. Babies and toddlers have it. Grade school children have it. Some just have more of it than others.

Joyce is an achieving Quester. She was one of those children who strove to master difficult tasks alone. She recalls: "When I was five, I went to the Ice Capades. I was so excited. I had to have a pair of figure skates so I could do all those fancy tricks, myself. The day after Christmas I went to the rink to do 'shoot the duck' on my new skates. It was freezing. I was the only person there. I practiced until I had it mastered. My bum was cold and wet and my feet and hands were frozen but I felt good. I did it! But I didn't tell anyone. I felt good inside and that's what it's all about for me."

And today, Joyce is still "shooting the duck." She loved her first job, teaching high school history. Teaching was fun. Joyce liked being around students and enjoyed trying to make her classes interesting and meaningful. Motivating poorly-behaved students taxed her, but the rewards were worth it. Besides her classes, Joyce had plenty of other interests. She was involved in a pilot project with her school's English, history and science departments. She also sat on a state committee that developed a values curriculum. But by the fourth year, Joyce's enthusiasm was waning. Teaching the same old stuff year after year was losing its excitement. A failing marriage added to her lethargy. It was time for a change.

So Joyce took time off to travel and think about her life. She returned to a job offer as principal of a junior high school. Part of the challenge was working with problem students. She plunged in with gusto. Joyce was determined to help teachers deal with difficult students and to help students confront their problems. She introduced humanistic teaching. Then she set up a student-staff liaison committee so both sides could do something about their beefs. Joyce liked having the freedom to solve problems creatively. By now, she's in her fifth year as principal. Joyce has mastered her job pretty well. She wants to move on. To shine, she needs a challenging job she enjoys.

Success and achievement breed even more success and achievement. Joyce and Jason know, from previous accomplishments, that they can do well. So they set even more challenging goals next time.

Every time they succeed, they are flooded with satisfaction. People who do well have the confidence to try and try again.

REVENGE MOTIVATES

Revenge can be a strong motivater. You know the feeling: "I'll show them I can do it!" Some Questers have been prodded to great achievements by people who rejected, mocked or wronged them. Evelynne, whom you met in Chapter One, had a desire to show the hometown snobs that she could succeed. This drove her to great success. "If someone says, 'You're wonderful, of course you can do that, you can do anything,' and someone else says, 'You can't do that,' you're going to work harder to show that you really can. You just want to prove they were wrong. Sometimes anger can be very constructive."

BOREDOM MAY BE GOOD FOR YOU

Boredom can be constructive, too. Oysters produce pearls to stop the irritation caused by trapped sand grains. People produce "pearls" to relieve the boredom eating inside them. Setting goals beats drinking, drugs or casual sex. Many Questers quit their jobs because the challenge is gone. Some women take jobs to relieve the boredom of being at home.

GROWING

Everyone needs to grow. Questers especially. They tend to welcome new experiences, personal or professional. Questers continuously try to improve themselves and the quality of their lives by enhancing these. Psychologists like Abraham Maslow would say Questers are motivated by self-actualization. They want to become all they can be. Once Questers master tasks, they tend to move on to other new and more challenging ones.

The desire to grow is partly biological. Your nervous system hungers for stimulation.

Looking for a job that uses all your talents will allow you to grow. Most Questers place the opportunity to grow ahead of position, title or salary. A peek at Renee's career history reveals how many Questers seek and develop growth from their jobs.

Renee, now in her late 50s, is like many Questers. She needs work in which she can grow. A speech pathologist, Renee began her career as a management trainee, then manager and head of ladies' fashions in a department store. By 36, she was a professional and had gained financial success. But the meaning and excitement of her work were gone. So, at 38, Renee ventured into speech pathology. With a masters in speech pathology, she went to work as a speech therapist for a school division. She loved it. Eight years later, she took a sabbatical for further training to prepare for private practice. Renee satisfied another interest in seeing that her community had access to quality education by sitting on the school board.

Happily married to the same man most of her adult life, Renee has balanced a career with a satisfying family life. She took a few years out to stay home when her son was young, but returned to retailing when he started school. Renee's family life hasn't always been idyllic. She admits to some pretty rocky times when she and her husband were in their early 30s. But true to her nature, she did all she could to save their marriage. Renee sought counseling. "I guess I wanted to know, in my own mind, that I tried everything possible before I gave up on the marriage." Fortunately, because Renee and her husband deeply cared for each other and wanted to make the marriage work, they resolved their differences. Not all Questers are so fortunate. Renee and her husband now have an intimate relationship. They share many things and have a few mutual friends. But Renee also has special friends of her own.

Renee likes serving her community. She wants to see positive changes in the educational system. Like many Questers, Renee feels good when she tries hard. She possesses many Quester qualities. Renee is her own person.

THE JOY OF INNOVATING

Most Questers like Renee like to find new ways of doing things. Steve, an 80-year-old Quester who paints, reveals his philosophy: "You remain young only as long as you experiment. When you are content with what you have already done, happy only to repeat yourself, you've reached old age."

Questers express their creativity in many ways. Renee loves to experiment with different recipes. When less creative colleagues complained that their productivity was being hurt, Aaron, an innovative young store manager, used his to do something about it. Dustin, a ski instructor turned entrepreneur, delights in dabbling in a variety of ventures. He went from a ski apparel and rental shop to a costume rental business, to a stationery store, to a toy shop. Now 38, Dustin is planning his next undertaking. Molly loves to paint, sketch and make candles. She just opened a craft shop.

OLDER IS BETTER

As Questers grow older, they improve. The accumulation of

many experiences has taught them to be realistic, accepting and caring. Many adults do not develop these traits until well after 35. A number of Questers develop these qualities earlier and more intensely because they dare to experience more.

YOU, TOO, CAN BECOME A QUESTER

Questers tend to possess many other common characteristics. They have come to terms with the transitions of their life cycles. They have dealt with developmental issues, struggled with whether to stay in destructive jobs or relationships. Questers have learned how to use life crises, like accidents, financial reverses, being fired or abandoned or sudden death, as maturing experiences to take stock and emerge as fuller, better human beings. Most Questers recognize the importance of a healthy lifestyle and strive to strike a balance between work and family, relationships and leisure activities. Questers aren't dependent on others for their well-being. They take charge of their own destiny. But they keep their options open, finding satisfaction and success in a variety of occupations and organizations. Questers know that surviving in uncertain times means being flexible and willing to risk. They have the courage to be open to new experiences, to let go of familiar people, places and ways of being. Questers have learned to push themselves ahead.

Which of the Questers' personality characteristics of purpose, autonomy, intimacy, self-confidence, androgyny, growth, achievement and risk are more important? They all are. They all complement one another. Mastering new skills helps them to gain the confidence to set their sights even higher. They grow and change.

You may not think you are a Quester. But you can become one by small acts of courage. You can move forward, too. Try *The Quester Questionnaire*. Dare to take the first step.

3: *Are you a quester?*

Are you a Quester? Could you become one? *The Quester Questionnaire* will help you find out.

Answer the questions that follow and read the interpretations carefully. Gaining a greater understanding of who you are and could become can be the first step to developing a more rewarding life. Contrary to popular belief, the personality which you developed through childhood and adolescent experiences needn't be a wardrobe for life. In fact, you can do a complete makeover any time you want. Naturally, before you do that, you'll need to draft a map of where you have been, where you are now, and where you are going. Once you have identified your strengths and weaknesses, you'll be better able to make the most of who you really are.

THE QUESTER QUESTIONNAIRE

The 146 statements that follow will help identify how your personality characteristics compare with those of the Questers. Indicate how much you *agree* or *disagree* with each statement by *checking* anywhere from *5* (very strongly agree) to *1* (very strongly disagree). Scoring procedures and an interpretation of the results are provided at the end of the questionnaire.

Make your responses as honest as possible. Don't choose the answer you feel others would expect of you. This is a test for you, and you alone. Since your attitudes about yourself can also be colored by how you feel at any given time, complete the questionnaire when you are feeling refreshed. For best results, find a quiet spot where you can devote two concentrated hours to completing and scoring it.

One final point: in the field of psychological evaluation, there are no absolute rights or wrongs. This questionnaire does not pretend to be infallible, but you will find it intriguing and revealing. In fact, you may never see yourself the same again.

		Degree of Agreement				
		V High 5				V Low 1
1.	Life always seems exciting to me.		4			
2.	I can like people without having to approve of them.	5				
3.	When I do a job, I do it well.	5				
4.	I am determined I will succeed in everything I do.		4			
5.	I often wish people would be more definite.	5				
6.	When I want something, I'll sometimes go out on a limb for it.		4			
7.	When I want to buy something, I rarely consider others' opinions.	5				
8.	It's easy for me to start conversations with strangers.		4	3		
9.	I don't often contribute new ideas.		4			
10.	Most of my misfortunes and successes were the result of things I did.	5				
11.	It's very hard for me to tell anyone about myself.			3		
12.	I have been doing quite a bit of stocktaking lately.	5				
13.	I have clear goals and aims in life.	5				
14.	I have had moments of extreme joy when I felt I was experiencing a kind of ecstasy or bliss.	5				
15.	I feel I have much to be proud of.	5				
16.	I feel good about doing a job well.	5				
17.	A well-ordered way of life with regular hours suits my temperament.	5				
18.	If the possible reward was very high, I would not hesitate about putting my money into a business that could fail.			3 3		
19.	I'm self-sufficient.			3		
20.	When I'm in a group, I hesitate to make suggestions.		4			

	Degree of Agreement				
	V High 5				V Low 1

21. I like a job which demands skills and practice rather than inventiveness. ___ ___ _3_ _2_ ___

22. I cannot really believe that chance or luck have played a very important part in my life. ___ _4_ _3_ _2_ ___

23. I always try to consider others' feelings before I do something. ___ ___ _3_ ___ ___

24. I have experienced at least one traumatic event in the past year. _5_ ___ ___ ___ ___

25. If I should die today, I would feel that my life has been worthless. ___ ___ ___ ___ _1_

26. I like to withdraw temporarily from the rest of the world. ___ ___ ___ _2_ ___

27. I have a great deal of confidence. ___ ___ _3_ _2_ ___

28. I don't have much ambition. ___ ___ _3_ ___ ___

29. I like to plan all of my activities in advance. ___ ___ _3_ ___ ___

30. I enjoy taking risks. ___ ___ ___ _2_ ___

31. I'd rather spend time and energy doing an interesting job than being successful at a job I dislike. _5_ ___ ___ ___ ___

32. No matter who I'm talking to, I'm always a good listener. ___ _4_ ___ ___ ___

33. I seldom bother to think of original ways of doing the same thing. ___ ___ ___ ___ _1_

34. My successes are the result of hard work, determination and some ability. _5_ ___ ___ ___ ___

35. I like to play with kittens and/or babies. ___ _4_ ___ ___ _1_

36. I'm very satisfied with my job. ___ ___ ___ ___ _1_

37. I am a very responsible person. _5_ ___ ___ ___ ___

38. I live only for the present. ___ ___ _3_ ___ ___

39. I believe that I am as successful or more so in achieving my goals as most of my graduating class. ___ ___ _3_ ___ ___

40. I will never profit much ___ ___ ___ ___ _1_

41. I like everything to be in its place. ___ ___ ___ ___ _1_

42. I would enjoy the challenge of a project that could mean either a promotion or loss of a job. ___ _4_ ___ ___ ___

43. I refuse to behave like everyone _5_

	Degree of Agreement				
	V High				**V Low**
	5				**1**

else just to please people.   5

44. I'm critical about the dress, manner or ideas of some of my friends.   1

45. I hope to develop a new technique in my field of work.   5

46. When I make plans, I am almost certain I can make them work.   4

47. I like to cook fancy dishes.   2

48. I feel that I'm passing through a life cycle transition.   5

49. I have seriously thought of suicide as a way out.   1

50. I can express honestly-felt anger.   3

51. I wish I had more respect for myself.   3

52. All I want out of a career is a secure, not-too-difficult job that pays enough to buy a nice car and home.   2

53. I like to work on problems that have ambiguous answers.   5

54. I don't fear failure.   5

55. Generally, I don't concern myself with what others think of my abilities.   5

56. I feel comfortable with all types of people — from the most wealthy and well-educated to the poorest and least-educated.   5

57. I usually continue to do a job in exactly the same way that it was taught to me.   1

58. There are many times that I feel that I have little influence over the things that happen to me.   3

59. I'm not afraid to take a stand even though it may be unpopular.   4

60. I believe the probability is good of finding an acceptable job elsewhere.   5

61. I regard my ability to find meaning and purpose in my life as prac- tically non-existent.   2

62. I will continue to grow best just by being myself.   3

		Degree of Agreement			
	V High 5				V Low 1

63. I feel that I am a person of worth at least equal to others. — 5 _ _ _ _

64. I would be very unhappy if I was not successful at something I seriously started to do. — 5 _ _ _ _

65. It bothers me when something that is unexpected interrupts my routine. — _ _ 2 _

66. I trust decisions I make spontaneously. — _ 3 _ _

67. What the general public thinks does not affect my standards or beliefs. — 5 4 _ _ _ / 5

68. I can take a joke when it's on me. — 5 _ _ _ _

69. I prefer activities which I know I will enjoy to ones I have never tried. — _ 3 _ _

70. It is often not wise for me to plan too far ahead because many things turn out to be a matter of good or bad fortune. — _ _ _ _ 1

71. I have male and female qualities. — 5 _ _ _ _

72. There is much to be gained by staying with this job the rest of my career. — _ _ _ _ 1

73. Facing my daily tasks is a source of pleasure and satisfaction. — _ 3 _ _

74. I feel that I would like to make a contribution to society. — 5 _ _ _ _

75. I am a useful person to have around. — 5 _ _ _ _

76. I have a tendency to give up easily when I meet difficult problems. — _ 3 _ _

77. I like things to be certain and predictable. — _ 3 _ _

78. In games I usually go for broke rather than playing it safe. — 5 _ _ _ _

79. I enjoy being a vagabond. — _ _ 2 _

80. I do not have a small circle of very close friends. — 5 _ _ _ _

81. I like trying different kinds of foreign foods. — 5 _ _ _ _

82. I take my horoscope seriously. — _ 3 _ _

83. I'm sensitive to the needs of others. — 5 _ _ _ _

84. My employer inspires me to do well. — _ _ _ _ 1

85. In thinking about my life, I see a reason to be here. — 5 _ _ _ _

	Degree of Agreement				
	V High 5				V Low 1

86. I believe that I am growing and developing personally and professionally. ___ ___ _3_ ___ ___

87. I certainly feel useless at times. _4_ ___ ___ ___ _1_

88. I must admit that I often do as little work as I can get by with. ___ ___ ___ ___ _1_

89. Once my mind is made up, that's it. ___ ___ ___ _2_ _1_

90. Skydiving is too dangerous for me. ___ ___ ___ _2_ ___

91. I find it very hard to work under strict rules and regulations. _5_ ___ ___ ___ ___

92. I can like people without having to approve of them. _5_ ___ ___ ___ ___

93. Few topics bore me. _5_ ___ ___ ___ ___

94. If I get a really good job in the future, it will probably depend a lot on getting the right breaks. ___ ___ ___ _2_ ___

95. I'm assertive. ___ _4_ ___ ___ ___

96. I never think of quitting my job. ___ ___ ___ ___ _1_

97. After retirement I would like to do some of the exciting things I've always wanted to do. ___ ___ _3_ ___ ___

98. I enjoy helping younger people both in and out of the workplace. ___ _4_ ___ ___ ___

99. I find failure difficult to accept. ___ _4_ ___ ___ ___

100. I set high standards for myself. ___ _4_ ___ ___ ___

101. I think I'm stricter about right and wrong than most people. ___ ___ _3_ ___ ___

102. I would prefer a stable position with a moderate salary to one with a higher salary but less security. ___ ___ ___ _2_ ___

103. When I was a child, I didn't care to be a member of a crowd or group. ___ _4_ ___ ___ ___

104. I feel certain and secure in my relationships with others. ___ _4_ ___ ___ ___

105. I like to participate actively in intense discussions. _5_ ___ ___ ___ ___

106. There are often times when I cannot keep my temper or hold back tears. ___ ___ ___ ___ _1_

107. Men and women should follow any vocation they desire, even if it violates tradition. ___ ___ ___ ___ _1_

108. I am very satisfied with the way

		Degree of Agreement	
		V High 5	V Low 1

things are going in my life. _____ 1

109. I can see past, present and future as a meaningful continuity. 5 _____

110. I believe that I know myself. _____ 3 _____

111. I welcome criticism as an opportunity for growth. 5 _____

112. I always try to do at least a little better than is expected of me. _____ 2 ___

113. I'm in favor of very strict enforcement of all laws regardless of the consequences. _____ 1

114. I try to avoid situations that have uncertain outcomes. ___ 4 _____

115. Before making a decision, I often worry whether or not others will approve of it. _____ 1

116. I would not dare to reveal my weaknesses among friends. _____ 3 _____

117. I always feel that I must look into all sides of a problem. 5 _____

118. Even when there is nothing forcing me, I often find that I do things that I do not really want to do. _____ 3 _____

119. I believe there are no genetic differences between the sexes in intellectual ability. 5 _____

120. I try to face reality even when its unpleasant. 5 _____

121. I feel that I have the knowledge and experience to be of great help to family members, friends and acquaintances when they ask me for advice. 5 _____

122. I enjoy doing challenging things. ___ 4 _____

123. I always see to it that my work is carefully planned and organized. ___ 4 _____

124. I probably would not take the chance of borrowing money for a business deal even if it might be profitable. _____ 2 ___

125. It's important for me to have a job where I have the freedom to perform

	Degree of Agreement				
	V High 5				V Low 1

the tasks my own way. _ _ 3 _ _

126. I have a very warm and caring relationship with my friends. _ _ 3 _ _

127. I think of myself as a straightforward, uncomplicated person. _ _ 3 2 _

128. What happens to me is my own doing. _ _ 3 _ _

129. It is possible for women to combine home and career, and do both successfully. 5 _ _ _ _

130. I would like a job that provides good opportunity for self-expression. _ 4 _ _ _

131. I can accept my mistakes. 5 _ _ _ _

132. I think I would accomplish almost anything I wanted to if I tried hard enough. 5 _ _ _ _

133. I take things very seriously. _ _ 3 _ _

134. I would enjoy a job where I have to adapt quickly to new situations and to emergencies. _ _ _ 2 _

135. I prefer to have a job where I am not closely supervised. _ 4 _ _ _

136. I am free to express both warm and hostile feelings to my friends. _ 4 _ _ _

137. It is important for me to have a job where I can create original things or ideas. 5 _ _ _ _

138. I feel free to *not* do what others expect of me. 5 _ _ _ _

139. It's ridiculous for a woman to run a locomotive and for a man to darn socks. _ _ _ _ 1

140. I would like a job where I can fully develop all of my potential. 5 _ _ _ _

141. I feel certain and secure in my relationships with others. _ _ 3 _ _

142. I set a high standard for myself and expect others to do the same. _ 4 _ _ _

143. I would take a job I enjoy even if strikes and layoffs are expected. 5 _ _ _ _

144. I would like a job where I can express my own creativity. 5 _ _ _ _

	Degree of Agreement	
	V High	V Low
	5	1

145. A college education is equally important for males and females.   _5_ __ __ __ __

146. I feel comfortable talking about very personal things with my partner or close friends.   _5_ __ __ __ __

SCORING

PART A: To determine your score for Part A, give yourself *3* points for each *5* (very strongly agree), *2* points for each *4* (agree) and *1* point for each *3* (uncertain or undecided) you recorded for the following questions. Place a 3, 2, or 1 in the blank beside each question. Now, add up your total score for each personality characteristic and place these in the blanks labeled Sub-Total.

INTIMACY

8 _5_	104 _4_		
32 _4_	126 _3_		
56 _5-_	136 _4_		
68 _5_	146 _5_		
83 _5_			
92 _5_			

15 +6+ 2

SUB-TOTAL _23_

CONFIDENCE

3 _5-3_	75 _5-3_		
15 _5-3_	111 _5-3_		
27 _3/_	121 _5-3_		
39 _3/_	131 _5-3_		
63 _5-3_	132 _5-3_		
	141 _3-/_		

SUB-TOTAL _27_

PURPOSE

1 _2_	85 _3_		
13 _3_	97 _1_		
37 _3_	109 _3_		
73	_1_		

SUB-TOTAL _16_

AUTONOMY

7 _3_	67 _3_		
10 _3_	79 _—_		
19 _1_	91 _3_		
34 _3_	103 _2_		
43 _2_	125 _2_		
46 _2_	128 _1_		
55 _3_	135 _2_		
	138 _3_		

SUB-TOTAL _33_

INNOVATIVENESS

45 _3_	137 _3_		
81 _3_	144 _3_		
93 _3_			
105 _3_			
117 _3_			

SUB-TOTAL _21_

ACHIEVEMENT

4 _2_	122 _2_		
16 _3_	132 _3_		
31 _3_			
64 _3_			
100 _2_			
112 _—_			

SUB-TOTAL _18_

RISK

6 _2_	66 _1_		
18 _1_	78 _3_		
30 _=_	134 _-_		
42 _2_	143 _3_		
53 _3_			
54 _3_			

SUB-TOTAL _18_

ANDROGYNY

4 _2_	23 _1_	43 _3_	107 _3_
6 _2_	27 _1_	46 _2_	119 _3_
10 _3_	30 _=_	55 _3_	125 _1_
16 _3_	32 _2_	56 _3_	129 _3_
19 _1_	34 _3_	59 _2_	134 _-_
20 _2_	35 _2_	71 _3_	145 _3_
22 _1_	37 _3_	95 _2_	

SUB-TOTAL _56_

GROWTH

WAYS TO IDENTIFY POTENTIAL QUESTERS

2 _3_	62 _1_	105 _3_	130 _2_	12 _3_	48 _3_
14 _3_	66 _1_	109 _3_	131 _3_	24 _3_	60 _3_
19 _1_	74 _3_	110 _1_	132 _3_		
26 _-_	81 _3_	120 _3_	136 _2_		
50 _1_	86 _1_	125 _2_	140 _3_		
54 _3_	98 _2_		144 _3_		

GROWTH SUB-TOTAL _50_

WAYS TO IDENTIFY POTENTIAL QUESTERS SUB-TOTAL _12_

PART B: To score Part B, give yourself *3* points for each *1* (very strongly disagree), *2* points for each *2* (disagree) and *1* point for each *3* (uncertain or undecided). Place a 3, 2, or 1 in the blank beside each question. Again, add up your scores and place the results for each characteristic in the blanks labeled Sub-Total.

INTIMACY	CONFIDENCE	PURPOSE	AUTONOMY	
20 _-_	51 _1_	25 _3_	22 _2_	94 _2_
44 _3_	87 _3_	49 _3_	58 _1_	106 _3_
80 _-_	99 _=_	61 _2_	70 _3_	115 _3_
116 _1_			82 _1_	118 _1_

INTIMACY SUB-TOTAL _4_

CONFIDENCE SUB-TOTAL _4_

PURPOSE SUB-TOTAL _8_

AUTONOMY SUB-TOTAL _16_

INNOVATIVENESS

9 ___
21 _2_
33 _3_
57 _3_
69 _1_
127 _2_

SUB-
TOTAL _11_

ACHIEVEMENT

28 _1_
40 _3_
52 _2_
88 _3_

SUB-
TOTAL _9_

ANDROGYNY

11 _1_
76 _1_
139 _3_

SUB-
TOTAL _5_

RISK

5 ___	65 _2_	102 _2_	124 _2_
17 ___	77 _1_	113 _3_	133 _1_
29 _1_	89 _3_	114 ___	142 ___
41 _3_	90 _2_	123 ___	

SUB-
TOTAL _20_

GROWTH

38 _1_
52 _2_
101 _1_
116 _1_

SUB-
TOTAL _5_

WAYS TO IDENTIFY POTENTIAL QUESTERS

36 _3_	96 _3_
72 _3_	108 _3_
84 _3_	

_15_

PART C: Now determine your combined, overall score by adding together your Sub-Totals for each personality characteristic under Parts A and B. For example, if, under Intimacy, you scored 9 in Part A and 21 in Part B, your combined overall score will be 30 (9+21=30). List each of these combined overall scores in the spaces provided below. You may want to compare your scores to the highest possible totals (far right column). Once you have determined your combined overall score for each personality characteristic, add them up and place the total in the space beside Overall Score. Do *not* include your score on Ways To Identify Potential Questers in your Overall Score. Read on to discover what your scores reveal.

PERSONALITY CHARACTERISTICS	SCORE	HIGHEST POSSIBLE SCORE
Intimacy	27	(42)
Self Confidence	31	(42)
Purpose	24	(30)
Autonomy	59	(69)
Achievement	27	(39)
Innovativeness	32	(42)
Androgyny	61	(90)
Risk	38	(75)
Growth	55	(75)
Ways to Identify Potential Questers	27	(27)
OVERALL SCORE	365	**(504)**

HOW TO BECOME A QUESTER

Your responses to the statements in this questionnaire reveal how closely you resemble the Questers. A high score means you have many Quester qualities. An intermediate score means you are a potential Quester. A low score means you are quite different from the Questers. Keep in mind that your scores are not fixed. When events are going well, your scores will probably rise. Under stress, they will be more inclined to drop.

Quester qualities are positive. However, if they become excessive, they lose their value. People with extremely high overall scores may be overly anxious, tense and unrealistic. People who seek intimacy compulsively may miss the joys of solitude. Those who have too much self-confidence are arrogant, unrealistic and may become blind to their own limitations. Those whose sense of purpose is all-consuming may become narrow and boring to others. Overly autonomous people may refuse help even when they need it. Those driven by too great a need for achievement have been known to be ruthless in their single-minded pursuit of major accomplishments. Occasionally, rampant innovators miss the value in the tried and true, and wrongly believe there is value in the new and novel. Some people, recognizing the trendy value of androgyny, may foolishly suppress some of the fine strengths of their own gender. A willingness to risk, when carried to extremes, may be hard to distinguish from irresponsible gambling. Obsessive preoccupation with growth can be found among boring people who are too absorbed in themselves.

What does *The Quester Questionnaire* say about you?

INTIMACY

28 or higher: If you scored 28 or higher on Intimacy, your feelings closely match the Questers. You tend to place great value on personal relationships and probably have a small circle of very close friends. Your friendships are emotionally rich. If you are married or living with someone, the relationship is close and loving. You have nothing to hide from family and friends, and readily reveal problems, foibles or concerns. You are candid and care deeply about others, and your excellent interpersonal skills allow you to empathize with and relate effectively to people in all walks of life. Your self-confident, trusting nature draws them toward you.

15-27: You are a potential Quester. Your dealings with people may fluctuate. For instance, you may be empathetic and have a caring relationship with your partner, but find it difficult to start conversations with strangers or hesitate to make suggestions in a group. Go back over the statements and see what you could change about yourself to enhance your ability to enjoy greater intimacy.

14 or lower: You are probably shy, have few close friends, feel uncomfortable being intimate with your partner, or feel ill at ease in social situations. Work on improving your intimacy skills. Your attitudes about love, other people, and yourself may be preventing you from enjoying intimacy. Like anything else, attitudes can be changed. By learning to become more outgoing and a more effective communicator, you can not only improve your intimacy skills, but also take better control of your own behavior. Here are some ways you can do this:

• **Get out and associate with others.** The act of mingling and making friends usually requires no more than suffering through the 10 or 15 awkward minutes it takes to get to know someone. Start a conversation. As soon as the conversation starts rolling, see if your shyness doesn't disappear. A hello, a smile, a handshake, a nod, a wink — any one of these tiny little communication devices can help overcome shyness. Force yourself to smile at and speak to someone you previously ignored. During an office coffee break, strike up a conversation with someone new. Go out into the world, even when you don't feel like it. Make small talk. Become more visible. Compliment others or, better yet, ask for their advice. Sit down next to a stranger or a new acquaintance on the plane, bus or train. Pick up the phone. Above all, communicate.

• **Enhance your social skills.** Try honing your interpersonal skills at a small task-oriented group, such as a PTA committee, or in a social group, such as a book club. A restricted, focused situation is much easier to deal with than the ambiguous, unstructured atmosphere of the party where words can, and do, easily fail most of us. Come to the group prepared to participate. Or, volunteer to collect for the cancer fund so you will feel forced to speak to strangers. Before the party begins, find something fresh to discuss by reading a newspaper or magazine. Seek out the host or hostess and ask for introductions. Most of all, be aware of your own body language. Don't close out others by looking away or crossing your arms. Look people in the eye. Set realistic goals. Talk to just a few new individuals each week. And don't feel hurt if someone doesn't respond. Move on to the next person. Introduce yourself to several strangers, then set out to discover three identifying characteristics about each. Next time you meet, you'll be able to put names, faces and facts together for a fun and fascinating conversation. Probably the biggest payoff from practicing these small steps is that they will help you to stop dwelling on yourself and to open up to the rest of the world.

• **Listen to what people are saying to and about you.** To avoid misinterpretation, listen not only to people's voices, but to the tone of their voices. Are they saying, "Notice me," "Help me," or "Care about me"? A good listener is an involved participant who shows that he or she understands and cares about the messages others are sending. A good listener hears feelings and probes for thoughts, intentions and actions, as well as statements. To become a good listener, you must learn to observe (to take special notice of non-verbal cues such as facial expression, body movement and breathing rates); to acknowledge (to let someone know you are really listening by paraphrasing or by reflecting your interest through nods, smiles, concerns and comments such as "Uh huh"); to encourage (to invite the speaker to tell you more); and to check out your interpretations so that you know that what you are hearing is what is being said. (You will want to recycle the message back and forth until what is being sent and received are identical.) As you practice these attentive listening skills, try to imagine what your speaker's experiences may feel like. Doing so will help you to better appreciate the message being spoken.

• **Say what you feel.** Learn to share your deepest feelings and to express anger without blaming or attacking. Learn how to express affection and discuss problems with friends as well as lovers. Express emotions indirectly or symbolically, perhaps through a gift. Emotions can also be expressed non-verbally through kissing, hugging, crying or even slamming doors. Such non-verbal demonstrations of emotion are certainly okay. Actions often have greater impact than spoken expression. But feelings and actions that are unsupported by words can be extremely ambiguous. Crying, for example, can express joy, sadness, disappointment, anger or relief. Direct statements of feeling are much more powerful. Next time you feel upset, say so. Next time you feel excited, tell someone. Most people will readily respond. Expressing those feelings honestly and directly can be done in many ways. Expand your emotional vocabulary by adding these powerful feeling words: pleased, calm, comfortable, satisfied, bored, fearful, confused, lonely, excited, uneasy, silly, surprised, eager, angry, weary, glad, gleeful, contented, confident, awkward, anxious, hopeful, sad, proud, relieved.

Using these techniques will help you connect with others more quickly and easily than you may ever have dreamed possible. All it takes is one positive response to send your shyness into seclusion. Being on the lookout only for Number One hinders communication. Remember that if you feel awkward and left out in social situations, so do many others. As you make a conscious effort to be pleasant, others will respond likewise. Pleasing others in this way can be reward enough.

SELF-CONFIDENCE

28 or higher: A score of 28 or higher on Self-Confidence indicates that you like and respect yourself. You have learned to accept both your positive and negative qualities. Because you feel good about yourself, you are happy and content with life. But being confident is quite different from being selfish and conceited. When you like yourself, you can accept life as a gift. Like most Questers, you can give yourself permission to tread life's path with enthusiasm.

15-27: People who score 15 to 27 are potential Questers. You probably feel quite confident in some areas of your life, while in others you may feel weak and vulnerable. Alternatively, your mood at the time you completed this questionnaire may have a lot to do with your score. Are you being overly hard on yourself? All too often achievement-oriented people set unrealistically high standards, standards that virtually ensure feelings of personal failure or inadequacy. Try to be realistic about what you can and can't do. Perhaps you are a perfectionist and just can't seem to give yourself the credit you deserve. Congratulate yourself on your accomplishments, willingness to risk and initiative. On the other hand, you may not yet have learned how to translate criticism or mistakes into learning experiences. Go back to the questionnaire and re-examine your low scores. Work on improving those aspects of your personality. Soon your level of self-confidence, and your career development, will begin to escalate.

12 or lower: Your low self-opinion may be taking the fun out of life. With this sort of attitude, you can't possibly hope to feel satisfied or happy, or to establish healthy personal or work-related relationships. The gulf between having an inferiority complex and recognizing your own limits is vast but not insurmountable. While a few of your limitations are genetically based, most are due to bad life experiences. Just as it is important to recognize and accept your limits, it is important to try to change those which you can. And to stop agonizing over those you can't change. You are never too old or too young. Here are some steps that will help you along the way:

● **Know and accept yourself.** Think of yourself as you really are, rather than as you think you should be. See yourself as others do. Be objective. Don't feel too bad if your clothes are two sizes larger than when you were in high school, or if your viewpoints are occasionally biased, or if you are developing wrinkles and a receding hairline. Compare the picture in your mind to the reality of your presence. You may not like what you see, but to avoid acknowledging these disparities can create immense disharmony, both within yourself and with the people in your life. Know what you can and cannot do and what you want out of life. If you can change your weaknesses, go ahead and do it. But, at the same time, be sure to maximize your strengths. Acknowledge and accept your accomplishments by preparing a list of positive achievement and personality characteristics. Post your list on a bulletin board or a door where you can see it and read it every day. When negative thoughts or experiences creep into your consciousness, look over your list. By competing with yourself, you will be learning how to accept who you really are, not who you think you should be. Don't limit your potential for achievement by only half-knowing yourself. Get acquainted with your strengths and weaknesses, then dedicate your life to daily improvements. It's almost guaranteed you will never be bored. Self-understanding and self-acceptance are assets.

● **Be yourself.** Don't be influenced by others who may reject your opinions. You don't have to change to please others. Opinions are extensions of your individuality. Even though others may not like what you say, most will respect your right to say it. Being overly concerned about what others think or trying too hard to please others can result in excessive inhibitions and poor performance. Be careful not to inhibit your creative self.

● **Reward yourself.** Start putting yourself first more often. A little self-indulgence is healthy for your ego. Start your morning by thinking of something positive you can do for yourself. Instead of going to the symphony because you are expected to, stay at home if you feel like it. Start dressing the way you would like to, not the way others say you should. Every time you pull through an experience you feared, give yourself a treat.

• **Enjoy success.** Measure yourself by what you have done, what you are doing now, and what you can do. Keep a daily, weekly or monthly record of your accomplishments and build on these. For example, develop an exercise routine. Start with five minutes of easy exercises every morning. Then get up three minutes earlier each week to work on it. Add a new routine each week. Mark this down. Be proud of yourself. Remember, change comes gradually. Strive each day to do something just a little better than yesterday. The exhilaration of achievement and growth will help you feel better about yourself.

• **Be image-conscious.** Your demeanor — the way you look, act, and express yourself — is your calling card; it's what you leave behind for people to remember you by. Act self-confident and you will be self-confident.

• **Use imagery.** Relax and slowly imagine yourself going through an anxiety-arousing situation without the accompanying fear and doubt. Picture yourself as competent and confident. Say to yourself, "I've done this before 100 times and I can do it again with no problem." Record any accomplishments you experience and your responses to them. Imagine yourself trusting all the positive feedback you receive.

• **Be heard.** Your speech is often a profound indicator of your level of self-confidence. Take responsibility for what you say. Be heard and be willing to speak clearly, not just loudly or aggressively.

• **Be flexible.** Welcome the new and the unexpected. Listen to your hopes, dreams and desires, and follow where they lead. Your creativity is challenged to the fullest by the new and unexpected. Open up, take a risk, explore new possibilities in your life. Refresh and revive your enthusiasm and sense of adventure.

• **Maintain your perspective.** Time and distance can make once seemingly insurmountable mountains seem like inconsequential molehills. Why let what happened yesterday affect what will happen today or tomorrow? Face each new day and each new challenge with an open mind. They may not be as difficult as you thought.

• **Persevere.** Into every life usually comes some turbulence. Weather it out. Power comes from persevering in the face of adversity. Remember, achieving your goals takes hard work.

• **Prepare.** Preparation gives you control and the strength to carry on. Keep your hands on the wheel and your road map before you. If you know where you are going, you'll get around the roadblocks.

• **Maintain your focus.** Don't look back; look ahead. Keep your energy focused on the problem and sooner or later, you'll find a solution.

     • **Become an expert.** Learn as much as possible about some subject. Take responsibility for your area of expertise, then enjoy the sense of accomplishment that comes from being an expert. An additional payoff will be the renewed confidence that comes from knowing a lot about your particular interest.

     • **Be responsible.** The more responsibility you assume, the more you will receive. Be responsible not only for performing your work, but also for maintaining your health, developing your personality and enhancing your lifestyle.

     Remember, you are an intelligent person who has succeeded in the past and can succeed again. Acknowledging that allows you to fully enjoy and appreciate your accomplishments without the doubt and anxiety that may have accompanied past efforts. Only you have the power to project a confident image. Exercise it, nurture it, delight in it. You can make anything happen.

PURPOSE

     20 or higher: A score of 20 or more on this section means that, like many Questers, you tend to be involved in activities that give you a sense of purpose, meaning and direction. You have someone or something to believe in, you probably have both short- and long-term goals and you are achieving them. Your achievements may be spread over several levels — they may be the result of work successes, achievements in your family life or relationships, or in your capacity to face up to the difficulties of life.

     11 to 19: You are a potential Quester. You may not be too excited about what's going on in your life and your goals may not be very clear. Perhaps you are having difficulty achieving them. You may benefit from the suggestions offered below.

     10 or lower: You probably have little meaning and few goals in your life. You seem to be suffering from boredom, frustration and a sense of aimlessness. To develop more meaning in your life, you will need to take action to change family, relationships, religious, occupational or other aspects of your life. Reconsider your philosophy of life. Here's help:

     • **Pick up a philosophy, poetry or history book.** As you read through it, you may discover a larger perspective on life. Think about your philosophy of life. In this "me" generation, it's easy to forget about the big picture. What is the real purpose of your life?

     • **Do something worthwhile.** Volunteer your time. Make helping others a goal. Giving away a part of yourself, within reason, makes you a harbor open to all of the good things going on around the world. Adopt a cause. Sign up to work in a senior citizens' home or with the mentally retarded. Make clothes that can be given away to social agencies. Join a citizens' action group fighting for a cause in which you believe. Take a look around your community. You may discover a wealth of ways to get involved.

● **Take constructive action to change at least one aspect of your life.** Determine what you want to change about yourself, then do it. Develop better interpersonal skills. Smile at a stranger. Help a senior across the street. Put more intimacy in your life. If your marriage is failing, learn to communicate better with your part- ner or go for counseling. If you are dissatisfied with your job, take steps to find another or to change what it is that is making you unhappy. Set short- and long-term goals for the changes you want to make.

● **Develop a personal philosophy of life — a statement of purpose, philosophy and ethics.** This will force you to be specific about what your life is all about. Having a personal plan of action can also commit you to taking positive steps to achieve it. Oral ex- pressions are fine, but the written word is a lasting testament of your decisions. Make it short and specific. Be realistic. Rather than setting yourself up for failure by developing a philosophy that doesn't address your needs and values, tailor this new philosophy to fit them. Weigh your requirement for economic reward, your desire for richer human relationships, your yearning for greater job satisfaction and your interest in participating more fully with your community. Nothing will help you more in clarifying your mission in life, and in enjoying the feelings of satisfaction and meaning that accompany a well thought-out philosophy of life.

AUTONOMY

46 or higher: A score of 46 or more on autonomy shows you are thinking like many Questers. You tend to be your own person. You believe in yourself, and are independent, self-sufficient and inner-directed. You honestly believe you are in charge of your own destiny and seldom blame others for bad experiences. You try to express your genuine self, your talents, interests and unique per- sonality. Rather than functioning as an adapted person, following someone else's script, you try to make your own decisions and, when need be, even swim against the tide. Far from being unneces- sarily unconventional or prone to illegal or socially-unacceptable behavior, you seem to have the courage to transcend your environ- ment when it infringes on your personal and professional growth.

24 to 45: You may be overly concerned with other people's opinions. Status, success or another's opinions may be controlling your life. Possibly you believe chance or luck play an important part in your life. Go back over the statements in this section. What kind of changes can you, or do you want to make?

23 or lower: You are quite dependent. Your levels of growth, creativity and self-confidence are probably quite low. You may believe what happens to you is determined by powerful others, fate or chance. You are influenced greatly by pressure from authority figures and peers, and probably lack clear goals. You may have decided early on to settle for quite a bit less in life than may be necessary. You seem to have chosen to take the path of least resistance by not facing up to the anxiety that accompanies growth. You can enhance your sense of autonomy and control by putting more faith in your own ability to make good things happen.

To become more independent, you must be aware of some basic principles. First, becoming more independent relies on your being aware of and accepting yourself, knowing that you have options in life, and taking action to achieve the goals you truly value. Self-knowledge and self-acceptance are the first steps toward constructive action. Getting to know yourself better is a process of letting go of old ideas about who you are or should be. Learn to accept yourself, flaws and all, for who you really are. Own your successes. Don't attribute them to chance; they are the result of your efforts and abilities. You'll also need to accept reality. Drive away those rigid or irrational beliefs that are blocking your expression. Accept the fact that your own decisions are just as good, and maybe better, than anyone else's. Besides, the wrong decision may just be a detour on the way to discovering the right one. Stop setting up self-fulfilling negative prophecies. Practice thinking positively about yourself and your abilities. Developing self-confidence can take time but the results can be phenomenal. Keep an open mind, learn to tolerate ambiguity and trust your own decisions. By seeking out new experiences, you may make some astonishing discoveries about yourself.

Understanding that you do have options is the second step. People trapped in bad marriages, relationships or occupations, do have options. Testing your options may mean trade-offs, but sometimes they arc well worth the inconvenience. Knowing that you have a choice in life can eliminate a lot of the distress and uncertainty that accompany difficult experiences. Studies have shown that the more freedom you believe you have, the more able you will be to meet and master the challenges of living.

Exercising your options is the third step to becoming more autonomous. Independent people have learned to act when they are afraid, when they feel like phonies, when they are certain they will do a poor job, when they think they are stupid and when they don't want to act at all. Independence requires action. Confront your fears. Speak up to your boss, take that vacation alone or approach your partner or spouse with your concerns. To increase your ability to be more independent, practice the following:

● **Anything worth doing is worth doing — even poorly.** Don't let your fear of not being perfect stop you from trying. If you are socially insecure, try settling for less than the perfect date. Learn to speak up, even if what you have to say isn't brilliant. Invite friends over to your home more often. Do what you want to do, not what others think you should. Rather than trying so hard to please others, learn to please yourself. Stop hiding your flaws or trying to get people to like you. You are who you are. Learn to become more vulnerable. Anxiety or fear can be major blocks to social independence. Instead of trying to protect yourself from potentially negative experiences, plunge in and see what the results are. You may even enjoy yourself. Accept the fact that you are afraid. Don't fight it. Instead of hiding your anxiety, which will only make you more anxious, tell others you are nervous. Most people will understand; after all, they've been in that position, too.

● **Experiment with confronting your irrational or distorted beliefs.** For example, spell out your negative predictions ("People will stare at me if I dine alone"), then devise ways to test them (venture out alone to a favorite restaurant). Now develop a way to measure the outcome (look around and see how people are reacting). Finally, draw a conclusion ("I can dine by myself"). Keep a record of irrational thoughts and devise experiments to challenge their validity.

● **Practice being more intellectually independent.** Follow your own beliefs rather than echoing others' opinions. Intellectual independence increases efficiency, which builds self-confidence, which leads to even more independence. This is the success cycle. As you learn to think more for yourself, you will see that you can start and follow through with those pet projects. You can do so by becoming more assertive and direct, by saying what you mean and want, by being concise and by letting your opinions stand on their own two feet. Learn to state your preferences, to speak up and to say what you want and feel. Just because others have opinions doesn't mean yours aren't valid. The same principle applies to your tastes in art, music, food and other cultural pursuits. Own your opinions and preferences. After all, there are few right or wrong decisions, just different results. Practice making your own decisions, and once you do make a decision, follow it through.

Changing distorted beliefs requires an open mind. Seek out and investigate facts that contradict your beliefs. Facts and experiences are the only way to test the validity of those long-held ideas. Instead of being a stereotypical thinker, be a creative thinker. No two people or situations are exactly the same, and just because you have had a negative experience in the past, doesn't mean it will happen again. Broaden your tolerance, develop creative outlets, take time out to think and reflect, and you will be on your way to a happier, more rewarding life.

Learning to become more independent is similar to learning to ride a bike. Repetition helps. Repeat to yourself: "It's better to do as much as possible for myself", or "I can do it, no matter what". Now practice this skill in different situations, starting with the most comfortable and then progressing to the least comfortable.

Being in control takes time, effort and transformation. But, chances are, you'll find taking charge of your own life makes you feel better about the direction of your life. Soon you will discover that you have more choices, more independence, more strength and more control than you ever thought possible.

ACHIEVEMENT

26 or higher: Is your score for achievement 26 or higher? Like the Questers, you tend to be motivated to achieve by an internal drive, such as the desire to do your best, or to accomplish tasks that require skill and effort, or to do a difficult task well. You may be determined to improve and do a better job. If you are predisposed to measuring your effectiveness in terms of achievement, you usually want to know how to improve your effectiveness. You tend to measure success by internal standards, rather than by status symbols or material wealth. You enjoy the whole process of learning, accomplishing and mastering. You are fortunate to find your work fulfilling, and are probably getting a chance to do things that you are capable of and really enjoy. Your work may also be your leisure. You would rather spend time and money at an interesting job than be an outstanding success at one that bores you. You want the best for yourself and are uncompromising about your standards of excellence. When you finish a project, you want to move on. While your work is obviously fairly important to you, you need to take more time for leisure. What can you do to put more fun into your free time?

14 to 25: You may be an easygoing, unambitious person who is quite satisfied with your work and lifestyle. Alternatively, you may avoid difficult tasks for fear of failing. Check your low scores for clues, then decide where you can make some changes in your life.

13 or lower: You may lack ambition. If you fall into this category, you tend to have a rather lackadaisical approach to life. You do as little work as possible and have a tendency to give up when the going gets tough. If you are happy with your lifestyle, then that's okay. If you are not, try accomplishing something you feel good about. Bake a torte or build a great recreation room. Learn to fix your car. Develop a respectable game of tennis. Perhaps you should be looking for a new job that will give you a better sense of accomplishment. Below are some additional points that may help:

- **Believe in the possiblity and desirability of change in almost everything, including yourself.**
- **Think in terms of action and consequences or results.**
- **Find a hobby or an area of interest and become outstanding at it.** Doing so will also increase your self-assurance.
- **Work hard and go the extra distance.** How can you improve your latest project? Set your own criteria for measuring your effectiveness.
- **Learn to manage your time better.** Good time management is good life management.
- **Assess situations from your own perspective.** Seek guidance, if you wish, but avoid leaving evaluation about situations that affect you entirely in the hands of others.
- **Assume more personal responsibility for improving those situations where you have some control.** Try to take the initiative, to demonstrate your energy and drive, rather than leaving the outcome to chance or to the abilities of others.
- **Identify a set of goals and develop strategies for achieving them.** Set high goals for yourself, goals that are moderately difficult but not impossible to achieve. Then strive for excellence. Goal setting works better if you decide in advance how you will measure your effectiveness, and include specific timelines for completing them. To determine how you are doing, seek constructive feedback from the people around you. Be persistent and patient. Instead of stumbling over roadblocks, seek alternatives or figure out how to improve the situation.
- **Take the initiative.** Demonstrate your energy, drive and decisiveness, but don't try to run the whole show yourself. Choose colleagues to whom you can delegate tasks with confidence.
- **Upgrade your skills.** Perhaps your employer will pay for additional management or technical training you could use.

● **Pinpoint something enjoyable in every task you undertake.**

● **Be amiable.** Try to show a sense of humor (particularly about yourself) and attempt to draw people to you. In stressful times, these people can be valuable friends and allies.

● **Try to place more emphasis on mastering a task, and on improving and innovating.** Don't just focus on avoiding failure. You can find your reward in doing a better job. Money should be a symbol of your success, not an end in itself. Start thinking today about what you could be doing tomorrow to develop a better product or service for your employer.

● **Reward yourself.** Pat yourself on the back for completing a task or sticking with a difficult project. Coax yourself along by setting aside time for enjoyable breaks, such as reading a favorite magazine or sleeping in. As you reach milestones along the way, reward yourself with an evening out or a day off. Major projects could be the impetus for larger rewards, like a ski weekend or a trip to the lake.

● **Keep a diary of every achievement you have accomplished or hope to accomplish.** Record your success and desires.

With success also comes a sense of purpose and satisfaction. Completing difficult tasks can be energizing. The exhilaration of achievement and growth will make you feel better about yourself. Soon you will be accomplishing even more difficult tasks.

INNOVATIVENESS

28 or higher: You tend to be an innovator. You like change, and use your imagination to find new ways of doing many kinds of activities, work-related or personal. Shaping fresh, new perspectives about yourself, life and the world around tends to bring you great joy. You are a complex, self-accepting person with many interests. You are generally independent, intuitive and capable of seeing many sides of a problem. To you, routine is boring. You would much rather tread new ground than follow in your colleagues' footsteps.

15 to 27: You may enjoy innovation in your personal life but dislike change in your work routine. Or the opposite may be true; perhaps you are very innovative at work, but conservative at home. To become a Quester, look back over the questionnaire statements and decide which aspects of your personality could use a little creative remodeling. For some ideas, read over the suggestions below.

14 or lower: You probably dislike change. You tend to enjoy the status quo, and prefer the tried-and-true way. If you are satisfied with your life, don't change. But if you want to add more excitement, learn to free and release the creative potential within so that you can express your real self. Learn to bring out the child deep inside of you. Creativity is a quality everyone possesses. Unfortunately, few know how to tap into it. You can live more creatively and intelligently by following the suggestions below. They are aimed at helping you to develop your creativity by quieting, within you, the voices of reason, disbelief, certainty, time. routine and social structures. In their rush to point out the rational and logical, these voices can often drown out your intuitive voice. Experiment. There is no right or wrong. Let ideas suggest others. Devise your own ways of freeing your creativity. But, remember, transformation doesn't happen overnight. Be prepared to give the process time. To release your creative blocks, try the following experiments:

● **Hurricane Thinking.** Suppose you had to give a talk or write a paper about Cape Cod or any place you choose. First, write Cape Cod in the center of a piece of paper and circle it. This is the eye of the hurricane. Now, write down the first thoughts that come to mind. Place these somewhere around the eye, or main topic. If this process generates related ideas, jot these down close to the parent thought. Draw lines to connect these related ideas. Should a completely unrelated association come to mind, record it on the opposite corner of the page. See if this new idea will produce offspring as well. Continue this process until the page is filled with major points swirling around the calm eye of Cape Cod. What is important in this exercise is not to evaluate your ideas, but to write down all of them that come to mind. Let your mind roam freely to produce as many ideas as possible. Now you will need to organize your cluster of ideas into a formal presentation. Link them up or circle them with different colored pencils to see where they logically belong. What sequences seem most appropriate? Extend Hurricane Thinking throughout your personal and career life. Be on the alert to those "crazy ideas" that could be the spark of genius.

● **Make friends with the imp inside you.** Jot down a list of those things that parents or authority figures always warned you about. Be especially conscious of what you went ahead and did any way and succeeded in despite their predictions of failure. Examine the attitudes and beliefs you developed as a result of these early teachings. Consider how, given your age and circumstances, these may no longer be appropriate. Admonitions such as, "Never question authority", "Boys don't cry", "Never eat in bed", or "Save for a rainy day" may have been useful at one time in your life but do they really apply today? Examining long-held attitudes and beliefs, particularly those that stifle creativity and change, can open you to new ways of being. No one is encouraging you to throw socially-acceptable behavior to the wind, but perhaps it is time you determined which attitudes and values are crucial to your current lifestyle — and which may be cramping your innovativeness.

● **Face-to-face.** Select two opposing tensions in your life. They may be two contradictory urges or feelings, incompatible goals, two roles you are required to play, perhaps even two duties or responsibilities that conflict with each other. Examples are: Independence vs. dependence; career vs. family life; male vs. female; freedom vs. security; friendship vs. solitude. Next, write down all the characteristics associated with each tension. Eliminate those that are shared by both. Then evaluate the remaining dissimilarities. These are the truly opposing forces in your personality. Explore your creativity. How can these contradictions be resolved? How can these tensions be allied? Keep in mind that there is often strength in diversity, but give some serious thought to how you can lessen some of the tension involved in the opposing forces in your life.

● **Other suggestions.** Learn how to accept and process criticism from your boss, clients, employers, friends or family members without becoming defensive and angry. Be open to new information about yourself. Play the devil's advocate by arguing the opposite side. Experiment more. Start with a new restaurant; order a dish you never tried before. Make your relationship more creative by surprising your partner with a small gift or favorite meal. Don't wait for a special occasion. Read an unusual book. Give those science fiction books you've been reading for the past eight years a rest and pick up an historical novel or pop psychology bestseller. As you become more comfortable with adding unusual touches to your life, you will find life will become more fun and rewarding.

ANDROGYNY

60 or higher: People who score 60 or higher on androgyny closely resemble Questers. If you are one, you tend to possess the best of male and female strengths. Regardless of your gender and depending on the situation, you can be both nurturing and assertive, competitive and cooperative, confident and tender. You are tolerant, broadminded, innovative, autonomous and free from stereotyped thinking. You have probably selected an occupation and lifestyle that suits you and feels comfortable. You don't consider your work to be either a man's or a woman's job.

35-59: You tend to have mixed feelings about what is appropriate for men and women. While you may tolerate some androgynous behavior, you may be more traditional about what constitutes acceptable gender-role standards. Back up. See which of your attitudes and behavior are androgynous and which are traditional. Were the statements that you scored low on related to assertiveness, achievement, confidence, intimacy or to traditional beliefs and values about what constitutes appropriate male and female behaviors? As you become more aware of your feelings, attitudes and behavior, you can take the first steps to becoming a Quester.

30 or lower: Do you have very traditional views about what is appropriate behavior for men and women? Chances are you attained 30 or less. A score in this range indicates you were low on one or more of the other Quester characteristics such as intimacy, confidence, achievement or growth. It can also indicate rigid ideas about gender roles that could hurt your health. The energy you are expending trying to deal with this conflict is incredible. Gender-role attitudes and behavior are learned responses that can also be unlearned. If you really want to change, take one step at a time. Read over the suggestions offered through these sections and see where you can broaden your mind to free yourself from preconceived notions about yourself and others. Learn to accommodate other people's values rights, feelings and perceptions. Being open-minded demands the ability to listen, to respond, to interact with others, to be free of the constraint of imposing value judgments on people. You might try developing this quality by becoming more empathetic toward your spouse or partner. Empathy is the ability to get into the other person's feelings and experiences. It requires being able to sympathize with their feelings (without getting your own bound up in the jumble of emotions). Try to put yourself in the other person's place. Would you want to do the dishes every day? Ask your partner how he or she feels about those household tasks they may be performing out of an outdated notion about men's and women's roles. If you are a man, offer to take some of the household chores off your partner's hands. Then try to understand her feelings about other aspects of her life. Women may want to try being more assertive, learning to say what they mean and feel without being offensive. Learn to be yourself. Practice being assertive first in situations which feel less threatening, such as with family and friends. For example, tell that aunt who plans a three-week visit that a weekend visit would be better for everyone. Test your new assertive behavior at home and at work. With practice and time, you'll feel more comfortable.

RISK

50 or higher: Like most Questers, people who score 50 or higher tend to enjoy taking risks. You are also autonomous, you like challenge, are confident, flexible and given to seeking out new experiences.

26-49: Potential Questers tend to score between 26 and 49. The higher your score, the more you resemble the Questers. You may be open to new experiences in some areas of your life, but overly organized or rigid in others. Or you may be reluctant to risk because of family commitments. Becoming a Quester requires determining what changes can help you to become more risk-oriented.

25 or lower: You are definitely not a risk taker. You prefer a secure, well-ordered lifestyle. You don't like ambiguity or trying out new things. It may be that you take fewer risks than you should because you misunderstand the meaning of risk. Risk-taking is not a sink-or-swim, do-or-die activity. Failure is only the beginning of growth, not the beginning of the end. Failure can be the impetus to move on to bigger, even better projects, jobs or relationships. If you are content with your lifestyle, then enjoy it. But if you want to grow and to develop to your fullest potential, you will have to make some changes. You must learn to be a little more flexible and to take planned risks. Make small changes first. Experiment with a different hairstyle. Men might try growing a moustache or beard. At work, offer suggestions about better ways of tackling a job. Change your daily routine. Take a bath instead of a shower, for example. When you feel you are ready to take a bigger risk, such as with your career, carefully read Chapters Eight and Nine to learn how the Questers do it.

Increasing your ability to take risks requires not only the desire to risk, but also attention to some do's and don'ts. Do have a goal. A risk without a clear purpose can backfire. Do focus on things you can change. Have positive expectations that you will succeed. Complete your homework. Ask questions. Investigate the risks. Do know the pros and cons and all of the choices. Don't be unrealistic. Figure out what your best effort will be, then aim for that. Once you have all the facts, act decisively. Remember, the first risk is always the most difficult. Taking risks gets easier each time.

Before you begin your adventure in risk-taking, try this fantasy risk exercise. On a sheet of paper, write your answers to the following:

1.   Think of an important risk that you would like to take soon, something that is within your control but that you are afraid to initiate.

2.   What appeals to you about taking the risk? What would you gain from it? (Be both objective and subjective about your response. That is, take into account, economic, family and other realities as well as your thoughts and feelings.)

3.   What is frightening about this risk? What holds you back from taking it? What do you stand to lose?

4.   What's the worst thing that could happen if it turned out badly?

5.   If the worst thing happened, then what would you do?

6.   If you need information to pursue this risk, where could you go for it?

7.   From whom could you get support?

8.   What could you do to make this less risky? What kind of measures could you build in to make it less urgent? Less irreversible? Less overwhelming?

9.   Suppose you were to break the risk into small steps? What would the first step be? How soon could you take it? What would the second step be? How soon could you take it? Proceed this way through each step.

GROWTH

52 or higher: You know and accept yourself. You tend to seek growth in both your personal and professional life by seeking opportunities to develop yourself to the fullest. Your perception of reality is good and you have fairly good tolerance for ambiguity. You can accept others as well as yourself. You are natural, spontaneous and innovative. You can also be altruistic. Self-fulfillment and achievement are important motivators for you. When you are no longer growing on the job, you move on to something else that will better satisfy your needs for challenge, autonomy, use of your talents and self-expression. You tend to possess most of the other Quester qualities.

26-51: You tend to be a potential Quester. You may enjoy challenge and be open to new experiences, but perhaps you can't take criticism. Or you may fear failure and have difficulty accepting your own limits. Look over the questions again and note where you picked up low scores. If you want to become a Quester, you must decide what you are prepared to do differently.

25 or lower: You probably like a very secure life with a not-too-difficult job. You may lack confidence, fear failure and be overly concerned with others' opinions. You don't need to change, but if you want to start small with easily-accomplished tasks, try the following suggestions:

● **Take a course in a subject you want to learn more about.** You can often get new perspectives or skills which may help you change your life. Learn how to learn, how to acquire new information and translate that information into constructive experiences. Whatever course you choose, whether it be assertiveness training or a master's degree in business administration, choose it because you are interested in it and believe it will help you achieve your goals.

● **Become more creative.** Take up painting, writing, macrame, gourmet cooking, photography, woodworking or carpentry. Creative expression helps you grow by giving you ready evidence of your creativity that can inspire you on to even greater performance.

● **Accept and encourage constructive criticism.** Don't take criticism too personally. Listen to what your critics are saying and then ask what to do differently. If you think the criticism is unfair, say so, but only after you hear out your critic. Especially helpful is criticism from people who have nothing to gain, and possibly something to lose, by giving you feedback.

● **Learn how to accept compliments.** Accept well-meaning remarks about your appearance or ability with grace and a simple "Thank you". Trust that the compliment is sincere.

● **De-personalize failure.** You don't have to score A in every subject. Failure is just a stage in becoming more fully you and a part of the world, a step towards, not away from growth. Failing at something means that you at least tried. Next time, you may succeed.

● **Develop a sense of humor.** Put some distance between yourself and your problems by thinking about how they will look 10 years from now. Learn to laugh at yourself.

● **Review the suggestions offered under confidence, autonomy, achievement, innovativeness and risk.** No matter what your score in these sections, the suggestions can be helpful.

● **Be persistent.** Once you have decided on a goal, put yourself into your positive thinking gear. Be determined enough to achieve your goal, but flexible enough to change directions if required. Don't stubbornly cling to habits, actions or beliefs that are damaging to your personal or professional life.

ARE YOU A POTENTIAL QUESTER?

If you agreed with statements 12, 24, 48 and 60, disagreed with statements 36, 72, 84, 96 and 108, and scored in the middle range or higher for most of the other personality characteristics discussed in the preceding pages, then you are definitely a potential

Quester. Potential Questers possess some Quester characteristics, but are usually Traditionalists who are engaged in some serious stock-taking, are shifting their attitudes, values and goals and are thinking about leaving dissatisfying jobs to become Questers. Read over these statements again. They might provide you with some additional insights into yourself and your feelings about your position.

PUTTING IT ALL TOGETHER

330 or higher: The higher your overall score, the more closely you resemble the Questers. A score of 330 or more indicates you are a Quester. You attained high scores on the personality characteristics of intimacy, self-confidence, purpose, autonomy, achievement, innovativeness, androgyny, risk and growth. You should also have attained high scores on *The Job Satisfaction Questionnaire* and *The Job Involvement Questionnaire*.

135 to 329: You are a potential Quester (particularly if you agreed with statements 12, 24, 48 and 60, and disagreed with statements 36, 72, 84, 96 and 108). You may have scored high on some Quester characteristics and low on others, or you may have scored in the middle range on all of them. Low scores on *The Job Satisfaction Questionnaire* and *The Job Involvement Questionnaire* and a high score on the *Burnout Questionnaire* indicate that, for your physical and mental health, you should seriously consider a job change. Chapters Eight and Nine should give you some ideas about how to accomplish this. The list of Suggested Readings contains a number of good books on job search techniques.

134 or lower: You are a confirmed Traditionalist, or at least for now. High overall scores on *The Job Satisfaction Questionnaire* indicate that you are probably a happy Traditionalist who is satisfied with your job. If your scores are low, you should think about changing your position or another component of your life. This book and good counseling should help you accomplish this.

You alone are responsible for your growth. You have enormous power to change who you are and what happens to you. Learn to use it slowly. Discard those old habits that are holding you back, like belittling yourself or taking unnecessary precautions. And if the tests you have just taken have shown you are either a Quester or a potential Quester, don't ignore that discovery. Dare to take the next step.

4: *Career change: up – down – sideways*

What makes the Questers different? Unlike most people, they have learned to ask themselves such questions as "What do I want out of life? What should I do next?" They have learned to do a little investigation into their needs and values. They get answers and then get going. Sound impossible in today's job market? Not so. Many Questers have learned you can't put a price tag on happiness. They understand that they alone are responsible for their career satisfaction and marketability. Most Questers have learned to monitor their careers and when staleness starts to set in, to look for new opportunities. By remaining open to alternatives, they are enhancing their ability to survive in tough job markets. You can do that, too.

Questers tend to take care of their careers by evaluating their development, tuning into their feelings and being aware of new opportunities. Questers see their careers as an ongoing opportunity for personal and professional growth. Their next career assignment is usually lined up while they still have a job, not while they are faced with the many stresses of being out of work. Life is like a tree that branches out before them. The assumption that an implicit social contract guaranteeing their work, status and income comes with the job just isn't realistic to Questers. Their careers are one long quest for more satisfying options.

Are you one of these people?

Finding excitement and satisfaction in a career requires understanding yourself — your needs, values and skills. You may enjoy a variety of career directions in the same occupation, or want to explore different occupations, or even work for yourself. Questers feel free to move up or down the career ladder. What matters is not what others think of your career direction, or what is socially acceptable, but what feels right for you.

Life crises often influence the direction of your career. Questers may have been through a divorce or experienced a death in the family, the loss of a job, job dissatisfaction, frustration with a boss, or even the desire for financial independence. Major or minor, these "determining events" usually lead them to reassess their lives. Events like these can be the catalysts for change.

Because of the influence of past generations, who usually trained for one occupation for life and stayed in it, many people. today are not prepared for the idea of change. Therefore, we fear change. But, today, career possibilities are almost endless. Not only are many traditional occupations still open but opportunities are also available in emerging occupations. Running your own business is yet another option. Just stop and think about it. The world is full of opportunities.

SAME OCCUPATIONAL FIELD

Almost 60 percent of Questers who change jobs stay in the same occupational field. Staying in a job that has a similar psychological climate, they move on to different work environments that provide them with a change, opportunities to grow, to learn something new, to try something different, to achieve greater challenge, responsibility or authority, to make a greater contribution to humankind. Moving on to a new position in the same field can be accomplished in many different ways. You could go from elementary school teacher to special education teacher to school librarian or art teacher. Or, you could progress from rehabilitation counselor to social worker to college placement officer. Or how about from bank manager to hotel manager to hospital manager? Even from bookkeeper to clerical supervisor to collection clerk. Why not from surgical nurse to special duty nurse to pediatric nurse? People who stay in the same field often rise to positions of greater responsibility, authority and autonomy, such as manager of a larger bank or hotel. With each move, they gain broader knowledge and experience. Questers, who found new satisfaction and success in the same occupational fields, often have fascinating stories to tell.

Helen, a physician, is a Quester who has found satisfaction by changing the focus of her attention in her original profession. At 50, still slim and youthful-looking, Helen is looking for answers to the mysteries of human pain. As head of her city's first palliative care unit, a hospice for the terminally ill, her quiet influence extends far beyond the hospital's walls. Helen has true compassion.

She has a tremendous amount of medical training, kindness, energy and consideration for her patients. She listens and cares.

Caring for and helping people was Helen's goal when, fresh from a nursing program, she entered medical school in England. Her career was interrupted only once. At 30, she quit to have two children. Three years later, in 1968, Helen moved with her husband and children to the United States. For seven years, she practiced family medicine in a mid-western city. Then, at 40, hoping to learn more so she could better help her patients, she returned to school for specialized training in obstetrics and gynecology. As a woman and a mother, Helen already understood many of the concerns of her female patients. She enjoyed her work, and her patients enjoyed her care.

But Helen's true professional calling didn't become evident until she helplessly watched a dying cancer victim writhe in agony while giving birth. Helpless and indignant, Helen became determined to see that terminal patients died in peace and dignity. Through the years, she gained a reputation for dealing sensitively with dying patients and their families. She also fought doggedly for the establishment of a palliative care unit at her hospital. Helen had the ability and tenacity to see her ideas through. It wasn't always clear sailing. While financial problems and uncertain government funding threatened the establishment of the unit, she continued to be optimistic. Now, in addition to heading the palliative care unit, she is conducting research into pain control. To promote palliative care, Helen schedules speaking engagements at least once a week. She also works actively to fulfill her patients' final wishes.

Helen changed jobs because she wanted to serve her patients better. She has all the qualities of a good physician: highly dedicated, selfless and self-disciplined. She is also healthy and can stand the pressure of working long days and nights, frequently on call. Helen's work gives her a great deal of satisfaction. In fact, her life is her work, although she also enjoys her family, her regular swims, cooking and gardening. Helen has combined her career and family responsibilities in an enjoyable, rewarding lifestyle.

Len is another Quester who has changed jobs several times in the same occupational field. As a business administration student, Len chose marketing. "It was a dynamic field, not routine. I thought it would be a challenge." Marketing research helps companies make decisions by determining what motivates consumers to buy a company's products, how and when products are used and how much people are willing to pay.

Len is 55 now, and he still finds marketing challenging. By now, he's had several positions in the field. His first was with a large consumer food products corporation. He took it because he wanted to get experience, learn about corporate life and apply his knowledge. "I learned a lot about these things," Len remembers. "I also developed greater confidence and became better at speaking up about my ideas." Five years later, Len moved on. He had mastered the job. Now, ready to explore other products and markets, he joined a large industrial marketing firm and stayed for 14 years. He was moved around sufficiently within the company so he continued to enjoy both new challenges and the opportunity for career growth. During the first four years, Len researched different products in the mid-west region. Then, he was sent to a foreign country for four years to open a marketing division. Heading up a training and consulting division in the United States followed that. Len liked his job but six years later he was ready to move again. He was no longer growing and the work had lost its challenge. If Len had stayed with the company, he might have been given the responsibility of heading a larger division. But the economy was uncertain and he would have had to wait his turn. Len decided not to wait. He was determined to take charge of his own career.

Doing so meant being responsible. Len knew he had to line up a new job before he could leave. That new job turned out to be general manager and marketing specialist for a medium-sized information systems firm. This time, Len was feeling the itch again after just four years. The fact he didn't agree with the philosophies of the other managers aided his decision. Len recalls being extremely unhappy; his co-workers were uncooperative and seldom agreed with him.

His next move was to his current position, general manager of special products for a medium-sized medical instruments distribution company. The work was exciting. Most important, he was in tune with the philosophies and values of the other senior managers. Len has been with the company for four years now and he still finds the work challenging. If he could start over, would he choose marketing again? "Very definitely!" Len asserts. "It's exciting and challenging."

That attitude explains why Len has been so successful in marketing. Both creative and detail-minded, he is well-suited to research. Len can see the big picture of shifting economic and social trends, political realities and changing lifestyles. He also has the right temperament to cope with competition, uncertainty, pressure, constant change and long hours. Above all, he is extroverted and amiable. Colleagues get along well with him.

Len's personality is what makes him a good marketing person. He knows from experience that many of the most creative and lucrative positions in marketing are the least secure. Being responsible for important marketing decisions leaves him open to both praise and blame. As he says, "In parts of our business, you aren't considered to be good if you haven't been fired at least once. Because, if you haven't been fired, you haven't had the guts to take the risks necessary to be successful." For talented, energetic and creative Questers like Len, marketing is a good career choice.

Zwirner began university in an architecture program. By the third year, he had switched to civil engineering. It seemed more practical. He's glad he did. Today, Zwirner is a structural engineer with a California consulting firm specializing in earthquake engineering. He analyzes plans of construction engineers and inspects building projects. He loves the challenge and creativity.

Zwirner held two other civil engineering positions before he joined his present employer. His first job was with a state department as a transportation engineer, planning, constructing and maintaining roads, bridges and airports. That position lasted seven years until he could no longer grow on the job. Then he accepted a job in hydraulic engineering. He designed and supervised the construction of artificial canals and reservoirs and directed water-control projects. His second job also lasted seven years. When the challenge was gone again, he moved to the west coast to specialize in soil research and earthquake engineering. What does Zwirner want to do in the future? "Perhaps become a freelance consultant or learn more about environmental pollution control," he says. "I'm keeping my options open." Zwirner does know that he wants to stay in civil and structural engineering. "I find it very creative. I enjoy seeing my work come to life."

Many Questers have turned hobbies and interests into rewarding careers. At 31, *Linda* switched gears to turn her interest in carpentry into a full-time occupation. Linda's job as an interior designer had already given her an entry into carpentry skills. But successful as she was, she found herself much more fascinated by the carpenters' work than by her own. She began to dabble. First, she put up a deck and helped friends and neighbors with odd jobs. Then, four years ago, pregnant with her second daughter, Linda got her first big carpentry job. The new addition to her family required a new addition to her home. As she and her husband worked on building an extra room, carpentry got into her blood. Soon, she was dreaming of building an entire house. Linda confided her wish to a neighbor. "I used to dream of things I wanted to do when I was young, too," he said, "but I didn't do them and now I can't."

Suddenly, Linda was seeing carpentry in a whole new way. Why should she, like her neighbor, just dream of the things she wanted to do? Why not do them?

Determined to find a more satisfying occupation, Linda enrolled in a carpentry program. Coping with the demands of the program was easier than coping with the resistance she met from well-meaning but dubious relatives and some bigoted union officials. "First, I had to fight with my husband and my mother-in-law. All I heard was, 'You should be home with your daughters.' But the more I fought, the more I knew what I wanted," says Linda. Getting accepted into the Union Brotherhood of Carpenters and Joiners of America was another hurdle. Fortunately, a senior administrator of the apprenticeship program helped Linda get a job with a construction company as an apprentice carpenter. Linda is now happily spending her days putting up walls, installing sheetrock and framing doors. Two nights a week, she also goes to school to complete her training as a journeyman carpenter. And, she still manages to find the time to be with her five- and seven-year-old daughters and her husband.

Linda's pay is good but the work is physically demanding. She ached all over for three months after starting her new job. "One day, we had to unload a whole truckload of sheetrock in the rain," she says. "I asked myself, 'Do I really want to do this?' " Even then, the answer was "Yes!" Linda's mother and mother-in-law still don't approve of her occupation but her husband now understands. He says she's more active and vibrant.

Linda is happy because she's working in a job she enjoys. Yet carpentry isn't completely different from interior design. Both are in the technical-crafts field and are suited to Linda's interests. Without changing occupational fields, Linda has managed to find a more satisfying and rewarding occupation.

Nick went from artist to art therapist. He began as a sculptor and artist, struggling to discover himself. He followed that with a teaching stint in a local high school. When he was 31, he realized art therapy could actually help people suffering from emotional or social disturbances, physical handicaps or neurological impairments. He entered a two-year graduate program and then created his own job by telling state prison officials about the benefits of art therapy. He's elated about the new direction his career has taken.

DIFFERENT OCCUPATIONAL FIELD

About 35 percent of job changers move to an entirely different occupational field. These adults move to jobs which have a different psychological climate and often require different temperaments, needs, values, interests and abilities. They usually change for one of two reasons. Some discover a poor match between their personality characteristics (such as interests, needs, values and abilities) and the requirements of their initial occupation. Others discover they have outgrown their first occupational choice. Their beliefs, or life experiences, which were initially compatible, have changed. Many, but not all, Questers who move to a different occupational field have prepared for their moves by taking upgrading or retraining, on-the-job training or by researching and reading.

THE JOB NO LONGER FITS

Some Questers have jobs that no longer fit their developing personalities and goals. Their first jobs were often chosen wisely and carefully. They were usually well-suited to their positions and were quite successful. But somewhere, over the years, they realized they had outgrown their initial choices.

Lynne became dissatisfied with her childhood career choice as she neared 30. As a little girl, Lynne's dream was to be a librarian. Soon after university, she landed a job as a high school librarian. "I always questioned whether this field was a lifelong occupation but I really never assessed my career goals," she recalls. Seven years later, at 29, Lynne realized she had to make a change. "It was like the seven-year itch," she says. Watching a play at a local theatre, she was struck by the protagonist's rhetorical question, "What am I afraid of?" She realized she had to answer that question, too.

She took a leave of absence. Sometime during that year, she discovered the intrigue of the stock exchange. After investing her money for several years, she was ready to learn more. "When I read *The Wall Street Journal* or *Business Week*, I felt like I was reading a foreign language. But, at the same time, the field fascinated me." Lynne signed up for a securities course, but began to wonder if there was an entry point for her in what was, in 1981, a male-dominated field. The idea of being in securities scared her somewhat. She wasn't used to taking risks. After working in a job with so much certainty, making such a radical move seemed difficult. "So I asked myself what could stop me. Fear of failure or of trying something new? What did I really have to fear?"

Her first step was to talk to the brokers who had invested her money. By 1982, she was ready to start work as a rookie stock-broker. "I knew I had to cross the line and give up security for growth," she reflects. While Lynne had enjoyed being a librarian, neither the routine nor working with teenagers really interested her anymore. These days, she fits a new baby and a job into a life-style that is "exciting and stimulating." Lynne's new position is well-suited to her shift in needs, values and goals. Like many successful brokers, Lynne is thriving on the excitement, tension and more-than-moderate dose of uncertainty.

Learning to be a stockbroker isn't the only lesson Lynne mastered. She has learned to re-evaluate her career choices regularly. She's thinking about her future, now. "Maybe there is a third occupation out there for me, too. When you find out what you're afraid of, you can overcome anything."

Ed also had difficulty making the switch to a different occupational field. As a young boy, Ed thought he had his life carefully mapped out. Because he loved mechanics, deciding on an occupation wasn't hard. After high school, he entered a civil engineering program. His first job was with an engineering firm in the midwest. Ed loved his work. But by the fifth year, his tasks began to seem too technical, detailed and narrow. Ed started looking around. Finding a suitable job took almost a year. Hired in the operations department of a manufacturing firm at 31, he spent the next several years working his way up to head of his division. Ed liked the work but not the new general manager. Their values and beliefs on policies and procedures just weren't compatible. Determined to leave before he was demoted or fired, Ed, now 42, again started looking around.

Opportunities at Ed's managerial level weren't plentiful. Ed and his family liked the city they had lived in for so many years. Rather than move, he began to consider a different line of work. Soul searching and research led him to real estate. The market was tight and Ed knew he would have to take a cut in pay, but his children were self-sufficient and his wife was considering a part-time job. Armed with a clear option, Ed resigned, took a short real estate course and joined a medium-sized real estate firm. He's happy he did. "I enjoy making a sale, not so much for the money, but because I get a kick out of pleasing my customers," he says.

POOR FIRST CHOICE

While some Questers discover they have grown beyond the challenges of their first occupational choices, others were never suited to their first occupations. Many plunged into jobs without assessing their own personalities, the job requirements, or the work environments they had selected. Making wise occupational choices requires time and understanding.

Bert is a good example. He went directly from high school to a university science program. He had always enjoyed science, and particularly research, so why not? Hired as a lab assistant while still in his master's program, Bert discovered a new interest, teaching. So, with a year of education behind him, he set off to teach science to high school seniors. To his surprise, Bert discovered he really didn't like teaching. "I didn't like policing and being a baby-sitter to students who didn't want to learn," he recalls. With a wife and young child to support, he could hardly resign. But he could bide his time while he searched for a more suitable occupation. He applied to a pharmacy program and was accepted but after further thought, he decided he wasn't suited. Then he took some night courses in real estate, "but it really didn't appeal to me." Frustrated, Bert decided to try to make a go of teaching. Just when he was about ready to give up, Bert found a new interest. He enrolled in a computer programming course. Bert suddenly realized he had found what he wanted to do with the rest of his life. Excited now, he studied by night and taught by day while he saved furiously for the day when he could study full-time. Two years later, with diploma in hand, Bert snapped up an offer from a small oil company to become a computer analyst. Within a year, he was working for a bigger company at a higher salary. His new position offered challenge, learning opportunities and a chance to keep ahead of the computer programming field. "I put up with the red tape because my job is challenging, never boring and there's always something new to learn," says Bert.

Surprisingly, Bert has also successfully managed to combine his new occupation with his old one. Teaching computer programming to adults helped him realize that he really did enjoy teaching — in situations where students wanted to learn. Now 41, Bert is very satisfied with his job, his lifestyle and his family. But you can be sure that when his job loses its challenge, Bert will once again be searching for a new position.

Jean discovered that dissatisfaction with a job exacts a high toll. Her break was more abrupt than Bert's. One day, Jean walked into her boss's office and quit her accounting and secretarial job on the spot. Jean knew career counselors usually advise against quitting one job before lining up another but she also knew she'd never be motivated to change directions if she held on to a steady paycheck. "One day I thought, 'I'm not going to sit here grumbling anymore.

I'm going to do something about it.'"

Jean spent the next 16 months discovering what her talents and interests really were and then searched for a job where she could use them. Her first step was to sign up at a temporary employment agency so she could continue to support herself. Then she went to the career counseling center at the local university. A battery of tests and inventories turned up a big surprise. Jean's real aptitude wasn't in accounting; it was in language. She had always enjoyed writing but had no idea her skills were so advanced. This discovery was a real ego boost. But Jean still didn't know what she wanted to do. While she floundered, temporary jobs were leading her from typing pool to typing pool. Discouraged, she complained to the agency and asked for proofreading or editing assignments. The agency was reluctant to send her for a job in which she had no experience. "I can read, so I can proofread," Jean insisted. Her determination paid off. A two-week proofreading stint led to an eight-month editing assignment. Jean loved it.

At the suggestion of a friend, she participated in a workshop on interviewing and job searching. She also got assistance with her resume. Finally, Jean made her first contact with an aerospace firm. Although her lack of a college degree was a handicap, her persistence got her an interview and an opportunity to take an editing test. She passed with impressive skill, but it was several months, and 40 calls later, before she got the job.

That was three years ago. With a recent promotion to technical editor, Jean doesn't doubt for a minute that her efforts were worthwhile. "I'm getting paid for doing something I enjoy," she says with a smile.

RE-ENTRY WOMEN

Homemakers are another group who often change occupational fields when they re-enter the work force. A few, like *Edie*, become Questers. Edie graduated from a university on the west coast with a bachelor of science degree. Her first journey into the work force was as a microbiology researcher. Shortly after her marriage five years later, she retired to raise children, run a house and do volunteer work. Twenty years later, the marriage was over, her children were growing up, and Edie was faced with the task of finding a satisfying occupation that would also support her and three teenagers. She had to earn money, but she wanted more than just a salary. She wanted an exciting, people-oriented job. "Unfortunately, like many women, I thought I didn't have the right to please my-self." At a women's career counseling center, Edie found encouragement to complete a master's degree in social work. At first, she was terrified at the prospect. "How would I support myself and my kids? What if I failed? How could I compete with younger people? Who would organize my family? What kind of a job could I get?"

Many married women who return to school or work have similar feelings and fears. Edie overcame hers. With child support from her ex-husband, a student loan and a part-time job as a sales clerk, she made it. Today, two years after graduation, Edie is doing excellent work as the executive director of a family social services bureau. She got the job because she had the personality, skills, experience and motivation to succeed. Some of those skills and experiences were learned as a homemaker and volunteer. A social work degree gave her the rest. Had Edie tried to re-enter research, she would have been bored. Instead, she is fulfilled.

FOLLOW YOUR DREAMS

Finding the right occupation is the key to success and enjoyment in your work. You shouldn't overlook the dreams of your childhood when you are contemplating an occupational move. But it isn't always easy to follow your dreams. Look at Ernie.

A talented singer in high school, *Ernie* grabbed the spotlight year after year at every musical festival. He loved singing and acting, but when it came time to decide on an occupation, he listened not to his heart but to his parents' advice. They wanted him to seek a secure occupation, like law. For nine years, Ernie practiced law, and didn't really mind it, but singing was still his first love. Every spare moment was spent singing in a nightclub production put on by a local group in his west coast hometown. Then it happened. One morning, as Ernie rose to go to work, he realized he no longer wanted to practice law. Within two months, Ernie was in New York taking singing and acting lessons. The money he had saved from practicing law and from singing in nightclubs helped finance lessons. Two years later, Ernie has landed his first small part in a television series. Will he make it big? Only time will tell. But, in the meantime, he is doing what he enjoys. He gave his boyhood dream a chance.

STRESS SYMPTOMS

A number of adults not suited to their original occupational choice develop stress symptoms. Some of these individuals became Questers.

Ted, a 48-year-old sales manager, had long been dissatisfied with his work. He stayed because he gradually became convinced he couldn't afford to switch jobs. "To be truthful, I was afraid to," he says. Suddenly, he developed a very strange illness. Abnormal lumps formed all over his body. Ted's doctor could find no physical cause for his malady, but was wise enough to refer him to a psychologist. Testing and career counseling revealed that Ted was more suited to literary arts than sales. He decided to pursue a library science degree although history also interested him. Returning to school was intimidating, but a student bursary and his savings saw Ted through. Now 53, he has been working as a librarian for two years. He loves his work and his health "has never been better." Ted is also researching and writing an historical novel. He's beginning to sound a lot like a Quester.

Ray developed ulcers when he switched from one civil engineering job to another. Career counseling and testing finally pointed out that he was in the wrong occupation. Ray had an average aptitude for engineering but little real interest. He also had highly-developed literary, artistic and creative abilities, however, which made him well-suited to advertising. The stresses he faces now as creative director of an advertising agency are far greater than any he faced as an engineer, but his ulcers are under control because, for Ray, it's positive stress.

RUNNING YOUR OWN BUSINESS

What do some Questers do when they find there is no ready-made place in the market for their skills? They go into business for themselves. Approximately one third of the Questers in my study established their own businesses. They seemed to be willing to go small in order to be in control of their lives and their careers.

Quester entrepreneurs typify the best spirit of American tradition. Inventive, bold, resolute, eager to meet the challenges that confront them, some become quite wealthy. Others find satisfaction in doing a job well. They prove that it still is possible for someone with a dream to succeed. Entrepreneurial Questers have very strong needs for autonomy and independence. Many are non-conformists who picture themselves as individualists and free thinkers. Resenting regimentation, they choose the business world to satisfy their needs. Their talents are very broad, and they have a great desire for variety and flexibility. More than any other type of Questers, they are not afraid to take chances. Their ultimate satisfaction comes from seeing something they have created grow and develop; money is secondary. Entrepreneurial Questers have the perseverance, self-discipline, energy and stamina necessary to work 12-hour days and forego weekends and holidays. Many are workaholics. They take it for granted that one of the rewards of their efforts will be financial independence. Entrepreneurial Questers get along with people. Not only do they have to motivate people who work for them, but they also have to solicit the support of customers and clients. This they do with customary skill.

BUSINESS CONDUCTED FROM THE HOME

Some Questers operate their businesses from homes. Here is what they have to say about it.

Eleanor started a children's discount clothing boutique because she needed the money. A single parent with two young children to support, she returned to work after her divorce by selling clothing as a manufacturer's representative, a job she had held before her children were born. But housekeepers' salaries, upkeep on her house and commuting expenses left little from her paycheck. And her 10-hour workday (including four hours of daily travel just to reach the center of her large midwestern city) was a strain on both Eleanor and her children. When she tried to give needed time to her children, she was fired. Sometime during the six months that she collected unemployment benefits, Eleanor decided to start her own business. The market for children's clothing was good, she had contacts in the fashion industry from previous jobs and she wanted to be home with her children. The result was a discount children's clothing boutique in her basement.

"For the first time in my life," she says, "I'm independent. I'm available for my children, can go to the school play, take them on holidays, and, because I'm in a child-oriented business, it's okay for them to be here in the background when I'm talking on the phone with suppliers or customers." In the first year, the discount business broke even. Eleanor credits much of her success to her marketing strategy. By dressing her children up in the clothing she sells, Eleanor acquires new customers from among friends and mothers of classmates. Now thinking of expanding her boutique into a full retail store, Eleanor is talking like a Quester when she says: "Everyone dreams of having a successful business — I know I can do it."

Ross, at 34, seemed a success. An accountant moving rapidly up the career ladder in a large firm for the past eight years, he seemed to have a promising future. But Ross was bored with working with numbers. He really wanted to work with his hands. Soon, Ross decided to turn his hobby into his occupation. He started taking pottery courses during the evenings. He loved it. He was also very talented. At first, Ross' wife wasn't too pleased to hear about his plans and hopes. With two children to support and bills to pay, the couple had some heavy responsibilities. But she could see that his dissatisfaction was making Ross irritable and lethargic. So, they decided to compromise. She took a part-time job to help pay the bills, and Ross stayed on part-time with the accounting firm. The rest of his time was devoted to pottery. Ross turned his basement into a workshop, bought a potter's wheel and built a walk-in kiln in his backyard.

Four years later, Ross is working full-time as a potter. Using his accounting skill to keep the books in order, Ross is selling his wares to specialty shops, galleries, department stores and private clients. His work is in so much demand that he works long hours just to fill the orders. But he doesn't mind. He's happy with his work and lifestyle. His relationship with his wife and children is better, too. Even though he is busy, Ross has more quality time to spend with them. Everyone appreciates the changes.

BUSINESS CONDUCTED IN THE COMMUNITY

Other businesses have taken Questers away from the home. Decorating windows gave *Jennifer* the start she needed to set out on her own. A former occupational therapist, Jennifer went from a window dressing job for a large department store to designing her own furniture. The frustration of trying to find furniture with clean, simple lines led her to create her own designs. The stark, uncluttered lines were so appealing that people soon began to ask about this young designer. From dreaming up eye-catching window displays, she went on to design inspiring show suites for apartment complexes. Soon she was getting commissions for private homes. Today, she not only does freelance designing, but wholesales her ideas to other interior decorators. Her biggest success came while searching for a carpenter. She could hardly believe her luck when she discovered Martin, a top-notch young furniture finisher, and then found he shared a shop with Peter, a first-class cabinet maker. The three have been collaborating ever since.

Melvin demonstrates you can take a calculated risk and win. When political hassles caused Melvin to quit his senior management job, he had $60 in the bank and a wife and two kids to support. Quitting was hardly a spur-of-the-moment decision — Melvin planned his moves — but illness forced him to resign earlier than intended. Determined to market a little-known line of sportswear, Melvin put his convalescence to good use, researching his idea. He even researched bank managers to find out who was the most liberal. Then, putting his idea on paper, Melvin approached the manager he thought would give him the best deal. His next move was to open a store. In four years, Melvin's business has expanded to 14 stores spread across four states and six cities. All smiles, Melvin still can't believe how quickly his idea caught on. He feels as if he's "in Disneyland. It's pure fantasy." Now he's researching a new venture, another specialty line.

INVOLUNTARY CHANGE

Boredom or the desire to do something different aren't the only reasons people start their own businesses. Some are forced to. Being fired or discovering that your skills are no longer in demand can leave a personal business venture as one of the few alternatives to unemployment. You are forced to begin the long process of learning new skills.

Carol headed a learning center at a mid-western university. But when the center closed down, she was forced to find a new job. As she searched, Carol turned a hobby into her sole means of support — operating a catering business from home. "I didn't anticipate what a drastic change it would be to go from Carol, the academic, to Carol, the cook." When the business became too big for her home, she rented space in a large warehouse and hired four assistants. Fortunately for Carol, a bad experience turned into a positive one. She never did return to the academic world.

UP OR DOWN

Up or down? Does it really matter which way you are headed on the organizational career ladder? Not to most Questers. When they change jobs, greater power, prestige or income are seldom the first questions on their minds. What Questers really seek are more satisfying jobs that offer opportunities for personal and professional growth, for service to others, for greater challenge, autonomy and use of their skills. Of course, many do end up with more power, prestige and money. Others don't. They tell us how they perceived their moves.

Don is a quiet, sensitive physician who, at 40, dropped several notches on the career ladder to switch from medicine to education. A caring and successful pediatrician, Don found that after 11 years of being a physician he just wasn't happy anymore. He felt hurt seeing children and adolescents suffer as he stood by, sometimes unable to alleviate their pain. The death of his father a year earlier had made Don realize that life is too short to spend in an occupation you don't enjoy. Despite reminders from colleagues that he had spent thousands of dollars building up his specialty, Don decided to go back to school to study education. Today, Don is in his third year of teaching biology to teenagers. He is still working with adolescents but these adolescents are not sick and suffering. He's discovered that teaching better suits his temperament.

For many, abandoning a medical practice to become a teacher may seem like a drastic drop in career status. But as a newly-emerged Quester, Don is happy with his new occupation and lifestyle, even though he took a substantial pay cut. When Don decides teaching is no longer right for him, he will probably change occupations again. His status on the career ladder will be much less important to him than his health, peace of mind and job satisfaction.

Interestingly enough, occupational prestige studies rank physicians in the top five percentile. Public school teachers, on the other hand, rank between the 25th and 40th percentile, depending on the study. At the bottom are shoe shiners, clothes pressers, waitresses, street sweepers and garbage collectors. But at least two people who moved from a high status profession to the very bottom of the occupational prestige scale are happier today because of it.

Until two years ago, *Dwight* was a lawyer with a prominent New York firm. These days, he can be found decked out in badly-soiled khaki pants and a grimy army jacket. Since last July, Dwight and 35-year-old *Timothy* a former administrative assistant to a senior government official, have been running a garbage removal truck in a town about 80 miles northwest of New York. Unlike many people who have been forced to make drastic career changes because of the recession, they are in a usually unpopular job by choice.

Why did Dwight leave law? Because, as he says, "I was getting pretty bored with being surrounded by so many high-powered lawyers working on legal refinements. It just wasn't challenging anymore and I had to wonder how much value I was really contributing to society. . .I don't want to give the impression that there is more social utility in garbage than in law but I'm satisfied with what I'm doing now. I wasn't before." Dwight and Timothy are intrigued by the possibility of expanding the garbage removal business into garbage disposal and recycling. After eight hours of guiding a nine-ton truck without power steering along the wooded roads that twist around the town, Dwight's body aches all over. "But I don't feel the strain of the long hours as I used to when I worked at the law firm all day."

A year after they bought the garbage removal business. Dwight and his wife, a graduate of a fashionable girls' college, gave up their Manhattan apartment and moved into an average-looking house nearby. Timothy, a bachelor, bought a townhouse. Both have taken substantial pay cuts — Dwight by 40 percent, Timothy by half that. Despite his smaller salary, Dwight says he has much greater peace of mind. "If you're traveling on a super-highway, but going in the wrong direction, you feel insecure. But if you're on a mud road, and it's going the right way, that's security."

That's how Questers differ from ordinary folks. Few move up the career ladder just for prestige or money. Instead, they change jobs for the opportunity to grow and develop in satisfying careers. *Ike*, a high school dropout who became a civil engineer, advanced from a low rung to a high one. But prestige and status were far from his mind when he left his construction job for engineering. Ike just wanted the chance to grow and develop, to use his mind, instead of his hands, to make a living.

THE CHOICE IS YOURS

Would it surprise you to learn that about 80 percent of the workforce is in jobs they don't like, and approximately 50 percent find their work unsatisfying? It shouldn't. You probably know many such people and maybe you are even among them. They're the ones who are exuberant Friday afternoon and depressed Sunday evening.

Having worked up to high-paying, prestigious senior positions, they feel as trapped and miserable as their subordinates. Poor matches between occupations and people cause much stress.

Why do people stay in jobs they hate and find unrewarding? For many, it's fear of change. They find it easier to stay in a comfortable rut and collect the gold watch upon retirement. Unfortunately, while the comfortable lifestyle may be materially rich, it doesn't always reflect what people believe is important in emotional life. Even surrounded with every symbol of the good life, they may be suffering from malaise and deep-rooted dissatisfaction. That malaise sets in because many of us have never been encouraged to stop and ask: "Am I doing what I want?"

Most people are suited to just as many occupations as they are wrong for. Anyone can change to a more suitable job when needs and values change. Even while still employed, you can be planning your escape. Remember, this isn't just a job change. This is your life!

Finding the right organizational fit is important too. Companies' personalities are just as different as people's. Your company's structure may be rigid or relaxed; it may treasure hard work and reliability, or new ideas and flexibility; it may insist on strict adherence to the hierarchy or form committees that include several levels of employees. In any case, checking out a company is just as important as checking out a job.

Deciding how radical a change you want, and what that change requires, is vital before you even begin to make a career shift. You will need to examine your needs, values and interests, as well as any transferable skills you already have. For instance, a minister looking for personnel work may be able to transfer many of the skills he has already developed. Teachers able to talk to people, help them develop and sort out priorities, would probably enjoy personnel work. But an artist who decides to become a banker will need a lot of additional training and may have incompatible needs and interests. The unstructured, free-flowing creative skills of the artist don't usually translate into the analytical, highly-structured skills required of a banker. Before leaving a job or investing time or money in further education, think over your career change carefully. Give yourself time to make a well-reasoned decision. Find out if you are, in fact, a Quester. Find out if you could become one.

5: *The career cycle meets the life cycle*

LIFE CYCLE BASICS

Adulthood is not a plateau. It is time of change. Much recent research describes adult growth and development as a cycle that follows an underlying, universal path. Many influences along the way may shape this course. They may produce alternate routes or detours, they may speed up or slow down the timetable, or they may stop the developmental journey altogether. As long as you live, this journey continues, following a basic sequence of stages, issues and concerns. This is called life cycle theory and it assumes you will pass through these stages as long as you are developing. It cannot predict how you will deal with them.

Your personality or identity is formed by many external and internal influences. Your culture, job, social class, family, interpersonal relationships, leisure activities, social roles, image and participation in the world are the external system. Your internal realm is composed of your genetic makeup — your body build, intelligence, temperament and vulnerability. Throughout life, your external and internal systems interact to influence your identity or personality. As events in the external system are interpreted by the internal one, crucial shifts in needs and values can throw you off balance. These are signals telling you to change and move on to the next stage. These shifts occur throughout life. Sadly, many people refuse to recognize them.

For each external system, you also have a corresponding inner sub-identity. Your identity is made up of several "sub-identities" representing your various life roles. You have an occupational identity, a family identity, a social identity, an interpersonal identity, a leisure identity and a religious identity. They may differ quite drastically. Some have large occupational and family identities, with smaller leisure, social and citizenship identities. With others, the balance is exactly reversed. Still others may have sub-identities that are almost equal in size. Moreover, the size of your identities changes as you mature. Those with small children to raise will have larger family identities in their late 20s and early 30s than before their children were born or after they leave the nest.

As the life cycle progresses, you move through alternating developmental and transition periods. Each presents tasks to be mastered and problems to be solved.

Between each developmental stage are transition periods that allow you to question who you are and where you are going. These give you time to re-examine your needs and values, to take another look at your external life systems, to explore and evaluate potential options and to make decisions to either deepen or alter earlier commitments. Each transition takes from three to five years. And each developmental period can take from five to eight.

The transition periods are times of disequilibrium and anxiety. But dangers arise both in moving and staying put. If you stay with a life component after you have outgrown it, you may betray yourself and limit your possibilities; if you break out, you impose burdens on yourself and may fail to find what you seek. Either way there are dangers and losses as well as gains. If you are growing, almost half your adult life is spent in remaking that life.

Every initiation is also a termination of what came before. The developmental periods are necessary for stability; the transition periods are necessary for growth. This process represents the overriding polarity you must integrate in your life, the polarity of change versus continuity, the problem of how to maintain a continuous sense of yourself while growing.

Developmental periods are just as important as the transitions. If your life consisted of nothing but transitions, you would feel as though you were being whirled in a centrifuge. But if it contained only developmental periods, you would experience yourself as an inert lump. At one pole, you risk anxiety; at the other depression. Your life must seek to veer between the two as you try to combine solidity with forward movement, security with risk.

Certain traumatic experiences may cause you to re-examine your life and come to terms with developmental issues. They can be positive, negative or even somewhere in between — marriage, the birth of a child, the death of a parent, serious illness, travel or divorce. All may cause you to shift your values and goals.

Adults in transition may be every bit as miserable as adolescents. But those of you who face up to the agonizing self-evaluation and who independently set future goals, will develop a healthier, happier and more mature identity. Failure to resolve the difficulties of transitions can cause severe problems. High rates of alcoholism, depression and suicide are often related to this inability.

Many of the problems and issues adults must deal with appear and reappear in new forms throughout the life cycle. They are not the exclusive property of any age group. Issues of intimacy and occupation, for example, haunt us forever. Compromises are found for a while, then renegotiated. And so it goes.

You may face five or more transition periods: adolescence, age-30, mid-life, age-50, age-60 and others. Of course, you may not face them exactly on schedule. Although the phases are normal, not all people pass through all of them. Some get fixated at one particular stage. They may spend the rest of their lives making futile attempts to work it through. Those who have difficulty making such transitions often resort to familiar, earlier behavior patterns. A three-year-old trying to adjust to a new baby in the family may forget toilet training or refuse to speak. A man in his late 30s may resume the dating behavior (now extra-marital) of earlier years to avoid the pain of advancing to another developmental level. While some adults fail to adjust to new stages, those who weather transitions often do so by finding new meaning in their work or by switching to more satisfying jobs.

Having realistic expectations about impending crises and transitions can ease the stress and the pain of their arrival. If you do some thinking about the transitions in life and prepare for them, you may be better able to cope.

THE CAREER CYCLE: ENTRY, MASTERY AND DISENGAGEMENT

Your occupational identity is part of your overall sense of who you are. If you are growing as a person and developing in your job, you will have several occupational identities throughout your career cycle. A healthy and vital occupational identity has three stages: entry, mastery and disengagement. During the entry stage, you make a commitment to the job, become involved and develop skills and personal meaning which make up your occupational identity. In the mastery stage, you work hard to achieve excellence, acquire experience and achieve a sense of accomplishment, enjoyment, challenge and purpose. This is the most productive stage for both employees and their bosses. You gain enjoyment and fulfillment; your boss gains a satisfied and productive employee.

During the last part of the mastery stage, you may become confident and even rigid. If your employer cannot or will not alter or expand your tasks, or if you cannot or will not move into another job, the quality of your performance will start to deteriorate. You may no longer be using your skills enthusiastically because you are no longer getting the perks you earlier enjoyed. The challenge, meaning and fulfillment are gone.

The formation of your career identity is a lifelong process. If, like a Quester, you are growing and developing, you will enter, master and disengage from several jobs. They may be sequential, each building upon the other in a logical sequence of increasing skills and responsibilities. For example, teacher, department head, supervisor, principal and so on, up the educational ladder. Or, they may be entirely unrelated — construction worker, teacher, accountant, musician, police officer. A healthy occupational identity occurs when you commit yourself fully to a set or work tasks and master these. When it is no longer rewarding, you move on. You move while your identity is still healthy.

Remember *Kathy* from earlier chapters? Her first full-time job was with a large insurance firm. At first, Kathy was enthusiastic about her position but four years later her feelings began to change. She no longer felt alert and enthusiastic. She had moved from the entry to the mastery to the disengagement stage of her job in just four years. By hanging on, Kathy wasn't doing herself or her employer any good. If she had been moved to another position where she could have learned new tasks, Kathy would have kept on growing. She would have been in the entry stage of another occupational cycle. If her employer had expanded her tasks, she might have stayed in the mastery stage for several more years. But Kathy left the company after working in the same position for seven years. Her occupational cycle had lasted only that long. Today, as an enthusiastic articled law student, she is in the entry stage of her second occupational cycle.

How long your occupational cycles last depends on your occupation and the strength of your intrinsic job needs. Many Questers in middle management have occupational cycles of five to ten years. Questers in occupations like teaching or air traffic control have similar occupational cycles. On the other hand, hairdressers who work for others generally change jobs every three years.

THE CYCLICAL PATTERN

Staying in a job just five to ten years is not necessarily an unstable career pattern. For many Questers, a cyclical occupational pattern is quite normal. Questers often reorganize themselves, their lifestyles and career goals every five to ten years. If they are not deriving satisfaction and challenge from their jobs or progressing in a way that complements their developing personalities, they tend to leave. Throughout their lives, they continue to experience the process of entry, mastery and disengagement. Most Questers set their own rhythm of change.

INTERACTION OF THE CAREER AND LIFE CYCLES

The career cycles of Questers often copy their life cycles. When most are in the disengagement stages of their occupational cycles, they are usually also facing transition stages of their life cycles.

Let's look at the Questers to see how their career and life cycles are intertwined. *Kathy* left her management job during her age-30 transition. The stocktaking she did during this transition was influenced by her growing job dissatisfaction. Feelings of depression over her father's death also affected her. As she looked more closely at her values and goals, she came to terms with the major issue of her age-30 transition − changing occupations.

Vern's occupational cycles also coincided with his life cycle transition. Vern started work as an ambulance attendant and loved it. Six years later, his enthusiasm gone, he decided to disengage. He knew neither he nor his patients would benefit if he stayed put. Vern returned to school to study physiotherapy. Soon after, he married. Vern's decision to marry and to change his occupation were the result of the stocktaking he did during his age-30 transition. Vern liked working as a physiotherapist in a hospital. Initially, he derived the job perks he wanted − challenge, variety, scope and autonomy. But during his fourth year, he became increasingly more frustrated and tense because he felt he had little input into decisions affecting his job. Three years later, he decided to take a year off to sort things out. Vern's "time-out" was part of his mid-life transition and was closely tied to his disengagement from his physiotherapy position. A year off helped him put life in perspective. He returned to school to get some upgrading in physical therapy and then established his own consulting business. Vern, now 47, is in the developmental period of his 40s and the entry stage of his third occupational cycle, a physiotherapy consultant.

Today, a number of managerial and professional workers are becoming even more involved in cyclical careers. Many top executives will set themselves a "time horizon" of five to ten years to tackle the tasks, see the results, then move on. Both executives and organizations benefit. The executive has the excitement and challenge of accomplishing a difficult set of tasks as well as maintaining his or her flexibility. The organization has an enthusiastic, innovative manager who can bring fresh new ideas into the company.

It's sad to see so many workers stay 30 or 40 years in jobs they are psychologically disengaged from, watching the clock as the days and weeks pass. With prestige or financial rewards their jailor, they abandon reality, living unfulfilled lives because the thought of starting anew seems humiliating or degrading.

THE BEGINNING CAREER

Your first developmental period begins with a commitment to your first full-time job. It is a critical time. As you take hold of the adult world, you have to make decisions, commit yourself to a whole new set of roles, and perform tasks that will have a strong influence in later life. Often, the lifestyle and occupation you pursue in early adulthood will be the framework for experiences throughout the rest of your life.

THE ADOLESCENT TRANSITION

Let's backtrack and look at the transition that marks entry into adulthood — adolescence. Later adolescence, which occurs from 17 or 18 to 22 or 23, is an important period. Many decisions made then about career and life goals will affect your potential growth during adulthood. Remember when many changes were taking place in your inner and outer worlds? Physical growth and sexual maturity were accompanied by the maturation of your thinking ability. Your ability to think in abstract terms multiplied as you struggled with problems, devised solutions, evaluated experiences and reconsidered your values. You looked at reality from many angles and considered the implications of your decisions. As you finished high school, you wondered what to do next — travel, continue your education or work.

Choosing an occupation is a crucial step. Work can be the source of pleasure, esteem and goal fulfillment or it can contribute to disappointment and feelings of failure.

Making decisions about a career and other life roles, such as family and sex roles, are major psychological tasks of adolescence. Erik Erikson, one of the pioneers of life cycle theory, called this the search for identity.

There are two essential factors in the attainment of a mature identity, according to James Marcia. First, adolescents must explore several options before choosing "among life's alternatives." Trying on different roles, adolescents struggle to make decisions about occupations, values and lifestyles. Second, adolescents must finally come to a commitment, an investment of themselves in their choices. They may be in one of four identity states: moratorium, identity achieved, identity foreclosed or identity confused. Not all adolescents achieve a mature identity nor do they achieve identity states at the same speed.

Moratorium. In this "time out" period, adolescents have not yet made commitments nor invested much of themselves in others, and they are still vague about their own values. Even while delaying their commitments, they are actively struggling to find the right roles. Experimenting by "playing the field" with the opposite sex, working at odd jobs or trying different courses in their first few years at college, they search for roles that fit. Ideally, adult demands can now be put on hold so that adolescents are free to experiment. Most young people in this state are vague about what they want to do. Kathy was in a moratorium before she committed herself to an insurance job. She "tried on" several jobs and then went for career counseling before she decided on an occupation. Vince also had a moratorium — he dropped out of his first year of college to travel in Europe for two years. When he returned home, he committed himself to a five-year geology program. Kathy and Vince were lucky. Both their parents helped with the finances.

Identity Achieved. Those who have reached the state of identity achievement have explored their options and have made commitments to desired values and goals. They know who they are and what they want to do. They have developed strong, healthy identities by experimenting, carefully evaluating various alternatives and making their own decisions. Efforts to resolve questions of identity may have taken these adolescents onto paths of overzealous commitment, emotional involvement, alienation or playful wandering. Flexible and inner-directed, they set realistic goals and are unlikely to subscribe to authoritarian values. They have committed themselves, at least for a while, to occupational goals. They have experienced a moratorium, and are often older than those in the other groups.

Identity Foreclosed. The identity foreclosed group have made commitments but have not explored their options. They seem very sure of what they want to be. James, a fourth-year medical student, studied hard to get good grades to enter medical school. His parents thought medicine was a good profession to be in — it paid well, had prestige and provided financial and job security. Judy, the daughter of a prominent New York banker, went to finishing school and then a prestigious girls' college because that was the family destiny. In many instances, the family destiny will define a certain value to strive towards — intellectual achievement, independence, power and status or societal contribution. James, Judy and other adolescents like them, made commitments without exploring options. They have passively accepted the identities their parents (or other significant adults in their lives) cut out for them. They have never seriously evaluated their own goals and values. People with foreclosed identities are generally more brittle, authoritarian and conventional than any other group. Adolescents in this group have not yet "broken loose" from the significant adults in their lives. They are "locked in". Until recently, most young women in our culture were part of this group.

Identity Confused. The identity confused group have not yet consciously explored their options nor have they made commitments. They have shrunk from the task of defining who they are or what they want to do. They perform well enough in school and social roles, but they often feel like misfits. They tend to "opt out" of situations to avoid commitment. Often, in the early attemps to define themselves, they become immobilized by feelings of inferiority. But unlike those in a moratorium, they do not seem to be compelled to do much about it. Many young women in their early 20s, who seem to live in a state of suspended animation, are in a confused state. They can't bring themselves to make career commitments, nor any extended plans for that matter, until they know whom they are going to marry.

As you passed through the adolescent transition to achieve greater maturity, you probably experienced confusion and depression. The task of bringing together the pieces of your life into a coordinated and clear self-identity is difficult and time consuming. Those who can consciously explore their options and make commitments to desired values and goals at this turning point often emerge stronger and more in control of their destinies.

Of course, your identity is never static. Each time you pass through a transition phase and re-evaluate your values and goals, you are re-formulating your identity. An identity foreclosed young adult may become an identity achieved adult — a Quester — as she comes to terms with the career decisions she must make during the age-30, the mid-life or later-life transitions. How you deal with the transitions in your life will determine whether you become a Quester.

DEVELOPING THE BEGINNING CAREER

Your need to expand and your career drive are likely to take precedence during the Beginning Career. Young people are busily engaged in the increasing responsibilities of career, marriage or relationships and acquiring knowledge. They do not have much time for stocktaking. The road ahead is exhilarating, conflicting and sometimes overwhelming. But most young people are certain they will have what it takes to overcome any difficulties. They want to shape a dream — to create a lifestyle and "make something out of their lives." They are getting started in occupations, learning the capacity for intimacy with spouses or partners, becoming involved in leisure activities and establishing circles of friends of varying degrees of intimacy. Career will play an important part in the realization of their vision, but young people must also strike a balance among work, love and leisure.

Two impulses, as always, are at work now. One is the need to build a firm, safe lifestyle for the future by making strong commitments. The other is to explore and experiment, to create structures that are easily reversible, to satisfy the cravings of the riskier self. Both can be easily taken to extremes. Like the identity confused group, young people who are too tentative tend to be transient and unstable. They spend their 20s hopping from one job to the next, one personal encounter to the next. On the other hand, young people who, like the identity foreclosed group, commit themselves too strongly tend to be fearful, rigid adults who cling too tightly to their choices. Striking a balance between tentativeness and commitment, exploring alternatives, keeping options open, avoiding strong commitments, and not clinging too tightly to the choices made, are all important to maintain occupational flexibility and adaptability.

The Beginning Career is more stable than the transitions that lead to and from it. It begins with a commitment to a full-time job to prepare for a life of work. For many, the process starts in the early 20s and ends with the age-30 transition. However, given permission to experiment, prolonged schooling and ample time out, it is not unusual for some Questers to be nearly 30 before they start on their Beginning Careers.

The Beginning Career is a mastery stage when young people gain positive feedback, achieve competence and become self-motivated. The positive feelings that flow toward them fill them with self-confidence. Devlin, a 25-year-old middle manager, says of his career goals: "Success and greater responsibility provide me with greater motivation to reach my career goals with my employer. . . I'm interested in obtaining more efficiency in all aspects of my personal and business dealings."

The future path of your career starts with the Beginning Career. Patterns that will affect your future lifestyle often begin here. Many older Questers in the Maturing or the Continuing Career started here. But these patterns can be changed. Some current Questers were Traditionalists or Self-Seekers in Beginning Career but moved to the Quester track as they acquired knowledge, experience and the will to risk.

Most Questers in Beginning Career have confronted the challenges of the adolescent transition. They have committed themselves to occupational goals and are working on implementing these. They have struck a balance between tentativeness and commitment. They have committed themselves to a career, but they know that technology and their own development will one day change the pace of their lives. Both Kathy and Vern were young Questers who recognized the need to be tentative.

A number of beginning Career Questers may seem quite like their Traditionalist and Self-Seeker peers but they have been through many broadening experiences. They may endorse several values, but personal and career development matter most. From their jobs, they want to get such valuable rewards as autonomy, challenge and opportunities for self-expression. They also desire quality from other life components. They are not afraid to work hard for what they want. Many put in long hours on weekends to achieve their goals. They may also make many material sacrifices to reach these goals.

Take *Aaron*. His goal was to own a jewelry store. To get enough money and experience to set out on his own, Aaron took a job as a management trainee with a large retail chain, and, at the same time, worked evenings sorting mail. During weekends, Aaron threw all his energy into designing jewelry. His wife didn't mind. Designing and making jewelry was one of her hobbies, too.

Rob is another Beginning Quester who sees work as a major source of satisfaction. After trying out a variety of courses and programs at the university, Rob wound up in physical engineering. He likes his first full-time job as an engineer for a large consulting firm. He enjoys the challenge, is involved in his work and relishes the positive feedback. Working gives him a sense of competence and confidence. Unlike many of his Traditionalist colleagues, Rob's sense of competence is inner-directed. Money and promotions come second to the feelings of accomplishment he gets from completing a challenging task. Moreover, he is less concerned with socializing just to get ahead. For him, the status, affiliations and external guideposts many rely on don't really count. He places more value on a self-defined lifestyle and career goals. To Rob, his job is an ". . .opportunity for challenge, freedom, a sense of identity, autonomy, involvement and creativity." His career goals are open-ended. He wants "to learn, to experience, to grow. . ."

Petite, attractive and 27, *Susan* is another young Quester with similar values and goals. A journalist for three years, she is happily involved in her work and has also managed to combine work and marriage successfully. Susan and her husband of two years have worked out a system of sharing domestic responsibilities. And like some young women approaching their late 20s who have postponed having children or anticipate not having any or decided against parenthood, Susan is more satisfied with her life than many of her Traditionalist contemporaries. Late motherhood is a bona fide pattern among some female Questers under 30.

Questers in Beginning Careers, who have been in the same job for four or five years, may begin to feel stale or bored. Company policies incompatible with their values may also trouble them. A few years earlier, they simply didn't care. But now, the excitement, romance and challenge which made their jobs something special are beginning to disappear. Questers who feel this way are in the late mastery or early disengagement stages of their first occupational cycles. A series of jolts in other areas of their lives are beginning to wean them from their earlier illusions. Their experiences with a career, marriage or the death of a parent, are preparing them for the age-30 transition. At the same time, their feelings, needs and values are beginning to change. So the Beginning Career ends.

THE DEVELOPING CAREER

THE AGE-THIRTY TRANSITION

The Developing Career is ushered in by the age-30 transition. Many people begin to question their past decisions. They may realize they have ignored important needs, interests and desires. Now, new choices must be made and commitments altered or deepened in all major areas of life. For some, this period may be marked by turmoil and confusion. For others, it may involve an intellectual inquiry into the past.

As you progress through this transition, you may feel confused, sluggish and dissatisfied. The desire to try new things is beginning to take precedence over safety needs. Apparent restrictions are the outgrowth of decisions made in the late teens or early

20s, choices that were perfectly appropriate at the time. Now the fit feels wrong. It may make itself felt suddenly, emphatically, sometimes precipitated by an external event. More often, it begins slowly, a vague but persistent sense of wanting to do and be something more.

Remember *Al*, the farmer in Chapter One? As he approached the age-30 transition, he began to feel that his life and his job no longer had purpose and meaning. Al's age-30 transition was tied to his occupational cycle. At 28, after working in computers for five years, he was in the early disengagement stage of his job. The meaning and excitement had disappeared. Negative feelings arose about his job. This, coupled with the birth of his child, began the stocktaking about his life and career goals.

How you look at time can also change. You will become aware that your life is finite. Death is still an abstract fear. You still have time to do it all. New experiences are waiting. You are impatient to get on with your life but the desire is not yet urgent.

The severity of the transition stage is reflected in the moratorium of one or more years many Questers took. *Adrian*, a happy entrepreneur, "walked away from the world" during his transition. He needed time to rethink the direction of his life. Adrian was particularly restless as he approached 30. While he performed his management tasks dutifully, he was in the disengagement stage of his occupational cycle. The job seemed frustrating and restricting. Adrian emerged from his moratorium with greater self-understanding and renewed confidence to move forward in his new, self-determined career. He and his wife became partners in a variety of entrepreneurial projects. Today, Adrian describes his job passionately: ". . .it represents a future — it gives me an economic base to pursue my own lifestyle." Now 34, Adrian (and his wife) is working on the goals set during the transition. When he is no longer challenged, he will probably seek greater challenges.

Janet also experienced a moratorium. A very creative and assertive young woman, she quit her job as a news photographer to travel in Europe for a year. She had no definite future plans. Even though she liked her colleagues, she no longer felt challenged. The marital problems she was experiencing aggravated her feelings of depression and lethargy. Counseling sessions with a psychologist gave Janet the necessary support and courage to "get away from everything for a while."

"While in Europe, I smiled for the first time in years. I returned home a different person. I felt happier, more at peace with myself, than I had felt in a long time." Janet changed both her job and her marital status. But it was a difficult process. "When I was in Europe, I prayed for help in making the right decision about my marriage in every church I visited as a tourist. . .and there were plenty of them!"

Questers who experienced time-out periods show it can be helpful. They emerged from their break with greater self-understanding, renewed confidence and courage to move forward in their self-determined careers and lifestyles.

Roman may become a Quester. Currently, he's recovering from surgery. He has a four-year business degree and has worked as a manager for the past seven years. Roman has some hard decisions to make about his career and life goals. Until now, he has been doing what everyone around him told him to do. That's probably why he's ill. Not feeling good about your job does have physical costs. You only deceive yourself if you think it doesn't.

Many Traditionalists in their late 20s or early 30s are experiencing similar thoughts and feelings as Questers. But they modify their lives to place higher value on family needs and leisure, building directly upon the past and making few real changes.

Men may feel anxious making it through the age-30 transition, but women face an even more turbulent time. Women have more options and, therefore, decisions to consider. The biological clock increases the pressure to make decisions about when and if they want a family and how long they are prepared to delay a decision to enjoy a career. For some, occupational change means dropping out of the work world to have children and stay home with them. Many say they would like to return to work in a few years. A few feel they have had enough.

Beverly, another Quester, is a good example. Beverly spent the married years of her early 20s as a graduate student engaged in occasional research projects. Her age-30 transition was accompanied by a strong desire to trade career for family. For the next seven years, Beverly was deeply engaged in the domestic life. Then, when she was 37, she began to think again about returning to work full-time. She felt she was "getting narrow". That's part of the complexity of women's development.

Clearly, the passage into the 30s stimulates a psychological changing of gears on all fronts. For Questers, this transition brings the desire to broaden their lives and make some changes. Many tear up the part of the lives they spent most of their 20s so carefully building. Those who have been in a corporate slot feel narrow and restricted. Some Questers decide to open their own businesses. Others return to school to prepare for new occupations. Yet others decide to enjoy life by traveling for a while. If they have been in training, such as graduate study, for a long time, now they eagerly look forward to starting a new job. If they have been single, they long for marriage and emotional attachments. Women who have been pursuing a career may decide to have a family and become more domestic. Moreover, stocktaking is often linked to other life crises, like divorce or job dissatisfaction. As experiences snowball, self-evaluation, a necessary prerequisite to passing successfully through the transition, takes place.

Transition problems occur whether people are entering or leaving jobs. But the solution most Questers found was constant. They were willing to listen to their inner voices and they were willing to risk. Even if no overt action is taken during the age-30 transition, there is often an unseen shift, a change in the way a person feels about his or her life, that will most likely lead to later changes. The equilibrium regained by reaching the other side of 30 makes it easier for people to re-examine their origins and gradually acknowledge parts of themselves that were left out by earlier choices.

THE DEVELOPING CAREER BEGINS

For the Questers who remained in the work world, the decision to make a commitment to another position marks their entry into the developmental cycle of the Developing Career – the entry stage of another occupational cycle. This is a very productive, fulfilling, exciting and creative period in their lives. Both their personal and occupational lives seem fuller and richer. Now, most Questers deepen their commitments and invest more of themselves in their work, family and other valued interests. They pursue their short- and long-range plans and goals.

The reappraisal of the age-30 transition leads a number of adults to shift their values, priorities and goals. Many adults become more self-aware and more interested in sharing their understanding of themselves and others. They place more value on the quality of life. Leading a more balanced life, becoming more family-oriented and developing relationships, may take priority. Job satisfaction suddenly becomes more important than climbing the corporate ladder or earning higher wages.

Questers also become more aware of their strong needs to become self-fulfilled, to derive challenge and independence from their jobs and to make use of their skills. They have outgrown their earlier choices. All want to avoid stagnation. Questers' reappraisals help them arrive at the decisions to leave their jobs when they feel stagnant. The age-30 transition is usually interrelated with a job transition. Many Questers have completed one occupational cycle and are eager to get started in another. But their decisions do not come easily.

Tall and well-built, *Mark* has blond curly hair and brown eyes. He is good-looking and well-liked by his peers. Mark completed his college degree at 22 and entered a management training program with an international banking organization in a large western city. His decision was largely influenced by the fact that his father was the president and major shareholder of a large manufacturing firm and his older brother was a successful executive in the family operation. Mark's goal was to become a senior executive. He enjoyed his work, especially the contact with his colleagues and subordinates. But over the next seven years he gradually came to realize he just wasn't "cut out" to be a manager.

"Two factors influenced my self-appraisal and consequent decision to leave management — the breakdown of my marriage and the fact that my father, who was in his mid-50s, was struck with two heart attacks. These events helped me realize that I wasn't going to live forever and that if I only had one life to live, I shouldn't be wasting it. I should be involved in doing something I enjoy." Then 31, Mark decided to enter broadcasting, a long-time love and hobby. The only experience he had was at his college radio station, years before. Combined with some initiative and his willingness to take a salary cut and change his lifestyle, it was enough. He got his foot in the door in a small town 100 miles from his hometown. Now a disc jockey and part-time announcer, he loves his work.

Some Traditionalists, who shift their work and life orientation dramatically as a result of the age-30 transition, may become Questers. Talking about the changes in her values and lifestyle over the past few years, Alice, a new Quester, said: "Position, status and power were extremely important to me in my 20s. Now I'm different. I'm more self-aware and I'm more interested in the quality of life, work and leisure. I also know that I need a job that gives me autonomy, scope and challenge. . .I have taken steps to do something about changing my status. I've made plans to enter a profession."

Brian is also in the mastery stage of his second occupational cycle. He dropped out of high school at the end of his sophomore year for a job doing office work for a railway company. He did well. Promoted to supervisor and then to management, Brian completed his high school diploma through night school. His first job lasted 13 years. Then he began to feel restless. He remembers feeling trapped as he rounded the corner to his 28th birthday. "I wanted to do something different. . .something I felt better about. Helping people meant more to me than financial rewards." But Brian had a wife and two children to support. Could he do it? The deciding factor was the death of his mother two years later. "Life is too short not to do what I wanted to do," he thought. So, at 31, he quit his job and went back to school to get a degree in occupational health and safety. "My wife was great about it," he says. A former dietician, she went back to work to support the family. By taking extra courses at night, on weekends and during the summers, Brian completed his degree in three years.

Two years into his new occupation, he admits to loving his job. "I feel very good about life in general. I understand myself better, I'm a better person, and I think I've become more broadminded and liberal. . .We have more conversations as a family, and I know where the children are coming from now."

Most women Questers marry later than their Traditionalist contemporaries and have fewer children — on the average, only one. Those who waited are usually happy. These Questers enjoy all three — marriage, career and motherhood. They have relished pleasure in love, family and work. Many are willing to spend extra time on their work, but they are not willing to allow their love or family relationships to disintegrate just so they can attain professional or business success.

Far from vagabonds, most Questers who set out to find more satisfying careers need roots. Questers who tore up the structure of their 20s are particularly keen to build a solid base. As he decorates his new apartment, Mark, the disc jockey who had to move to a new town, says, "I want to feel I'm a very stable citizen."

Many Questers aren't bothered by work pressures. They don't feel helpless in the face of continuing distress. Instead, they feel a sense of exhilaration from a challenging job well done. They feel in control of their work and lives.

Bill, a Quester, is currently disengaging from his second occupational cycle. A sensitive, reflective, diplomatic man who describes himself as "a loner and a lover of people," Bill worked in a government department after he completed his master's degree in forestry. He was promoted up the ladder at regular intervals but at a slower rate than he would have liked. Gradually, Bill became bored, disinterested and disenchanted with his job and lifestyle. When an offer arrived to teach forestry at a two-year college, he willingly accepted. "Teaching was something I always wanted to do. I thought it would provide me with more meaning, interest and freedom than the government job and it does." Four years later, Bill was still teaching but was thinking that in the future he might like to devote his time to writing. He had been married for 12 years, but was not particularly happy. Bill and his wife had been through two separations and it looked as though their relationship might not survive the next few years.

Bill is in the process of disengaging himself from both his marriage and his second occupational cycle. The unhappy marriage and his desire to try something new are precipitating and aiding the stocktaking that accompanies a transition. For Bill, it will be the mid-life transition.

Many Questers who have been involved in their new occupations for a few years are also making transitions. They are beginning to think about what they want to do next. They have mastered their second set of tasks and are enthusiastically looking forward to conquering new ones. Bill, for example, is still interested in writing. Others, like Melvin, are pondering expanding their businesses. Still others are considering returning to school to make more dramatic occupational shifts.

THE MATURING CAREER

THE MID-LIFE TRANSITION

The mid-life transition acts as link between the Developing Career and the Maturing Career. The transition can occur anytime between ages 35 to 45, and, in some cases, even later, depending on when the earlier transitions began and ended, how many life crises occurred and how they were dealt with — and where a person is in his or her existing occupational cycle.

This transition is the beginning of what many authorities have called "the crossroads of life" or "the halfway mark". We become aware of advancing age and death. Time seems scarce. We begin to think about time left to live, rather than time already lived. We become aware of our lost youth and our faltering physical powers. We question the stereotyped roles we adopted and we realize that we do not have all the answers. We may wonder: "Is this all there is to life?"

Our source of identity moves from outside to inside. It causes men and women to switch from one set of goals in their 20s to a different set by their 40s. We begin to notice previously hidden masculine and feminine aspects of our nature. Men are caught by surprise as a more tender, feeling side emerges. Women are amazed to discover a more aggressive, rational side surfacing. We become aware of developing a more ethical self. An old part of us is dying — and we are troubled.

During this transition, we question every part of our lives. To pass through this "authenticity crisis", we must listen to our inner voices and critically evaluate ourselves and our goals. We must identify and accept our suppressed and unwanted parts and integrate them into our real selves. Now we must shelve the phony self we created just to please others. This is also a time when we must master other tasks. Commit ourselves to goals which have meaning and value to us. Come to grips with the decline of our bodies and eventual mortality. Feel free to express what we previously considered foreign.

Psychologists and psychiatrists, who have helped investigate adult development, believe failure to resolve the difficulties of the mid-life transition helps explain the high rates of alcoholism, depression and suicide that occur during this period. It explains why many creative and industrious people burn out in their mid-30s and why others blossom only after that age.

Quite often, people who considered themselves successful during young adulthood become disenchanted with their work, spouses or lifestyles. Many will question how important and fulfilling their work really is. Earlier career stages may have required compliance with demands at work which may have interfered with the development of an achieved identity. If you have been in a job for 10 or more years without promotions or lateral moves, you are probably already in the disengagement stage. You may be feeling stale, tired, anxious, unattractive, restless, old, burdened or even unappreciated. You may be thinking of getting back to your original career "dream" after being nudged away from it through the adaptational demands of earlier career experiences. Ulcers, anxiety or other emotional problems may be taking a toll. Being in charge of your life and your career is important. You want to be able to produce something lasting and worthwhile. Many who did nothing about their careers in their early 30s may be feeling panicky. "This is my last chance!" they cry. Some are forced out of their jobs by obsolescence or technological change. Other adults also flee from well-established bases, like marriage. Or, they may decide their life is just fine as is. Any of these alternatives are okay if they feel right for you.

Daniel Levinson and his colleagues pointed out that this is a time of paradox. They describe the dilemma a man faces when, on the one hand, if he doesn't make a switch, he will never become his own person; if he does, he risks hurting the people he loves by failing. "Having made his bed (marital, occupational or other), he cannot continue to lie in it. Yet to change is to tear the very fabric of his life, to destroy much that he has built over the last 10 or 15 years."

Now you can see that you must evaluate your life not by external symbols of success (for example, prestigious job, big house), but by internal symbols (for example, feelings of satisfaction and accomplishment).

Bertrand, is one Quester who is thinking of changing jobs again. For the past six years, he's been teaching law school at a mid-western university. Before that, until boredom came calling, he practiced law in the same city for seven years. Now 43, Bertrand likes his job. He has independence and variety. But he is beginning to feel stale and restless. In a few years, he would like to do something else. Maybe start a business, something he can be enthusiastic about. A very creative man, Bertrand's needs for challenge and growth are stronger than many others. Because he understands himself, Bertrand knows he will need some changes soon to keep his occupational identity healthy.

Ill health or misfortune forces some people in this transition to make changes that cause them to become Questers. *Kit*, a brilliant man of 42, was the controller of a large corporation. He worked his way up with a master's degree in accounting. Kit's position, salary and lifestyle were the stuff dreams are made of. He had a beautiful wife, well-behaved kids, a large home with a swimming pool and sauna and could afford luxurious vacations. But he was frustrated and uneasy. Psychiatric counseling was necessary. His doctor referred him to a career counselor. It was apparent that at least some of Kit's frustrations were related to his career. He was in a figures-and-paper job. He belonged in a selling and people-persuading job. Kit was lucky. He could ask for a move to a sales department where he could use his accounting skills. By night, he studied marketing techniques and strategies. Two years later, he was sales manager.

Martha has a similar story to tell. A married woman of 38 with three children, she was feeling "out of sorts" and didn't know why. The feelings came on gradually. Night after night she lay awake. Her relationship with her husband and children faltered. She had everything she needed — a loving husband, well-behaved children, a nice home and enough money to buy the things she needed. Martha let a friend talk her into counseling. It was a wise move. During the counseling sessions, she learned she was letting her own needs play second fiddle to what she thought her husband and children wanted.

Martha's whole world revolved around her family. She deprived them of nothing — she gave them her time and even sacrificed many pleasures. A year later, Martha had the courage to talk about her feelings. To her surprise, her family understood her needs and supported and encouraged her to pursue a long-time goal — to become a dietitian. Soon after, Martha began to follow her dream. As a young woman, she was not motivated to complete the home economics program she began because she was too busy having a social life. Today, Martha is in the final year of her program. She is talking like a Quester. She feels great.

For many adults, the mid-life crisis is so great that they fail to make a smooth transition. A long period of frustration and failure follows. A women whose children no longer seem to need her may become depressed or decide to have another baby. To bring back the excitement of years long past, many men will try to reassert their masculine prowess through vigorous physical activity or invest in risky stock ventures. Alcohol can become an escape route leading nowhere. Many of these problems are a result of job dissatisfaction and disengagement. Staying on the job physically, while far removed from it intellectually and emotionally, causes many dissatisfied workers to wither. Those adults who weather the crisis often do it by finding new meaning and purpose in more satisfying positions or leisure activities.

THE MATURING CAREER BEGINS

For many Questers, the Maturing Career begins about age 40. Relatively stable and content, they understand themselves a little better. They are in tune with their needs. They are more real, happy, warm, mellow. They feel alive! Their families are still important to them, and so are their friends. But having some time to themselves is becoming more important.

A number of Questers are in the mastery stage of their next occupational cycle. Their job satisfaction is high. So is their productivity. They are creative but their creativity is more "sculptured" than in earlier years. They form and fashion a product, work and rework the material, act and react to what they are making. Rather than the intense, spontaneous and often unconscious, creativity of the 20s and early 30s, the creative process is more deliberate, conscious and analytical. It may continue for years. The creativity of leadership peaks during this life period. Leadership abilities in education, law and industry are at their highest in the 40s, 50s and 60s.

Along with leadership ability, the need to make a lasting and significant contributon to a profession or organization is strongest in middle age. Since development of a future generation of leaders is a significant and highly satisfying contribution, interest in helping the young blossoms now.

Betty, a Quester politician, radiates a star quality that belies her age of 50. She refused entreaties to run for a seat in the Senate because, as she stated, "I want to be a mentor rather than a power broker." Betty and other Questers like her become role models to the young women who will succeed them.

Men and women in the Maturing career may also become interested in people-related work. Adults in people-oriented occupations, such as teaching, social work, sales and politics, find immense satisfaction in helping others.

Erik Erikson called adults who have dealt with the mid-life crisis "generative". They are paternal, productive and creative in a new sense. They feel voluntarily committed to guiding new generations as parents, as mentors of an occupation, as members of society. In contrast, those who haven't dealt with the tasks of the transition successfully are egocentric, non-productive, self-indulgent, depressed and lack the ability to truly care for others.

Peter left his senior management position to teach accounting in a two-year college. He traded his plush office — its deep pile rug, brown leather sofa, windows overlooking a lake and private secretary — for a cubbyhole with no windows, no rug and a secretary shared with seven others. Peter seemed to make the decision to leave his career of seven years quite suddenly. It happened when he spotted an ad for a business administration instructor. He phoned. Several hours later he was interviewed. There was no hesitation when the offer came. "I was ready for a move," Peter said. "It was a matter of time. . .I was beginning to feel stale in my position. . .Even though I like and respected my colleagues, I couldn't see myself spending the next 20 years of my life there." Peter, now 45, did considerable stocktaking during his mid-life transition and discovered he really did want to change positions. He was in the disengagement stage of his managerial cycle and was ready to change when the teaching opportunity presented itself. Now in the mastery stage of his teaching job of four years, Peter muses that he would like to do something else in a few years — perhaps work in staff development with his previous organization, or consult. Like a typical Quester, Peter is keeping his options open

Evelynne (you met her earlier) is another 45-year-old Quester who is keeping her options open. Evelynne made the decision to start over during the self-appraisal she did at 40. Today, in the mastery stage of her entrepreneurial cycle, Evelynne is thinking about getting involved in something new a few years from now.

By the time Evelynne, Peter and many other Questers in their mid-40s reach their 50th birthday, they will probably modify or change their plans again if they feel they are no longer growing. These shifts in careers will be associated with their age-50 transitions. Many adults will be trying to come to grips with recurring issues, such as jobs, and issues they haven't dealt with, such as faltering relationships.

Murray came to terms with his growing dissatisfaction when he was 51. Principal of a junior high school for eight years, Murray was tired of political hassles. Art and interior design had been long-time hobbies, and, for many years, he had dreamed of spending more time on his leisure activities. So he decided to open a furniture store in the suburbs of a medium-sized, mid-western city. At last, Murray could put his interests and knowledge of art and interior design to use. The management and people-related skills he developed and used as a principal were invaluable in his new venture. Murray had begun his working life as manager of a retail organization. His age-30 transition found him returning to school for teacher training. In seven years, he was principal. A Quester throughout his working life, Murray has found his disengagements from occupational cycles always coincided with life cycle transitions:

Like Murray, *Brady* has undergone the same transitions. He left his dentistry practice when he was 47, traveled for a year, then returned to America to take a lower-paying job as a researcher. Brady felt he was getting stale. He needed to expand, personally and professionally. "I feel more alive now, and believe I am a better husband and person. I'm also more productive as a professional." His family and colleagues agree.

Brady is a good example of the growing number of professionals in their late 40s and 50s who leave secure positions to pursue new interests.

For Traditionalists, the era from age 40 to retirement is often called the maintenance period. Established in their careers, they enter a plateau. Usually holding their own at work, they can maintain what has already been achieved.

Many women in Maturing Career, who have been homemakers, can't get their children out of the nest fast enough so they can return to work. Some studies of American women between 35 and 65 indicate they are feeling extra-ordinarily good about themselves, their lives and their futures. These feelings are shared by women in all kinds of roles, from housewives to executives. Some are just now becoming Questers.

Many are the beneficiaries of a new social climate created largely by the women's movement. Not so long ago, the common perception was that women over 50 were over the hill and unemployable. Today, the numbers alone challenge the old stereotype. Women who have reached or passed 50 are frequently regarded as glamorous and desirable. Women such as Jacqueline Kennedy Onassis, Lena Horne, Sophia Loren and Joan Collins have popularized the appeal of "older" women.

Many women of 50 are going back to school and literally starting new lives. Kate, who has six children, went to school to study economics at 50 and now works in the trade department of the federal government. Anne is becoming a student again. Being 50 can be a special time for a working woman, too. Gloria Steinem and many other women in their early 50s set goals they hope to realize over the next 20 years. These women are aware of how much age has to do with state of mind. Studies show women who are homemakers tend to be physiologically 10 years older than women in the work force. It's not the work. It's a result of the lack of control, dignity, respect, stimulation and company. Today, diet and exercise are changing the way women look and feel about themselves. Nowadays your only limits are energy level, drive, motivation and goals. At 50, you've just begun to come into knowledge and experience you've spent a lifetime piecing together. Many women over 50 feel a new sense of independence and strength. They feel good because they're doing the kind of work they want to do. They are keeping young. That such changes are commonplace even into the 60s surprises many young women. Yet this bloom in the middle of the female life cycle is a signal that it's never too late to find wholeness.

Looking for jobs to replace the outlived purpose of mothering is particularly difficult for the middle-aged women of today. Their generation was never adequately prepared, emotionally or educationally, for the reality that paid work is central to the self-confidence of middle-aged women. And yet, they rally. All at once, a "sense of accomplishment" becomes vitally important. Middle-aged women who point the way to younger women's futures are the only ones in recent studies who rate accomplishment as their most important long-range goals. Mobilizing their strengths and pouring their energies into doing paid work is one way of handling stress. This sudden, strong emphasis on work and achievement brings exhilaration and a renewed sense of purpose.

Moreover, most Traditionalist women don't do much about

achieving their identity until after their mid-40s. Now, at 46 and older, they begin to establish a firm sense of their own identities for the first time. Many women who have weathered the crises of the mid-life and age-50 transitions see their 50s as the happiest times of their lives.

The developmental period of the 50s comes to an end when we start wondering what to do about retirement. Should we work full-time or part-time if we have a choice? Or should we disengage ourselves completely from the marketplace?

THE CONTINUING CAREER

THE AGE-SIXTY TRANSITION

The age-60 transition marks the boundary between the Maturing Career and the Continuing Career. As we progress through this transition into late adulthood, we again question and explore our inner selves in relation to our external world, examine our careers and other options and settle upon a course which will give us opportunities for continuing growth. If you can come to terms with issues that lie before you now, you will acquire a clearer and fuller sense of who you are. You will develop greater inner strength and become more capable of pursuing your goals.

One issue almost all of us must deal with is whether or not we will accept the compulsory retirement included in the employer-employee contract of a number of organizations. Despite new attitudes towards aging and medical advances that have prolonged life expectancy, many still hang on to outdated beliefs about retirement and aging. Sixty-five was the magic number most industries once used to formally disengage us. Now mandatory retirement is usually 70. In the future, people may be expected to work even longer.

Retirement means different things to different people. For some, loss of work means a loss of part of themselves — they feel as if a piece of their inner self has disappeared. Retirement raises the spectre of unwelcome inactivity. To others, retirement means escape from a dreary and frustrating job — freedom to do things they had no time to do before. Yet others consider retirement an escape from suffocating pressures. Decisions about your post-retirement life may be related to how long you want to live.

For many Questers, retirement means continuing growth and revitalization. During the age-60 transition, many are in the late mastery or early disengagement stage of their fifth, sixth or seventh occupational cycles. Some cycles have been sequential, a logical succession of increasing skills and responsibilities. Others have been as unrelated as athlete, artist, mechanic, teacher. Questers are continuing to find work in which they can grow.

Fortunately, at the same time, some Traditionalists are also becoming Questers. *Wally* worked for the same bank for 40 years until recently, when he began to think like a Quester. His retirement plans are still tentative, but he can hardly wait to get started. Wally believes retirement will give him a chance to do something different, to be more flexible and autonomous. For Wally, compulsory retirement doesn't mean disengagement or diminished activity. It means greater challenge, scope and freedom.

Some people who seem to be Traditionalists are retiring early. *Cliff* spent his life in a white-collar world as a senior executive in the insurance business. Now 55, Cliff retired early from insurance but decided not to give up business. Instead, he started a new occupation selling real estate-related investments. "One of my strengths is that I'm a creative person, and that type of individual always searches for new experiences," he says.

But for most Traditionalists, retirement can be difficult since it often requires dramatic changes. Having nothing to do or feeling you are just in the way can be devastating when you have been a good provider or wage-earner for 35 years. Death rates increase dramatically for retired men and women. So do illnesses that have no physiological causes.

THE CONTINUING CAREER DEVELOPS

When many Traditionalists are retiring, most Questers are in the entry or early mastery stage of their next occupational cycles.

Phyl is a good-looking man with grey hair and sparkling blue eyes. He walks with a spring. Now 70, he has had an amazingly diverse career — news photographer, newspaper reporter, school principal, magazine and newspaper editor, politician, writer and television producer. Phyl dropped out of school after repeating the 10th grade and managed to get a job as a photographer's assistant with a local newspaper. From there he moved to newspaper reporting. During the age-30 transition, he went back to school. Phyl earned his education degree and got married in the same year. He taught school for six years, then became principal of a school in the same city. At 45, he was off to work as editor of a newspaper and then magazine. By age 60, when most men are planning for retirement, Phyl ran successfully in state elections. He left politics for writing and working as a television producer.

When Phyl is asked which job he enjoyed the most, he replies: "I enjoyed them all. I have enjoyed whatever I was doing when I was doing it. My various positions have a common thread running through them. . . .I need to work with people and to communicate to others."

Phyl has some regrets. Most involve interpersonal relations: "I have been so immersed in what I'm doing that I have neglected friendships and family at times. Much of my success is due to the energies that I have put into the work at hand. . . .I have sometimes wondered why I work with such single-mindedness. It is not for the financial rewards nor is it for the renown. . .If there has been a dominant drive, it has been a deep need for challenge. . .for variety, scope. . .for personal satisfaction. However, I would still lead a similar life if I had my life to live over again."

Phyl has this to say about his career goals. "I am by no means certain what I will do next. I will certainly continue to write." Like many Questers. Phyl's career goals are still open-ended.

Growing old is not a death warrant for mental activity. Many outstanding people did not reach their prime until long after 50. Pablo Picasso was still painting at 91, Grandma Moses at 101. Arturo Toscanini gave his last performance at 87 and Guiseppe Verdi composed *Falstaff* at 80. Konrad Adenauer was Chancellor of West Germany at 87. Artur Rubinstein excited audiences with his piano artistry well into his 90s. So did the late centenarian Eubie Blake.

Sociologists say that with more people living active, youthful lives well past 60, public perceptions of later adulthood are changing. College students fresh from high school share classrooms with 65-year-olds. Grey-haired athletes enter marathons. Retired workers become entrepreneurs. Artists become world travelers. "A few years ago," laughs a fashion expert, "the sight of a woman over 40 dressing in jeans and riding a motorcycle was thought bizarre, or at least, inappropriate. Now women are expected to be fit into their 70s — and jeans have become so haute couture that only women over 40 can afford them." Nowadays, who can we tell to "act your age?" The rhythm of life has changed in other ways, too. A man and woman can become father and mother again at the same time they become grandparents. Puberty arrives earlier and menopause later. Grandparents are getting younger and living longer. You truly are "as old as you feel."

Attitudes are going through immense changes and people have many new and interesting alternatives. *Kay* was a principal until she retired at 65. Everyone was amazed at her energy level and wondered how she managed to find time for skiing. singing and other projects, in addition to her heavy work schedule. When she retired, Kay and her husband spent a year traveling around the world. Six months later, she was bored and restless. To keep challenge and meaning in her life, she approached the school board and asked for a job. Her first project was to coordinate a group so that it could attack the problems of inner-city schools. This was followed by the evaluation of private schools. Kay, now 72, is still working on educational projects. She also has time for social activities. She is feeling great and hopes to continue with her present lifestyle.

Frank worked for the railway for 42 years, first as a mechanical apprentice, next as a tradesman, then as a supervisor. He climbed the organizational ladder until he was in his mid-50s. Then his career reached a plateau. To keep involved and enthusiastic about life, Frank volunteered to do first aid with the Red Cross during his spare time. At 61, he retired early to become a full-time, first-aid worker. When most of his railway friends were retiring, Frank opened up a practice in reflexology (a form of therapy based on manipulation, anesthetization or cautherization). Now 70, Frank is still a vital man. "Age," he says, "is a matter of attitude more than years." Frank plays tennis and skis during his spare time. He's remarrying.

Contemporary career development is a continuing quest to improve the fit between your occupation and your developing personality. Only you can establish your rhythm of change. It's never too late!

6: Job satisfiers

What Questers get from their careers depends on their personalities. But most are seeking higher-level needs: freedom, growth, independence, challenge, achievement, variety, involvement, altruism plus a sense of purpose and identity. They tend to enjoy their jobs as indicated by their use of such adjectives as "fun," "excitement" and "pleasure". Phyl, the energetic 70-year-old, now in his seventh occupational cycle, says it best: "There is nothing more thrilling than creating something out of yourself. To follow a strong drive toward a goal and find yourself, to work at what you want to do and do it successfully, to risk everything when the chances for success seem so small, to give everything to your work and get everything back from it, this is the ultimate satisfaction."

How different they are from many Traditionalists. Lorne, a 50-year-old writer in the civil service, is thoughtful when he considers why he works. Then he says: "For bread and butter. It's a necessity, a way of making a systematic life for me in that it gives me a place to go, even though it's no longer fulfilling because it is no longer challenging. I'm not learning anything. I'm not reaching." Lorne acknowledges that he misses the challenge and stimulation his career earlier provided. Now in the disengagement stage of his occupational cycle, he has, quite simply, outgrown his job.

The sense of resignation in Lorne's voice is echoed when we hear Jessica describe her job. A 40-year-old bookkeeper and former homemaker, Jessica sees her work as "an escape from housework and doing routine tasks." Her job may be more rewarding than housework, but she's far from satisfied.

Unfortunately, while a number of Traditionalists do derive a sense of identity and sometimes challenge from their jobs, their careers tend to satisfy little more than lower-level needs: money, security, prestige and something to do. Many Traditionalists are missing the intense feelings of satisfaction that drive Questers on to further challenges. Ultimately, they will pay for it.

HOW SATISFIED ARE YOU?

Because your job needs are dynamic, they usually reflect your reactions to your current work environment. For example, as you gain competence, a job that first seemed challenging may become boring.

Why, then, do some people seem satisfied to do the same work over and over again, day in and day out, without complaint? Because their need hierarchies may be very different from most Questers'. Less-important needs can be satisfied much more easily than higher-level needs. So, for instance, if you have a high need for social contacts and your job gives you many opportunities to satisfy that need (assuming other important high-level needs are also met), you will have a high level of job satisfaction. But if you took a job that offered few chances to make social contacts, you would be very dissatisfied.

As you grow and develop, your needs constantly jockey for position. As a result, in middle age, you may seriously consider changing the direction of your career. A young person with a job that demands extensive travel may be very satisfied. But once married and with children, being away from home may become so displeasing that a new job with limited travel demands will be sought. Whether or not you're satisfied with your job depends upon the degree to which your needs are being met.

A look at the job satisfiers many Questers seek will give you a better idea of where your career fits into your need hierarchy. Here is a summary of what many Questers consider in the often-difficult task of finding true career satisfaction.

EMERGING IDENTITY

Part of the search for career satisfaction is finding an occupation that will fit your personality and self-image. Your career is a statement about you. Knowing who you are and what you want to become and getting recognition from your work are essential to satisfaction. The desire for self-understanding and recognition will last all your life.

Your career plays a major part in how you represent yourself to society. The recognition you get from your job is an important part of your life. A career charts your path in the human community.

Asked who they are, many people will respond by telling you what they do. Children also face this. Who hasn't been asked, "What do you want to be when you grow up?" The proper answer, of course, is "a doctor" or "a police officer" or "an astronaut". The explosion of expectations has left many people more interested in what they do than what they are.

The importance of a job to one's sense of identity is evident when speaking to the unemployed. Many feel worthless without a job. *Grace*, an assistant vocational rehabilitation counselor, was depressed to find herself out-of-work even though she puts her husband, her 12-year-old son and her home before any job. "When I was working, my husband was proud of me, my son was proud and then all of a sudden, I had nothing," she recalls. "Though I never really blamed myself, I felt emotionally worthless. There's more to life than staying home and it's bad when getting your un-employment check is your big day out."

You are judged not only by what you do, but also by the industry in which you do it, your responsibilities and your company's reputation. A person who craves responsibility might be quite happy working in a small company. But someone who iden-tifies with prestige and status may accept a much lower position just to join a large, renowned company in a prestigious industry. Much job dissatisfaction can be traced to the mismatch between a worker's identity needs and his or her employer.

Of course, as you grow and develop, your identity will change too. In fact, most Questers are constantly reshaping their identi-ties. They commit themselves to occupations only as long as the jobs fit their personalities.

FINDING PURPOSE IN WORK

Everyone needs something to believe in. People who feel they have a reason to exist are healthier, happier and live longer. Your career can give you a sense of purpose.

Brock exudes happiness and good health. A politician now, this 55-year-old Quester has been an actor, salesman, market re-search analyst and stockbroker. When it came time to retire, he just couldn't do it. After a year of being idle, Brock decided he pre-ferred to work even though he didn't need the money. "After a year, I felt parasitic and indolent. I have to be involved in some-thing I can enjoy, can get involved with, from which I can know that I have been of use to humankind. To energize myself, I needed something that would make me push myself to the limits." He moved into politics and now Brock feels he is making his country a better place to live. "It's a wonderful feeling to be involved in something you love," he says earnestly after election to the provincial legislature. "It gives you a feeling of being needed."

THE NEED FOR CHALLENGE

Questers usually need more challenge than most. As soon as most master one challenge, they are off to tame yet another. Why? Differences in genetic makeup and early socialization experiences give some people a greater thirst for challenge. But the workplace can also play a big part.

HOW THE WORK ENVIRONMENT INFLUENCES YOUR HAPPINESS

Learning new tasks, having control over your work and being responsible for decisions all involve mental challenge. But what happens when your work doesn't provide enough challenge or opportunities for mastery and achievement? The result is usually boredom. Employees who enjoy sufficiently challenging jobs are enthusiastic and involved. Those who feel responsible for the actions and outcomes of their work will strive harder because their total personalities are involved. Coping with challenge also requires effort and commitment to your goals in life.

Challenge, of course, is dynamic. Once you have mastered a difficult task, you need new challenges. The quest for challenge corresponds to a growing person's occupational cycle.

Psychological Success

You can get a better understanding of the cyclical relationships among challenge, achievement, involvement, self-confidence, goal attainment and job factors from the diagram illustrating psychological success.

Achieving your goals leads to feelings of psychological success. The prerequisites for feeling good about your job are:

- challenging work
- autonomy
- support from others
- feedback

As mastering each task pushes you to newer levels of competence, your satisfaction increases. So does self-confidence. As a result, your involvement in your job will probably increase, too. These increased

PSYCHOLOGICAL SUCCESS

feelings of success, confidence, involvement and commitment will usually lead you to set more difficult goals. When this cycle is occurring, you feel "turned on" by your work.

To set work goals, you will need a healthy degree of autonomy. Close supervision may make you feel that your performance reflects more on your supervisor than on your own efforts.

However, getting support when you try a difficult task (regardless of whether you succeed or fail) spurs you on; it also facilitates the development of your creativity. Feedback is necessary to help you evaluate your performance. This tends to give you feelings of accomplishment.

Glen is a good example of what happens when an employee receives support and encouragement. As an accountant for a meat packing plant, Glen persuaded his boss to allow him to plan and install a new management information system. Extensive research went into his plan. Its success was overwhelming. His confidence bolstered by this success and the discovery of a whole new set of skills, Glen asked for a transfer so he could develop his management potential. Now general manager of a division, Glen is again happily involved in the entry stage of a new occupational cycle.

The good feelings of success and satisfaction that Glen and other Questers derive from their jobs come because they tend to have challenging jobs that are interesting and meaningful. They are able to set their own goals, work independently to achieve them, gain support from supervisors and get useful feedback about their performances. Because of this, Questers are satisfied they are doing good work.

DIFFERENT STROKES FOR DIFFERENT FOLKS

Challenge comes in many different forms. At one end of the stimulation spectrum is the commodities broker who makes potentially disastrous trades every minute. At the other end is the product researcher who may develop a new product only once or twice a year. Both are challenged — with different timing.

Just as too little challenge may cause you to be dissatisfied, so can too much. If the level of challenge is so great you can't cope with it, you are in the wrong job. Moderate challenges that make success difficult but possible will give you the most pleasure and satisfaction.

Questers who understand how to match their needs for stimulation to the right job could find challenge in many different occupations. What do you need to find challenge? And how much is right for you?

VARIETY ADDS SPICE TO LIFE

Questers tend to enjoy work that allows them to accomplish many different tasks. They appreciate jobs that require some thought, have some unexpected challenges and allow them to use their own ingenuity.

Sandy gets plenty of variety in the Peace Corps. A broad range of experiences, skills and interests have prepared her to succeed at this often-frustrating job. Before she married, Sandy, now 51, was an agricultural agent. While she gave up her career for motherhood and marriage, Sandy kept busy with volunteer work. She headed a political campaign, lobbied successfully for a home for battered women, organized a youth employment center and chaired many committees seeking better facilities for the mentally retarded. "I love challenge and variety. I want to help others."

Her husband died when she was 49 and Sandy needed a job to support herself. She was well qualified for the Peace Corps. Although her position as a director is often difficult, she treasures the variety. "Every minute, every hour, is different. I get to work for world peace, to travel, to meet people from all walks of life and to help with all kinds of projects in agriculture, education, social work and medical care. I even answer phones for the African relief hotline."

THE NEED TO ACHIEVE

Understanding why many Questers are so involved in their work requires knowledge about the need for achievement. People who derive feelings of accomplishment from completing a difficult task feel satisfied and proud. How successfully they cope with a task determines how competent and proud they feel. Psychological growth only occurs when there is opportunity for achievement.

To see how important achievement really is, you must meet *Omar*. He raised $275,000 to start his own Italian ice cream store, the first of its kind in a large eastern city. The store drew 160,000 customers in just six months. Strange as it may sound, Omar didn't really care how much money he made or how famous he became or whether he could beat the competition. What he cared about was his product. "I had a product that I loved and believed in and I wanted a perfect gelato store that looked attractive and authentic and gave people something wonderful." To achieve that, he was willing to pay his employees well.

PERSISTENCE IS THE MOTHER OF INVENTION

Inner toughness. the ability to stick with a dream or an ambition even when it's not going well, tends to set Questers apart from a number of Traditionalists and Self-Seekers. Instead of panicking and packing it in when their dreams seem about to fall apart, they size up the problems and figure out alternative solutions. As they have discovered, there are many paths to success.

Bernadette learned that when she decided to go to college. Divorced and with two children to support, she worked day and night just to make it through her program. By the time she had obtained her BS, she had to face facts. She was just too poor to afford her long-time dream of becoming a doctor. So she took a job as a junior biologist, then as a technical writer, moving from a computer company to a small medical electronics firm. While she seemed to be drifting, Bernadette was actually questing, constantly "fine-tuning" her abilities.

By 1975, Bernadette had saved enough money to start her

own company making electrosurgical equipment, the same product her last employer had specialized in, only better. Her company's best seller, a high-tech scalpel, made her rich. Bernadette's interest in medicine had finally paid off, but in a much different way than she had envisioned.

HARD WORK IS ENERGIZING

The accomplishments of many Questers usually take a tremendous amount of hard work. Omar held a full-time job at an investment firm while working nights to research gelato recipes. His new position still keeps him going day and night. Bernadette went to night school and studied weekends. Getting ahead as they did without succumbing to exhaustion or self-doubt takes enormous determination and single-mindedness.

What Questers know is that hard work can be very energizing. Hard work has its own rewards, like positive feedback and the feelings of satisfaction that accompany a sense of accomplishment. Like many Questers, as you gain competence and become more fulfilled and involved, you will also gain energy. You may even learn to approach your job with verve, as if you are playing an exhilarating, although serious, game.

Successful activity, no matter how intense, leaves you with comparatively few scars; it causes stress, but little distress. Work wears you out mainly through the frustration of failure or boredom. Many of the hardest workers in almost any field live a long life.

INFORMATION IS POWER

If many Questers don't know something, they tend to find out, pronto! Omar tells his employees that "there's no such word as 'can't'." While some salesclerks sit around waiting for customers, many Quester salesclerks hound their bosses to teach them how the businesses operate. Questers know that every bit of know-how they pick up can only help to make them more resourceful.

When they're not studying, a number of Questers are evaluating what they've learned. This thirst for information heightens their chances for succeeding when taking risks. Omar found market research invaluable when he approached possible financiers. While the banks had a million facts and figures to show why another ice cream store just wouldn't make it, Omar had the research to prove it would. "I might have stopped right there, but I had done my own research and I just had a feeling that gelato would go."

FEAR OF FAILURE

Questers seldom risk their resources on impossible dreams.

While they take chances, their actions are based on sound knowledge of the facts plus planning and intuitive feelings. Omar's friends were appalled when he left his well-paying position. But he had done his homework so well that opening the store felt like the next step in a well-conceived plan.

Risk takers have to confront the fear of failure. Losing job security and possibly pride is risky. Questers tend to deal with this by waiting until the signs look good — and then plunging ahead. They work out their anxieties by acting, not agonizing. Since setbacks are inevitable, Questers train themselves to look at reversals as learning opportunities, not signs of personal inadequacy. "Failure is good for you," Bernadette says confidently. "It's a kind of bruise that makes you tougher. If I've done my absolute best and still goof, I say, 'Okay, I'm human.' I forgive myself. Then I sit down and take a look at what went wrong."

ENHANCE YOUR POTENTIAL

How can you develop your achievement potential? Set personal and professional goals and then start realizing them one step at a time. For example, start and stick with a training or savings program. At work, figure out how long a single project will take you to complete, then try to do it 10 minutes faster, then 20 minutes faster. Not only will increased efficiency raise your feelings of competence, but it could prompt your boss to give you even more responsibility and challenge.

While you are raising your own sense of competence, try to avoid competing with the experts around you. Instead, enlist their help and support. Many Questers are backed up by efficient and loyal support teams. When you are generous with your own talents and time, your efforts are usually rewarded many times over.

BE SELF-CONFIDENT!

Confident people stand out. They seem so comfortable and so in control of their lives. But self-confidence is often the result of accomplishing something. It also stems from learning to accept one's negative qualities.

Many Questers don't feel rejected for long if they have been passed up for a promotion or some other form of recognition. Because they are self-confident, they tend to have the courage to move on to occupations that do satisfy their needs. Their confidence also gives them the courage to take other risks leading toward goals that are important to them.

Studies in the workplace have found that most managers and professionals select "feeling that my work is worth doing" as the most important factor contributing to their sense of self-confidence and self-respect. Other contributing factors are:

- an equitable salary
- a sense of accomplishment
- growth opportunities, such as freedom, independence, authority and creativity
- sufficient feedback and recognition
- ability to advance within the company
- two-way communication
- enjoyable work
- company security

Highly self-confident employees get more pleasure from succeeding at their work than from any other factor. They are more likely to:

- value challenging tasks
- find the pleasure of achievement to be very intense and enduring
- want promotions for reasons of justice
- desire responsibility over status

And they are less likely to:

- value prestige, approval and verbal recognition as sources of self-assurance
- be emotionally affected by criticism
- experience fewer conflicts and feelings of anxiety on the job
- be defensive and employ defense mechanisms (Less confident employees will often project their failures onto other people and circumstances.)

How did they become self-confident? Few were born that way. Instead, they developed it through work, practice, determination and achievement. You can develop self-confidence in the same way. Start by realizing that at your core is an inner strength that you alone have the power to bring to the surface. The ability to top that resource is what long-distance runners call "digging down". Once you've grabbed hold of your own power and felt the magical quality that you possess, you'll see that self-confidence can truly turn your world around.

Bette learned that lesson while she was still young. A shy, quiet little girl, she stayed pretty much to herself. "If you had known me then, you would have said that I was one of the most unassuming and unambitious kids you ever met." But Bette had a secret. While other kids were outside playing, she was pouring over her mother's magazines and trying to copy the high fashion togs on her sewing machine. "I wasn't too successful at the time," she remembers, "but I knew somewhere deep down inside me that as long as I could play 'dress up' in my life, I would be happy. As I look back on it, I realize that even then my career was growing inside of me."

Bette's interest in sewing was translated into the desire to become a good dress designer. "Not to say it was a piece of cake. It wasn't!" She studied and worked very hard. Though still just a frightened little girl at heart, she traveled to Paris and New York to learn her trade. She took risks. "But the important thing is that once I made my decision to work toward this goal, I gave myself every opportunity to achieve it." These days, when she recalls her past insecurities, Bette thinks that she, like the legendary glass of water, was half-full, not half-empty. "Now, I design dresses that other little girls dream about!"

Bette didn't acquire self-confidence overnight. Nor will you. Self-confidence develops as you work on and achieve small goals. Like learning a language, developing self-confidence may sometimes leave you feeling awkward and uncomfortable. You will make silly mistakes and you will feel as though it's someone else, not you, doing those things. But the more you practice, the easier it becomes and the more natural you feel.

Ultimately, you alone are responsible for the decisions you make. The final results — self-confidence, knowledge and success — are the results of those decisions. To become more like the Questers, you will have to act like the Questers.

AUTONOMY IS BEING IN CONTROL

Questers tend to have a strong desire to control their own work. They perform best in jobs where they have the freedom to use their own ideas and knowledge, pioneer new procedures, take responsibility and prove their competence. Questers need the freedom to persist, to take risks and to fail without fear of being reproached or fired.

Few large organizations today provide employees with the opportunity to be autonomous. That's why so many Questers go into business for themselves or work for small companies. A National Science Foundation study showed that small firms produce about four times as many innovations for each research development dollar as medium-sized firms and about 24 times as many as large companies.

Mauro, now 55, owns one of these small companies, a factory that manufactures statues, fountains and tombstones. During his career, he's been a copywriter, salesman and middle manager for a large manufacturing firm. He left the last position because he was frustrated by the bureaucracy. Unable to use his own ideas, he felt stifled. "I had little input to decisions affecting my job and little creative input. The position was becoming really watered down." Feeling emotionally drained and physically ill from his lack of power, he soon developed ulcers. "I felt like I was wearing a strait-jacket." When Mauro decided he just couldn't take the feelings of powerlessness anymore, he left. Friends who knew him when he worked for his old employer are startled by the way he changed. His wife, Sandra, is happy with the new Mauro. "Mauro is more relaxed now. He was an old man 10 years ago. Now he's young again." In control of his life and his health, Mauro feels good about himself again.

Nothing breeds success more than success, nothing blocks it more than frustration. Frustration caused by lack of work autonomy can lead to serious consequences. Unrelieved tension or distress, usually accompanied by feelings of helplessness, is a threat to your health and self-confidence. Ongoing frustration can weaken the body's immune system and result in physical and psychosocial illnesses such as peptic ulcers, migraine, high blood pressure or back pain. Low self-confidence, job dissatisfaction, lack of creativity and low aspirations usually accompany the feelings of general ill health and malaise associated with lack of autonomy. For employers, the cost is measured in high turnover, dissatisfied employees with low levels of motivation and morale, reduced productivity and creativity and ineffective management. Some organizations are now involving their employees in decision-making and providing human relations training. Employees are taught to alleviate frustration and stress through relaxation training. They are also encouraged to talk to a trusted friend, counselor or relative when they feel tense.

FITTING IN

Corporations often fail to tolerate creative Questers who are the force behind many innovations. In an organization's eyes, these highly creative people may seem impatient, egotistical, obnoxious and perhaps even a bit irrational. As a result, some Questers may have a difficult time convincing prospective employers to hire them. If hired, they may not be promoted or rewarded. The frustrations of seeing creative efforts go ignored is what causes some Questers to move on.

Fortunately, some Questers can continue to be themselves

and find autonomy in large companies. Some organizations give employees plenty of autonomy. These companies encourage employees to take practical risks and, even if they fail, support good tries. They know that many Questers have to be allowed to experiment and even fail. The companies have learned that "turned on" employees can accomplish miracles. By creating small, independent divisions which give managers control over hiring, firing, finances and purchasing, these organizations breed loyal, dedicated managers who make better decisions than centralized departments ever could. The absence of paperwork and over-planning is as conspicuous as the internal competition. Unlike many organizations, managers who take on additional responsibilities outside their own divisions are even rewarded.

Jack is a bright, young Quester who works for a progressive company. Encouraged to take risks, he has the freedom to persist and the freedom to fail. At 32, this enthusiastic chemical engineer developed a new medical adhesive product. Supporting and protecting Jack in the development of his product, his manager sympathized with Jack's occasional failures and celebrated his successes. Jack appreciates the support he received. "Without the freedom to persist and fail, I never would have discovered the product." Once developed, the product has been so successful that Jack's employers have given him even more autonomy and incentives to promote further development and marketing.

COPING WITH FORCED AUTONOMY

Not all Questers find a company they can fit into. But unemployment has motivated many a Quester to become more independent and autonomous. Carol, the educator turned caterer, is just one Quester who had to learn to cope with forced autonomy. Today, these Questers are adamant that they will never again let anyone else control their careers. Simone, manager of an insurance agency, is another who learned coping mechanisms.

Five years ago, *Simone* found herself suddenly unemployed when the insurance company folded after she had advanced from policy typist to branch supervisor. It didn't take long for Simone to turn a crisis into an opportunity. "I realized there were only two ways to do things: work for somebody else or work for myself." She decided to open her own agency. She had already prepared for the change by taking night courses. Most Questers are thinking ahead long before fate or fortune causes them to move on.

Among many Questers, the yearning for independence is a

familiar feeling. Hasn't everyone, at least once, dreamed of owning a business? These dreams come true more frequently now as the economy and various job frustrations prompt more and more employees to strike out on their own. But can you really do it? Of course you can, if you're willing to put in the time and work and to take the risks involved. Most Questers have — and very successfully, too. Why can't you?

INVOLVEMENT IS EXCITEMENT

Questers are generally very involved in their jobs. Psychologically, they identify closely with their work. They take their positions seriously and their moods and feelings are significantly affected by their work experiences. Their jobs must satisfy the needs and values that are important to them. People who are highly involved in their jobs are more likely to feel either extremely satisfied — or dissatisfied, depending on what's happening at work. On the other hand, uninvolved employees tend to have less extreme emotional reactions to the same job experiences. If carried to extremes, such job involvement can become a neurotic compulsion. While wise Questers want to immerse and enjoy themselves in their work, they have learned to balance their jobs with the many other dimensions of their lives.

Job involvement is related to job satisfaction. Some authorities say the orientation to work is learned early in childhood and is hard to change; others think it may be related to biological make-up. Most agree that while work orientation can be developed, it is also related to certain personality characteristics and work environments.

ENTHUSIASM IS GOOD FOR YOU

Involved employees have an infectious enthusiasm about their work that employers can't help but admire. One company president remarked that he'd forgive just about any mistake, at least once, that was made out of enthusiasm. The president came away from his first meeting with the new company lawyer (a woman selected after much hesitation) glowing with admiration. He was involved in a legal battle which his company was almost certain to lose. Did she tell him he could win? "No," he said. "I know better than that and if she had, I'd have fired her. What she did do is to outline the steps she could take to limit our loss and all the ways she could press the other side to settle and she was so enthusiastic about it that I came out of our meeting feeling pretty good about the whole thing. Any lawyer who can make me feel good about losing a $1-million case is unusual. Given a case she can win, this lady is going to be a real tiger!"

The excitement of being involved in your job communicates to other people. Joyce, the school teacher from Chapter Two who left her job to become a principal, moved on because she was no longer enthusiastic about what she was doing. "Enthusiasm is catchy," she says, "and if I can't be enthusiastic about what I'm teaching, neither can my students." The intensity of high-energy performers and actors is the result of their deep involvement in their work. They can't be boring. They're too interested in what they're doing.

Enthusiasm is no less valuable in your private life. More love affairs and marriages die from lack of enthusiasm than any other reason. Nothing is more wounding than indifference or boredom. Even in sex, how much energy or interest you put into it pretty much determines how much pleasure you get out of it. Sex is a need like other needs and often is treated only as such. But the real need could be fulfilled by masturbation or routine intercourse. An interesting sex life is one in which people share their feelings, energy and passion. It's surprising what a satisfying sex life can do for your image. And why not? The better you feel about yourself and your life, the better your image will be. Same with your job. The real secret of having an exciting image is enjoying what you do.

PASSION

For some Questers, work is a passion. Gerald, the eye specialist from Chapter Two, calls himself a work addict, but a happy one. "I love my work," Gerald remarked. "Helping people see is rewarding. On occasion, I've met my wife at a party at six in the evening when I've been working since six in the morning. I haven't had time to wash or change to black tie, even if that's what all the other men are wearing. I might be completely exhausted, but when I think of what I did with my day, I feel good inside."

This passionate involvement in their work helps many Questers deal with problems that do arise. Gerald says even if he starts the day feeling sick or out of sorts, he forgets about it. "When you are working at your best, you forget your negative feelings. At that moment, nothing else exists."

MONEY IS A BY-PRODUCT

Financial reward is often the result of a growth process that begins with a real interest in your work and a love of accomplishment for its own sake. After all, earning power is just the by-product of doing a good job. Even in today's turbulent society, a number of people without family money or social connections are growing rich on their own initiative. They are not hotshot investors, intellectual geniuses, money grubbers or ruthless competitors. In fact, studies of the personalities of financially-successful people claim that these traits actually impede money-making potential. The successful are involved in careers they like and value.

Andrea, vice-president of a western investment firm, was divorced and unemployed with two children to support when she discovered her life's work. From secretary to administrative assistant for a financial services company, she has blossomed into a six-figure employee. Andrea used position as a springboard to learning what was previously foreign to her — finance. Studying largely on her own, she borrowed money for some night courses that helped her earn a broker's license. "I learned a lesson that I wanted to get across to other women whose husbands left them," Andrea says with determination in her voice. "When you're on your own, you can't afford to be a financial sleeping beauty." Andrea's financial planning series for women is an ongoing success.

THE JOY OF HELPING

Many Questers have little interest in financial rewards or prestige. What they do value, however, is an occupation that will give them opportunities to contribute to the welfare of others. Feelings of altruism or concern for others' well-being usually develop around the mid-life transition. The middle-aged become more committed to being mentors — guiding and helping others. A number of Questers seem to develop the need to be altruistic early in life and many look to their careers to satisfy this need.

Take *Christopher*. Until two years ago, Christopher, now 31, was doing extremely well as a lawyer for a large insurance company in a midwestern city. Then, suddenly, he quit and took off to do some wandering and to put his life in perspective. He turned up two years later in a store-front legal office funded by the Office of Economic Opportunity. Christopher explains that his insurance position, defending the company against plaintiffs who had been struck by cars, was the first rung on the career ladder. His next move would have been to become a personal injury lawyer. Had he stayed with the company for the usual — "heaven forbid!" — 25 years, Christopher would have retired with almost $400,000 in profit-sharing receipts. He laughs. "Once the novelty wore off, spending 10 hours a day defending an insurance company was a waste of time. With the education I've got, I might as well do something useful."

Today, Christopher is satisfied that he is doing something more useful. He's still a lawyer but now his clients include single parents, senior citizens, new Americans and people struggling to overcome landlord-tenant disputes. He represents juveniles in trouble, blacks abused by police, inmates caught in the state penitentiary system and people dumped into the streets as a result of overcrowding in state hospitals. Happily involved in a challenging new position, he charges one-tenth of the going legal fee. "Every day is different," he says with real pleasure. "I can work four days straight, 16 hours a day, and never feel tired. Until my eyes start falling out. . .then I know I have to go to bed."

Unlike his new position, the insurance company was all competition. "Everyone was trying to push the other guy down and crawl all over him to move up. If you didn't, you knew he was going to do it to you. God, the days dragged! I'd have a stack of 100 files on my desk, and all I could do was make checkmarks or go into court and make the same motions, day after day. And why? To save the company money."

Legal problems aren't the only ones that concern Christopher. If a client has an emotional problem, Christopher calls a psychologist. If the problem is lack of job skills, he encourages the client to go back to school. "They're so pushed down, so depressed. You get to know them intimately. I call them by their first names. We've been to each others' homes. After five o'clock, I never even saw the people I worked with at the insurance company. I would never have shared my thoughts with those people. But I would with my clients."

These days, money or fame are the furthest things from Christopher's mind. Helping his clients is reward enough. But he also realizes the immensity of his task. At times, he feels over-committed, over-extended and powerless, but Christopher has few regrets.

Many Questers feel the same way as Christopher and commit themselves to helping others. Some are even able to work happily within the bureaucratic constraints that Christopher finds so frustrating.

Soft-spoken *Meagan* has been called the Indiana Jones of her province's child welfare system. Each day, she slashes through a jungle of red tape to safeguard the rights of government wards. Why did Meagan, a former political scientist, abandon a prestigious consulting career to become a community social worker? "I think, more than anything else, for the challenge of developing something new that might have a chance of helping deprived children," she says thoughtfully.

TIGERS RARELY REACH THE TOP

Popular myths aside, wealth and success don't have to be achieved at the expense of others. Wealthy and successful Questers didn't claw their way to the top, heedless of whom they hurt along the way. Many Questers have made their contributions through inspiring others, promoting teamwork and developing other people's abilities. Of course, Questers must be competitive to succeed. Those who own businesses know the importance of being acutely aware of how their products and services stack up to their competitors'. But most Questers are less intent on getting ahead at the expense of others than they are on achieving. This is what Ryan, a factory owner, says about competition: "I know what my competitors are doing and I keep 10 steps ahead of them. I can meet them any way they want. But not to cut their hearts out. We all have to make a living." Other more ruthless competitors have come and gone. Ryan is still in business.

GROWING ON THE JOB

Whether or not a job rewards you depends on what you want from it. For most Questers, this equation is easy — they seek occupations in which they can thrive, develop and mature. They want to develop their own personalities, to exploit their talents, to innovate, to get the job done without having to follow rigid regulations. Questers' drive for growth is closely related to such other job satisfiers as challenge and autonomy.

Nicole has left several jobs that didn't offer the rewards she wanted. Petite, vivacious, with expressive brown eyes, Nicole at 38 is a magazine editor. Before that, she was a staff writer for an institution that published health care literature. And long before Nicole began her writing career, she was an elementary school teacher. Loved by her fourth grade students, Nicole was flattered by the power she wielded as a teacher, "but I felt I wasn't really using enough of me." So she took a writing job. Much as she loved reading and writing, that occupation just wasn't right for her either. "When I first got my job, I came in early and stayed late," she recalls. "I would work a project to death and get it really done right and then ask for more. But I found I was out of place. No one else was devoting as much passion to their jobs as I was and they didn't want to be reminded of it." So, she settled down and conformed, divorced her mind and spirit from her work. Like her colleagues, who were just as capable as she, Nicole ceased to care. I played cards for three hours at lunch or went sunbathing or shopping," she says. "It was a very comfortable job and it was despicable." Because Nicole's company expected less than she offered, she felt she was forced to play the game by its rules. "But I couldn't. At the end of the day I felt that I had not accomplished anything. I was furious, I felt humiliated and used." Predictably, it wasn't long before she quit.

The difference between her last position and her new one shows in Nicole's face. Blossoming as an editor, she is delighted that her new job offers her the freedom to develop her writing, editing and other skills. The magazine's readership has doubled since she became editor, but Nicole is constantly concerned about improving its quality.

Nicole, always highly independent and innovative, will change jobs again, if necessary, to avoid stagnating. Like many Questers, she is more concerned with acquiring a job and a lifestyle that matches her interests, needs, values, abilities and goals, than with seeking material rewards.

Brad satisfied his love of challenge by opening his own business. His success story started with a belt and a buckle. While in second year college, Brad received a beautiful belt buckle as a gift. Intrigued by the possibility of designing his own belt, Brad splurged $50 on leatherworking tools and materials. Soon he was selling his unusual, handmade belts to friends. "The business really snowballed from there," he remembers fondly. As his belts began selling at art shows, Brad expanded his work to include caps, wallets, key cases and other small leather products. Suddenly, Brad realized that he could be a business success. "The more involved I became in running the business, the more I realized how much I enjoyed the challenge." Today, he has 25 stores and is a multimillionaire.

PERSISTENCE

Genius or a natural talent such as Brad's isn't the only prerequisite for success. The word persistence crops up again and again when Questers talk about their accomplishments.

Ryan is a 64-year-old entrepreneurial Quester who, like Brad, loves to innovate. He, too, has kept expanding his business for the sheer joy of seeing it grow. From a newly-built factory on the outskirts of a large industrial city, Ryan manufactures coin and vending machines, vending machine parts and video games. He's thinking of expanding into computers.

With $100 borrowed from a bank, Ryan started his first business, a pinball game parts factory. As he kept adding new products, his business developed into a successful enterprise. Ryan admits he's not an engineer but he does love to create mechanical parts and products. "I love to see a piece of iron do some work," he says with a sparkle in his eyes. "I have an idea and then I see if I can make it work. "I love what I do," he explains. "I persist, and I keep on top of things."

BEING INNOVATIVE

Many Questers understand that the difference between being creative and being innovative lies in the ability to bring ideas to life. Innovators *do* things; creative people *think* up new things. While there is no shortage of potentially creative North Americans, there is a shortage of people who have the courage to innovate. Innovative Questers have the know-how, energy, daring and staying power to venture beyond convention. They may — and usually do — fall somewhere along the road to success. But their determination drives them on to bigger and better projects and eventually they will succeed. They are not geniuses. They are merely persistent and willing to fail. That willingness is what separates creative people from innovators.

KEEPING OPTIONS OPEN

Having the ability to succeed is one thing. Deliberately setting out to do so is another. Questers tend to succeed because they set career goals related to their needs, values, interests and abilities. Careful to keep their options open, they have the freedom to develop and to find challenge. Their career goals may range from open-ended goals to five- or seven-year plans. But all represent an active and independent commitment to career management. Questers are in control of their lives. Most Questers will move on to new goals that better satisfy their developing personalities. Having made at least one occupational move, they are not afraid to make others when they are no longer growing.

And a good many, aware that they might be approaching a dead end, have searched for and found a new road. They are usually adept at anticipation — imagining future bends in the road and preparing to shift gears in advance.

The willingness to manage their own careers and to anticipate their future needs is what tends to separate most Questers from many Traditionalists. Questers have learned to maintain a balance between tentativeness and commitment. Committing yourself to and becoming actively involved in a job that satisfies your goals is admirable. But Questers are usually the masters, not the slaves, of commitment. With a clear understanding of their own needs and goals, they can balance the two with skill as they travel tentatively along the sometimes-rocky road to career satisfaction.

In today's economic climate, being open to change is the best protection against obsolescence. Most Questers have learned to ignore the dangers and focus on the opportunities. Open-ended career goals permit them to react quickly to the changing market place and to high unemployment.

Having a satisfying career and life isn't always easy. But to most Questers, the easy life is usually not worth living. Consider your own career and lifestyle. What kind of life are you leading?

7: Rate your job satisfaction and adjustment

Are you satisfied with your job or do you feel it makes you moody, depressed and discouraged? It's normal to experience career ups and downs, but if your lows become much more frequent or last a lot longer than your highs, you probably need to give serious thought to whether or not you are in the right position. You can find out by asking yourself specific questions about your job and work habits. The three questionnaires in this chapter, *The Job Satisfaction Questionnaire, The Job Involvement Questionnaire* and *The Burnout Questionnaire*, are designed to help you do just that. The questionnaires will also help you determine whether your work attitudes and habits may be leading to burnout and what you can do about it. Directions, scoring procedures, interpretations and suggestions are provided.

As you read the items in each questionnaire, think them over carefully. The more honest you are, the more you will benefit. Let your feelings be your guide.

THE JOB SATISFACTION QUESTIONNAIRE

Each of the 38 items in this questionnaire evaluates one job facet. Understanding how well your job satisfies these facets will give you a good picture of your overall degree of job satisfaction. For each facet:

1. Place *+2* under the *VS*, if you are *very satisfied* with that facet.
2. Place *+1* under the *S*, if you are *satisfied* with that facet.
3. Place *-1* under the *U*, if you are *unsatisfied* with that facet.
4. Place *-2* under the *VU*, if you are *very unsatisfied* with that facet.

5.   Place *0* under the *?*, if you are *not sure*.

6.   Place *0* under the *N/A*, if the facet is *not present* in or appropriate to your job.

Grade each facet with your present job in mind. Scoring directions and an analysis of your responses follow.

FACET	RATINGS					
	VS	S	?	U	VU	N/A
	+2	+1	0	-1	-2	0
1. Personal growth and development	—	—	—	—	—	—
2. Working alone	—	—	—	—	—	—
3. Security	—	—	—	—	—	—
4. Appropriate salary level	—	—	—	—	—	—
5. Self-esteem or self-respect	—	—	—	—	—	—
6. Participating in decision-making	—	—	—	—	—	—
7. Accomplishing something worthwhile	—	—	—	—	—	—
8. Having a position of authority and/or leadership	—	—	—	—	—	—
9. Assisting others	—	—	—	—	—	—
10. Social status and prestige	—	—	—	—	—	—
11. Time to pursue leisure activities	—	—	—	—	—	—
12. Money to pursue leisure activities	—	—	—	—	—	—
13. Desirable locale	—	—	—	—	—	—
14. Opportunity to develop friendships	—	—	—	—	—	—
15. Varied responsibilities	—	—	—	—	—	—
16. Professional development	—	—	—	—	—	—
17. Seeing results of work	—	—	—	—	—	—
18. Feedback on performance	—	—	—	—	—	—
19. Fringe benefits	—	—	—	—	—	—
20. Merit promotion	—	—	—	—	—	—
21. Paid study leaves and/or time off for courses	—	—	—	—	—	—
SUBTOTALS	—	—	—	—	—	—

FACET	RATINGS					
	VS	S	?	U	VU	N/A
	+2	+1	0	-1	-2	0

	FACET	VS	S	?	U	VU	N/A
22.	Opportunity to change jobs within the organization	—	—	—	—	—	—
23.	Special skills and abilities used	—	—	—	—	—	—
24.	Respect and support from subordinates	—	—	—	—	—	—
25.	Personal goals and values compatible with the organization's	—	—	—	—	—	—
26.	Resources to do adequate job	—	—	—	—	—	—
27.	Respect, fair treatment and support from superiors	—	—	—	—	—	—
28.	Physical surroundings	—	—	—	—	—	—
29.	Interesting work	—	—	—	—	—	—
30.	Lack of pressure	—	—	—	—	—	—
31.	Relocation possibilities	—	—	—	—	—	—
32.	Esthetic contribution(s)	—	—	—	—	—	—
33.	Using own ideas	—	—	—	—	—	—
34.	Time to spend with family	—	—	—	—	—	—
35.	Amount of job involvement	—	—	—	—	—	—
36.	Amount of unrelated/clerical work	—	—	—	—	—	—
37.	Ability to organize/regulate work	—	—	—	—	—	—
38.	Clients' and/or customers' appreciation of work	—	—	—	—	—	—

SUBTOTALS — — — — — —

TOTAL SATISFACTION SCORE _____
TOTAL DISSATISFACTION SCORE _____

**OVERALL JOB SATISFACTION
    SCORE** _____

(Job Satisfaction minus Job Dissatisfaction)

SCORING

To evaluate your score:

1. Determine your subtotals, for VS, S, U and VU scores and write them in the spaces provided under Subtotals.
2. Determine your Total Satisfaction Score (add the VS and S ratings) and your Total Dissatisfaction Score (add the VU and U ratings) and write these in the spaces provided.
3. Determine your Overall Job Satisfaction Score by subtracting your Dissatisfaction Score from your Satisfaction Score.

The highest possible score you can get is 76. The lowest score you can get is -76. The higher your score, the more satisfied you are with your job. The lower your score, the more dissatisfied you are.

INTERPRETING YOUR SCORE

32 or higher: If your needs and values are being met thoroughly in each job facet, your Overall Job Satisfaction Score will be 76. This rarely ever happens. But if your score is over 32, you are still quite satisfied. However, there probably are some aspects of your job that could stand improvement. Find out what they are by reviewing your low scores. Then think about how you could better satisfy these needs.

16-31: If your Overall Job Satisfaction Score lies between 16 and 31, you are moderately satisfied with your position. Your job situation is in need of some changes. Can the facets in which you got negative scores be improved? If you answered yes, you need to assess your current job in relation to your career goals. Exploring other career options should be considered. View your work as a continuing opportunity for growth and development. Some jobs are good; they are regenerative and the longer you keep them, the more they increase your value. Other jobs diminish your value; they are repetitious. The longer you do them, the older you get, the more you lose your flexibility and opportunity to grow, and the more easily you can be replaced with someone who is younger and cheaper. Making a job change may be the best way of revitalizing your working life.

0-15: A score between 0 and 15 indicates you are a candidate for a job change. You are tolerating a number of on-the-job conditions that make you unhappy. Seriously consider moving on. Don't remain in a deadening work situation. Circumstances often force people to take jobs that fall far below their true abilities. Selecting a job out of economic necessity is understandable, but choosing to remain year after year in a blind alley is detrimental. Don't put off for long your resolve to do something about this situation. If you do, you might end up in the next category within a few months.

-1 or lower: If your Overall Job Satisfaction score is -1 or lower, you scored yourself VU or U for most job facets, indicating that you find many of your job conditions dissatisfying. You have a serious case of job blues. Obviously you need a change, perhaps even a dramatic shift to a totally new field. Considering that you have so few satisfiers in your position, it's amazing you can even motivate yourself to go to work. If you suspect that you would have answered this quiz in a similar way six months or even a year ago, you may also be a procrastinator who is waiting for someone to force you to make a move. Wait no longer. Put your career back in your own hands.

Appraising your career development should be an ongoing process. Do it whenever you need to clarify where you are in your career and what your next step should be. Do it to get to know yourself better. Do it to get ahead. The key to an ever-evolving career is to monitor your own career development and stay attuned to new opportunities.

FURTHER CONSIDERATIONS

The Job Satisfaction Questionnaire should have helped you pin down your major sources of job frustration. Now you have to decide what to do with this information.

Many men and women hope their discontent will go away on its own. It rarely does. Others throw themselves into their work in an attempt to compensate for their feelings of self-doubt. Some distance themselves from their work, which often leads to poor performance or problems with the boss.

All these reactions to job dissatisfaction are part of a "survival mentality". Too many of us often put up with unhappiness in our work that we wouldn't tolerate in other areas. Although some people might be content with a nice safe rut, most eventually realize how dissatisfied and frustrated they are.

With time, a certain fear sets in with some people — fear of the unknown. Rather than try something new, they adjust to the old. They don't select, they settle. These people keep going but regret that they never even tried to find out what really might have been right for them.

This is the big question. You may tolerate your work because it pays the bills. You may even like it because it's familiar and easy. But is it what you want to be doing years from now?

What can you do if you feel stuck in a position you dislike? If you could create the ideal job for you, what factors would you want to include? *The Job Involvement Questionnaire* and *The Burnout Questionnaire* should give you additional insights into the feelings you have about your work.

THE JOB INVOLVEMENT QUESTIONNAIRE

Answer the statements below by checking either Yes or No. If you are uncertain about a question, check the response that most closely describes your feelings. If neither feels right, check the statement that seems most appropriate. Once you have completed the questionnaire, add up your scores. Scoring procedures and an interpretation follow.

1. The most important things that happen to me involve my job. ( ) Yes ( ) No
2. I am really a perfectionist in my work. ( ) Yes ( ) No
3. Most things in life are more important than my work. ( ) Yes ( ) No
4. My work is one of the most rewarding and fulfilling parts of my life. ( ) Yes ( ) No
5. I would probably work just as hard as I do now even if I did not have to support myself and my family. ( ) Yes ( ) No
6. Most of my friends would probably agree that I usually have a great deal of energy and I get much of my energy from my work. ( ) Yes ( ) No
7. I never work on weekends and holidays. ( ) Yes ( ) No
8. I am so involved in my work that it is hard for me to take vacations. ( ) Yes ( ) No
9. I would never think of breaking a date or cancelling an appointment so that I could get more work done. ( ) Yes ( )No
10. My work is so much a part of my life that distinctions between work time and play time get blurred. ( )Yes ( ) No
11. My involvement in my work never causes problems for my family and friends. ( ) Yes ( ) No
12. I never bother making a daily list of things to do to help me make the best use of my time. ( ) Yes ( ) No
13. I often do some extra work for my job which isn't really required. ( ) Yes ( ) No
14. Even though I'm efficient, I work harder than most other people doing the same type of work. ( ) Yes ( ) No

15. I live, eat and breathe my job. ( ) Yes ( ) No
16. I feel depressed when I fail at something
connected with my job. ( ) Yes ( ) No
17. I'll stay overtime to finish a task, even
though I'm not paid for it. ( ) Yes ( ) No
18. For me, mornings at work really fly by. ( ) Yes ( ) No
19. How well I work does not affect the way
I feel about myself. ( ) Yes ( ) No
20. Sometimes I'd like to kick myself for the
mistakes I've made in my work. ( ) Yes ( ) No

TOTAL POINTS ___Yes ___ No

SCORING

POINTS

Give yourself one point for each Yes answer
to questions 1, 2, 4, 5, 6, 8, 10, 13, 14, 15, 16, 17,
18 and 20. _____

Give yourself one point for each No answer
to questions 3, 7, 9, 11, 12 and 19. _____

Add your points.

TOTAL POINTS _____

ARE YOU HAPPILY INVOLVED IN YOUR WORK?
The maximum possible score is 20. The higher your score,
the more involved you are in your work. Some people would call
you a workaholic. If your score is 12 or higher, you are quite involved in your work. Your work is probably central to your identity. If you can truthfully answer Yes to six of the seven questions
below, you are probably happily involved in your job.

1. Does your family support your work habits? ( ) Yes ( ) No
2. Do you have autonomy at work? ( ) Yes ( ) No
3. Do you have variety at work? ( ) Yes ( ) No
4. Do you get positive feedback from your
job? ( ) Yes ( ) No
5. Does your job make you feel good? ( ) Yes ( ) No
6. Is there a good match between your needs,
values, interests, skills and job? ( ) Yes ( ) No
7. Are you in good health? ( ) Yes ( ) No

TOTAL POINTS ___Yes ___No

TOTAL YES POINTS

Work addicts who answered Yes to six or more of these questions generally feel good about themselves. But if you responded No to three or more questions, you are a prime candidate for job burnout.

The word "workaholic" may have negative connotations but fortunate indeed are those who find work they passionately want and do successfully. After all, you will spend more than half of your time on the job or commuting to and from it. The label, "workaholic," for those who are happily involved in their jobs, is a positive, not negative, word.

ARE YOU A HAPPY WORKAHOLIC OR A NEUROTIC?

There is a distinction, of course, between happy job involvement and neurotic compulsion. Determining whether you genuinely enjoy your work or are being driven by a neurotic need to control and manipulate is an important first step in rating your job involvement. People who are happily involved in their work are usually flexible and can cut loose from a work addiction to enjoy the many other dimensions of their lives and relationships.

The workaholic's biggest problem usually isn't the job itself, but the inability to do or enjoy anything else. Most really don't enjoy leisure pursuits and feel uncomfortable in social settings. They may feel distressed, anxious and dissatisfied when they are not working. The hook is sunk when this drives them to work harder and longer in an increasingly anxious and isolated lifestyle. If your family life is crumbling or you can't sustain a good interpersonal relationship, you may not have the resources to call upon for support and help when a crisis looms. Extreme workaholic tendencies need to be balanced out with the other parts of your life. Here's help:

- **Think about the parts of your work you enjoy most and delegate or reduce the parts you dislike.** Decide how much time you want to spend working and limit your work accordingly.
- **Schedule free time into your work life.** Breaks can actually improve your performance.
- **Learn to say no to new demands on your time.**
- **Lean towards the positive aspects of your job.**
- **Place a value on the time you spend away from work.** This will give you the opportunity to reassess your life values and to make decisions about changes and directions.
- **Most of all, remember to appreciate your friends and family.**

If you are a workaholic, you are lucky. Not only do you love your work, but the cure for your problem is quite pleasant. Just learn to relax. . .do more of what you like to do and less of what you don't. Spend more quality time with friends, family and yourself.

ARE YOU ONLY MODERATELY INVOLVED IN YOUR WORK?

If you scored between 6 and 11, you are probably only moderately involved in your job. In the right work environment, you could probably increase your level of job involvement by taking charge of your job. Don't just react to your boss or other people around you. Instead, take the initiative and create your own ways to reach your department's goals. With your boss' help, see if you can shape your position so you are doing more of what you are good at and shift or delegate the other duties and responsibilities to coworkers with complementary talents. Don't hold back or be afraid of being thought of as too enthusiastic.

ARE YOU REALLY SUITED TO YOUR JOB?

A score of 5 or lower indicates you are not even slightly involved in your job. Perhaps other aspects of your life are more interesting to you. Good! But really low job involement indicates a lack of interest and enthusiasm in your work. It may even suggest poor health.

If your scores on *The Job Satisfaction Questionnaire* and *The Job Involvement Questionnaire* indicate you are dissatisfied with your job, you should probably do something about changing jobs or even occupational fields. To find an area in which you'll excel naturally, do some self-analysis. Just why do you dislike your position so much? What would you rather be doing? To help you do that, complete the inventories in Part A of Chapter Nine.

THE BURNOUT QUESTIONNAIRE

Do you experience chronic fatigue? Are your thought processes dulled? Are you irritable? Are you progressively withdrawing? Do you feel physically unwell? Is your work always with you? Do you wonder why? If you answered yes to more than two of these questions, you may be headed for burnout. Psychologists and physicians consider career burnout a chronic stress syndrome.

Burnouts are often successful in their fields — that's what burns them out. Some bright women and men work terribly hard, make tremendous sacrifices, soar to the top of their occupation or profession and then seem to run out of fuel.

To find out if you are on the path to burnout, complete the

questionnaire below, then read over the explanation that follows. Check Yes for the symptoms of burnout that apply to you and No for those that don't.

1. Are you increasingly irritable and impatient? More disappointed in the people around you? Are you having more arguments with your spouse, friends or even strangers lately? ( ) Yes ( ) No

2. Do you feel irreplaceable? Do you go to work even when you feel ill? Do you accept extra duties out of obligation? ( ) Yes ( ) No

3. Do you tire easily? Feel fatigued rather than energetic? Does sex seem like more trouble than it's worth? ( ) Yes ( ) No

4. Do you have very little to say to people? Are you seeing close friends and family, even if you live in the same city, less frequently? ( ) Yes ( ) No

5. Do you fail to establish an enriching and satisfying life separate and distinct from your work? ( ) Yes ( ) No

6. Do you take work home only to find you don't complete it? Do you find that even though you don't do it, the work dominates your environment, provoking guilt? ( ) Yes ( ) No

7. Have you overtaxed yourself at work or home? Do you feel persistent pressures — too much to do and too little time? Are you too busy to do even routine things like make phone calls, read reports or send out Christmas cards? ( ) Yes ( ) No

8. Are you increasing your use of drugs, such as aspirin, sleeping pills, tranquilizers, alcohol or tobacco, to cope with job pressures or to unwind from work? ( ) Yes ( ) No

9. Are you preoccupied with thoughts of self-blame, guilt, self-recrimination, anxiety? Do you feel powerless about certain aspects of your job? Do you lack feelings of success or challenge? ( ) Yes ( ) No

10. Do you feel as if nothing is going well? Do you find yourself talking mostly about work and are your conversations mostly

negative?   ( ) Yes   ( ) No

11. Are you developing uncharacteriically
     rigid ways of thinking and/or losing the
     ability to adapt to change? Are you adopt-
     ing rigid "by the book" approaches to
     problems rather than developing indi-
     vidual solutions?   ( ) Yes   ( ) No

12. Are you turning excessively to colleagues
     for help in coping with emotional or
     physical problems or with business and
     professional responsibilities?   ( ) Yes   ( ) No

13. Do you use more ditto/board/workbook
     activities, audiovisual materials or support
     staff lately to remove you from direct
     contact with subordinates? Have you
     taken a large number of sick days lately?   ( ) Yes   ( ) No

14. Are you forgetting appointments, deadlines
     or personal possessions?   ( ) Yes   ( ) No

15. Are you suffering physical complaints —
     aches, pains, headaches or a lingering cold?
     Have you had severe physical or mental
     illness — ulcers, high blood pressure, hyper-
     tension, colitis or nervous disorders —
     lately?   ( ) Yes   ( ) No

16. Is joy elusive? Are you often invaded by a
     sadness you can't explain? Are you unable
     to laugh at a joke about yourself?   ( ) Yes   ( ) No

17. Do you hate going to work? Do you turn
     off as you enter your workplace? Do you
     feel as if you are operating like a robot that
     doesn't care enough to care? Do you get a
     knot in your stomach when you realize the
     next day is a work day?   ( ) Yes   ( ) No

18. Do you constantly say, "Is this all there
     is?" about your job?   ( ) Yes   ( ) No

19. Do you fail to achieve desired professional
     goals (for example, "cures", financial gains,
     attainment of status, perception as an "ex-
     pert", respect from others and validation
     from patients)?   ( ) Yes   ( ) No

TOTAL POINTS   ___Yes   ___No

INTERPRETING YOUR SCORE

Give yourself one point for each Yes. The maximum score is 19. If you answered Yes to 11 or more, you may be a candidate for burnout. The higher your score, the greater your chances. A score of 12 or higher indicates you need to take quick action to change your work habits or job. While no one sign of burnout is important on its own, when many are present, you may already be well on your way to burnout. Burnout is not only preventable, but can be temporary and treatable.

If you are prone to burnout, you probably have several of the following symptoms:

- feelings of recrimination about work problems
- cynicism
- long work days to compensate for diminished productivity
- loss of energy combined with emotional fatigue, strong ambivalence about work (Why am I doing this?) and feelings of being overwhelmed
- use of drugs as an escape from stress
- a tendency to postpone vacations
- anger and hostility towards anyone — friends, colleagues, children, even your pets
- a chaotic family life
- a loner lifestyle
- a sedentary lifestyle
- a continuing restlessness that drives you to constant activity

On the other hand, people who thrive on long work hours have the following in common:

- the ability to postpone thinking about problems
- prompt reactions to signs of fatigue
- avoidance of drug abuse
- enjoyment of scheduled vacations
- stable domestic situations
- the ability to organize and manage time
- the ability to make a distinction between their personal and professional lives
- the ability to set realistic work goals
- the ability to maintain friendships
- a regular exercise program
- a belief they have control over their lives rather than feeling controlled
- a thirst for novelty and challenge rather than familiarity and security

PREVENTING BURNOUT

Most Questers stay healthy because they are committed, challenged, have control over their destinies and feel supported by family and friends. Surprisingly, these people tend to be challenged most by adversity. Many have learned to use stress as a constant source of energy that helps them get things done and feel good about what they have accomplished. Perceived this way, stress can be valuable. But it must be managed wisely. If you can adopt attitudes like theirs. you may cut your chances of becoming ill in half. To survive, you need to recognize the possibility of burnout and act to stop the syndrome before it strikes or becomes worse. Here are some ways to manage stress·

● **Find something to stimulate you each day.** Make your life full and rich. Seek out interesting ways of viewing life and take time each day to learn something new. Make your career a cherished exciting, living and developing part of you.

● **Build your self-confidence.** Make your accomplishments a form of personal expression so you feel good about what you do. Realize that you don't need to perform to prove anything or to beat anyone. because you already know and like who you are.

● **Don't try to control everything.** After all, you are in control from within. Stay on top of your work, but don't let it overwhelm you.

● **Seek challenge.** You will grow wiser and more skilled if you let each day bring new, manageable opportunities for growth.

● **Look on the rosy side.** Reinforce the positive in yourself and others. Most of all, keep your sense of humor; learn to laugh at yourself once in a while.

● **Keep problems in perspective.** Mistakes and setbacks, even outright failures, can be learning experiences. Accept responsibility for your actions.

● **Get away from it all.** Have other interests besides work. Make family, leisure and relaxation times fun. These activities are necessary to maintain physical and mental health. Burnout can become so serious that psychologically just "getting away from it all" becomes extremely difficult. But you can do it if you learn to balance your life.

● **Learn to relax.** Relaxation techniques can help to emotionally rejuvenate your weary mind and soul.

● **Seek professional help.** Many good books and articles on both burnout and relaxation techniques are available in your local bookstore or library. If you can't cope on your own, most hospitals or mental health professionals can give you good advice on how to deal with burnout.

8: *The will to risk: psychological aspects of decision-making*

The will to risk is a difficult quality to cultivate. It requires great strength, strength that is built on wounds, failures and losses. People who become Questers tend to draw their strength from every dimension of their lives so that they can become resilient and enduring.

Making a change requires letting go of the familiar. You will feel exposed and vulnerable. But that very stress gives Questers the determination to go through with change. It provides the heightened awareness that offers hope that change will be worthwhile.

Questers' sense of inner control determines their success in new ventures. The link between a sense of inner control and the willingness to risk is a strong one. Having some plans for the future strengthens Questers' assurance that they can have a positive impact on future events in their lives. Moreover, because most Questers believe in what they are doing and expect that they are going to succeed, they generally do. They usually have realistic expectations.

PART A: STYLES

How do Questers go about making risky decisions? What is their decision-making style? Most Questers take planned risks. The majority do not move on impulse, but give careful deliberation to their decisions. Making decisions rarely comes easily to them. They often harbor numerous doubts about themselves and their work options. Many will struggle with doubts and uncertainties about their futures, their jobs and the consequences of their actions. They will evaluate their personal characteristics, as well as their occupational alternatives. But once they make a firm commitment to change, the rest of the process becomes easier.

Questers tend to be flexible risk takers. The risks they take are a response to feedback from the environment, colleagues, friends and their own emotions. Questers do not discount security. Most take measures that carry them through a crisis.

Most Questers try to establish a balance between the intellectual and emotional, between the rational and the intuitive aspects of decision-making. Although they will consider a broad range of alternatives, Questers will eventually select one. They are realistic enough to know that there really is no one right decision, only one that feels good for them at a particular point in time. They anticipate both good and bad outcomes of their decisions. Doing so often requires from six months to several years. Even after they arrive at a probable decision, Questers will remain open to new information and ideas. But once they have made the big decision, Questers usually stick to it. Most evaluate the results after they act. Questers tend to learn from mistakes.

MELISSA'S STORY

Small, dark-haired, attractive, energetic, intense, warm, Melissa belies her 44 years. Dressed in a dark grey suit and a becoming gold blouse, she projects a businesslike, yet feminine, image. Melissa is impulsive and intuitive but she plans her risk-taking. Today, Melissa is director of training and development for a large retail outlet. After her first full-time job as an airline stewardess, Melissa returned to school to study education. She had grown tired of her nomadic existence. Her desire to challenge her mind led to three years of college, then to a job as a high school English teacher. But six years was enough of that. Now, her desire for new challenges led her into a management training program for a large retail outlet. Melissa was an extremely good manager. A promotion to manager of women's fashions in a large department store gave her a chance to exercise her flair for fashion and well-developed people skills. But by the time six years were up, the old familiar, uneasy feelings were back. Increasingly restless and tired, she looked around for other opportunities inside her company. Nothing seemed particularly attractive. Melissa knew she needed a change, but to what?

Now 43, she was anxious about her future. An amalgamation with another retail chain had resulted in regressive policies and procedures. Incensed with her lack of control over purchasing and personnel, and frustrated by a lack of autonomy yet total responsibility, she quit. Resigning may not have been very wise, but Melissa chose to trust her instincts. "I felt like I was in a strait-jacket." Unemployed and scared, Melissa turned to friends and family for support, but there was none. "They thought I was crazy to give up this position, even after I told them why I had to leave." With no support from friends and family, sticking to her guns took real guts.

Actually, the decision to change jobs had germinated some time before. Long before she quit, she had begun salting away large chunks of her salary. A full year before she left, she attended a seminar on career change that helped identify her abilities and transferable skills. It was no accident that Richard Bolle's book, *What Color is Your Parachute?*, rested on her bedside table. Still there is a difference between leaving one job for another and quitting with no prospects. Quitting was an impulsive (and perhaps even irrational) act, something Melissa had never before done. Only the knowledge that she was at the breaking point propelled her forward.

What to do? First, Melissa assessed her net worth. By giving herself permission to live off rainy-day resources, Melissa could manage for 10 months. The next move was a call to a talented career counselor who could help sort out her feelings and priorities and set some definite career goals. Within an hour, the counselor had helped Melissa to see that staying on would have been a mistake. That gave Melissa courage to carry on. The six months that followed were some of the best months of her life. "It was very stimulating," she says. "I felt completely in control. I loved setting up my own schedule. I took 'me' on as a new project and worked like a dog!"

Melissa was determined to keep moving and in touch with her network of friends and former associates. Good fortune stepped in when a former colleague called to offer her a chance to conduct some workshops in retail management. The $5,500 contract put a little more distance between Melissa and the poorhouse. She used some of that $5,500 as seed money for her career search, investing in a typewriter, an answering service, calling cards, attractive letterhead and a handsome resume.

Her next move was to set tentative career goals. Melissa decided to target her career search into three general areas: management, self-employment and training and development. Systematically, she explored her network of friends and associates, applying for job after job, until she had sent out over 52 job enquiries. Some merely involved a letter. Twenty-one reached the interview stage, and one, a job in the food processing industry, required seven interviews during a single day.

For each interview, Melissa diligently researched her prospective employer and product. During one interview for the executive directorship of a community welfare agency, Melissa launched a series of tough queries to decide if she and the company were a good career match. Who really held the power in the organization? What kinds of skills did the director need? What was the director's scope of authority? The silence that met her questions was uncomfortable. Her interviewers decided that they would have to postpone the search until they had determined what the job really entailed.

That wasn't Melissa's only fruitless job interview. But then another promising management opportunity, this time with a large flour milling company, slipped past. So Melissa took a cue from a job search book and fired off a letter to the mill's vice-president of public affairs. Instead of the usual "Thanks for your time," it said:

> *I'm sorry to hear that the position has been filled. I thought I'd be good for it. I also very much appreciate the time you spent talking to me. Because you know so much about the food processing industry, I would like to keep in touch with you from time to time as I continue my search. Would that be okay?*

With an approach like that, who could turn her down?

Melissa's time-out period gave her the opportunity to seriously consider an idea that had long intrigued her: going into business for herself. The possibilities tempted her. Should she become a freelance retail consultant? Establish a fashion boutique? Or buy into a publishing position with a regional women's fashion magazine? The options were exciting. But Melissa decided her bottom line, at this point, was a regular paycheck. Although these options weren't right for her now, Melissa promised to reconsider them later on.

Having ruled out going into business for herself, Melissa was now ready to explore a third possible avenue: training and development. Her self-appraisal had revealed that she had knowledge, skills and experience in retailing, teaching, managing, coordinating, communicating and public relations. Further testing told Melissa what she already knew: She had high abilities in English comprehension and expression, analytical reasoning and supervision. An interest inventory gave her top scores in leadership, business, supervision, human relations and teaching. Other inventories revealed that she had high needs for autonomy, variety, achievement, challenge and creative expression.

Wedding these personal characteristics into a satisfying union took planning. Melissa did it by accepting a senior training and development position with a large retail enterprise. The marriage didn't happen overnight. Instead, with a friend's help, Melissa explored the options by reading and talking to people already in this field. She then drew up a list of five firms that seemed compatible with her own personal characteristics. Melissa began a serious, high-gear job search with letters to the vice-presidents of personnel and phone calls to top managers. When all five responded that they had no immediate openings, she shifted the nature of her campaign. She then chose a young, growing, people-oriented, flexible organization that offered profit-sharing and competitive salaries. Most important, the organization didn't yet have a fully-developed training and development program. Melissa was armed for her attack. First, she made a series of phone calls to the company's top managers. Finally convincing them she was serious, she landed an interview with the vice-president of personnel and the senior vice-president. It lasted four hours. The company brass were impressed, but the only job available was a junior position training sales clerks. Melissa persisted. What the company really needed, she asserted, was a more ambitious training and development program. A second interview was all it took to convince the company to hire her as the new director of training and development, at a higher salary and with six weeks grace so she could finish up her contract work and take a well-earned vacation.

How has her job worked out? "Very well," Melissa reflects one year later. Although the job hasn't grown quite as quickly as she hoped, and she doesn't yet have the size of staff she needs, Melissa is content. "I'm glad I didn't take the jobs that I thought would be dead ends. I'm glad I avoided traditional corporations. And, I'm glad I took a chance with a growing, progressive organization because now I can grow with it."

Does she have any regrets? "Absolutely none." In fact, Melissa says, quitting without having another job lined up was lucky. "I might not have conducted such a thorough job search if I hadn't felt so pressured." A good job search, she now knows, is a long process. Melissa was lucky; she found her position in five months. "But, of course," she says wryly, "I had to work like a demon to do it."

Besides the obvious reward of a new job, Melissa's job search had other benefits. One was self-confidence. "I love my work," she says, "I feel good about myself and, at the end of the day, I have lots of energy left over." While being 44 seemed like an added pressure at first, her age was no barrier in the end. What hasn't changed is her cautious approach to relationships. Since her divorce, Melissa has had several relationships that just didn't work out. "I wish I could change my personal life as easily as my work life," she admits. But Melissa has the maturity to understand that while she may be quite venturesome in her career, slow is the right speed for her personal life right now.

WHAT CAN WE LEARN FROM MELISSA?

Melissa's experience is a good lesson. It demonstrates that while confidence and willingness to risk can be positive qualities, job searchers also need to protect themselves by reducing some of the risks involved in an occupational change.

Melissa's success was partly due to investing in herself. By realizing that this was the very rainy day for which she had been saving, Melissa could allow herself to buy the time she needed.

Taking time out allowed Melissa to learn five important lessons. First, she learned the importance of trusting her instincts. Far from being disastrous, quitting a job before she had another one gave her more time to devote to a job search. Second, she discovered that the most satisfying positions are often ones that allow you to tie together the threads of past experiences and interests. Third, she found that mature age can be an advantage. Having reached the age and level of experience that demanded the opportunity to call her own shots, she discovered that the best job is often the one you design. Creating your own job doesn't require that you be self-employed, only that your self be fully employed. Fourth, was the discovery that her options were numerous. Because people become tied to certain jobs and skills, they forget just how vast their actual choices are. Finally, Melissa's job search demonstrates that the tremendous investment of energy that every successful job search demands is what allows people to look back and say, "Win, lose or draw, I gave it my all." Being able to say, with satisfaction, that you risked for a dream is the biggest prize of all.

UMBERTO'S STORY

Success doesn't always come easily. When it does, the experience can be astonishing, invigorating and a little frightening. Those are the emotions Umberto, a former social worker, experienced when he turned restaurateur. At 40, this handsome, sensuous, dark-haired entrepreneur with brooding eyes and deep voice has mixed emotions about the success of his Italian restaurant and his highly-popular cookbook. A cautious risk taker, Umberto is in his fifth job, but first "real occupational choice." Despite his cautious nature, experience has taught this west-coast entrepreneur that once the first risk is past, the rest follows naturally.

Umberto enjoys talking about career choices because he feels his own risk-taking pattern is fairly typical. "More and more," he explains, hands slicing the air around him, "I see people who, 10 or 15 years ago, would have been expecting to take a long, steady climb up the career ladder to the top of their fields. But they've tumbled off and now they're beginning to rethink what they want, and it's not just to change jobs within their field, but to change occupations completely." Umberto has tried both. For the first 12 years of his professional life, he experimented with moving around in the social work system. Then he made a drastic move that changed not only his career, but his entire life. This is the story of that process.

Like many, Umberto greeted university graduation with uncertainty. The year was 1960. With a BA in social sciences, he was not sure what he wanted to do. He took a job as a social worker for a small school division about 100 miles from his home city. The job promised to combine his desire to do socially-useful work with an interest in adolescents. Weekly meetings with the school division's psychologist and evening courses and workshops led naturally to a BSW degree. The job was especially gratifying because Umberto liked working with people. "Until then, as an only child, I had led a fairly protected life. The job exposed me to a lot of life that I hadn't seen before and I was forced to do a lot of soul-searching to clarify who I was and what I valued. You can't discuss values with kids without looking seriously at your own." The next few years saw him working tirelessly during the days, then, instead of spending time with his new wife, Brenda, he wrote reports endlessly during the evenings. Even in his sleep, Umberto was still writing reports and rehashing problems. But while the job was challenging, it was also frustrating. "You were supposed to help change the students' behavior but you only saw them once every three weeks."

Five years of frustration were enough. Soon, Umberto was off to get his MSW and into the probation system where, with a smaller workload, he could work with delinquent youth. Now that Umberto had the opportunity to work intensely with his young charges, he felt he could make a real impact. His sense of progress was short-lived. No matter how effective he was, a rigid probation system thwarted his good intentions. Feeling disgruntled, he searched again for a position in the same field. His third job was the draining task of investigating child neglect and abuse. "What I saw literally made me sick." By December, 1974, Umberto had been a social worker for 15 years. "It felt like 30." His career growth had been agonizing and what he had seen depressed and infuriated him. "I saw people who didn't rock the boat get promoted. Those who did and were their own persons didn't have a chance to advance. I was very good at my job, but there was no incentive to be creative."

Umberto had to maintain some balance in his life. So he took up painting and cooking to relieve his career pressures. But the tragedy of his life didn't fully strike Umberto until he watched his father dying. He recalls: "It was a funny thing. Here you are, watching a beautiful man with white hair lying in his bed, dying of a heart attack. You hear him ramble and wander, and talk about his life and what he wished he had done. You watch death. Then you say, 'Wait a minute. What's going on with him is going to happen to me. What am I doing between now and my death?' You begin to assess yourself and that's a shock. 'Am I going to do this for the rest of my life? Isn't there another way to earn a living?' That's what you wonder."

Suddenly, Umberto had to do some serious self-evaluation. After a long discussion with his wife, she turned to one of his paintings and said: "Umberto, you're a very creative person, but this job is wiping you out. You're miserable, you have migraines. Please quit." The time had come. With his father's death and Brenda's permission to quit, Umberto's unspoken dreams could surface. Consumed with joy and relief, he burst into tears. "I didn't know what I wanted to do, but I just knew that I had to get out of social work. I saw that I had interests and talents, intelligence, creativity and energy that, if I directed them toward the goals I cherished, I could make it." Umberto also realized that he had never really made the choice to be a social worker. Chance and circumstance had led him into an occupation that filled him with misery. He wanted to be able to choose an occupation right for him.

That took time. While his wife encouraged him to quit right away, Umberto was reluctant to leave her carrying the burden of a hefty mortgage. Since he could do his job effectively in just six hours a day, he could devote the rest of the time to exploring his options. Gradually, he discovered what he didn't want. Umberto enjoyed making pastry, but he didn't feel it would be profitable enough to pay the family's bills. And the artist's life was too solitary. Then, at 38, Umberto realized that what he loved most was cooking and entertaining. As a child, he had cooked while his parents worked. Now a grown man, he was still cooking. Maybe this talent could be turned into a profitable venture.

There were other reasons Umberto wanted to succeed on his own. One was his hostility toward authority. He also wanted to rise on his own merits. Excited now, Umberto realized that he didn't want to be a chef, confined to a hot kitchen all day. He wanted to be a manager. Too impatient to return to school for the business and management skills he needed, Umberto took the direct approach. He talked to the manager of a fast food outlet about entrepreneurship. The die was cast when he discovered the outlet's parent company had an excellent training program. Within a day of being accepted, Umberto had quit his job. His co-workers were envious.

Quitting was easier than he had thought. True, his salary would plummet to less than half of what it had been, but his family was prepared to skimp for a while. The next 18 months were among the hardest and happiest of Umberto's life. He quickly advanced to become manager of one of the largest-growing outlets in the chain.

Soon Umberto began fantasizing about his own place. During the months of training, he had discovered that he really loved the restaurant business, that his counseling skills could be put to good use in dealing with employees and customers and that he could get the immediate rewards he so desired. This time, quitting was even easier. "Having quit once before, I had finally managed to overcome my fears."

Within a month, Umberto had found the perfect location, a large, old house overlooking a river. Raising the money was more difficult; the lowest interest rate he could find was 22 percent. Umberto thought it over carefully, then decided instead to remortgage his home and borrow the money from friends and family. With cash in hand, he then decorated the house and designed the menu, using the motif of a typical northern Italian restaurant. Il Palazzo opened with a staff of 20. In a city noted for sophisticated palates and numerous restaurants, Il Palazzo soon accumulated a dedicated following. As demand for the secrets of his fine cuisine grew, Umberto followed up his first success with a guide to Italian cooking. With astonishing pre-sales of 40,000 copies, it, too, was a hit.

Achieving that elusive mix of culinary and financial success was no mean accomplishment. Long before he launched his new occupation, Umberto had researched the market and the pros and cons of the restaurant business. He says, "This just felt right. I knew what I was getting into, so I felt ready to take the plunge." Even though, through preparation, he had reduced the risks of failing, this new entrepreneur still experienced the usual anxiety. Today, he says, "I can hardly believe that this is the new me! I did have a difficult time leaving social work. But I remember by father's regrets. I didn't want to have similar ones."

WHAT CAN WE LEARN FROM UMBERTO?

Umberto learned to be a risk taker and a Quester by moving carefully at first, researching his options and taking into account the needs and desires of those close to him. But as he grew more confident, risk-taking became easier. Umberto's decision-making style also changed from that of a cautious, play-it-safer to that of an enterprising entrepreneur.

Had Umberto examined his career goals sooner, he may have fulfilled his dream much earlier. His unhappy work history was partly the result of entering an occupation out of expediency rather than conviction. It was also the result of a desire to make a difference.

The right pieces to Umberto's puzzle eluded him for a long time. Finally, he found that running a restaurant satisfied his needs for control, for creativity and for dealing with people.

Umberto's story punctures the fallacy that you can't change the direction of your career in mid-life. To be truly satisfying, your occupational choice should allow previously disregarded aspects of yourself to finally emerge.

PART B: PROCESS

In their planned risks, many Questers proceed through a series of steps or stages as they move toward their goals. The steps Questers pass through do not always occur in the precise order outlined here, and Questers may pass through some more than once. For instance, many will experience ambivalence (Step Three) even while they are preparing for risk (Step Four). But if Questers omit one of the stages, they can end up in trouble. Moreover, in dealing with different problems, Questers may be at different stages. Since a decision in one life component (career, marriage, leisure) affects the processes in another, decisions need to be thought out carefully.

Decisions are based on knowledge about yourself and your environment and are influenced by societal pressures and realities. Most are made with an element of uncertainty and subjective probability, but all involve emotional and intellectual processes. Unconscious, pre-conscious and conscious thoughts should be considered in evaluating the information that goes into making a decision. A proper balance of both commitment and tentativeness is crucial in today's work world.

Making decisions is seldom easy. No one can tell you if you should change jobs. To grow and develop to your fullest potential, however, you have to be willing to make changes.

By learning how Questers tend to plan for risk, you can change the direction of your life. Even now you could be planning the moves you would like to make, rather than waiting until the situation is so awful that you are forced to change.

STAGE ONE: UNEASY FEELINGS

Petite and 55, *Gloria* is a clinical psychologist in private practice who just completed her Ph.D. Her ambition and ability are inspiring. Obvious intelligence is balanced with a magnetic beauty. Stunning green eyes glitter with excitement and the worldliness of experience. For all of her success, Gloria hasn't had an easy life. Her father died when she was eight. By her early teens, Gloria was burdened with an alcoholic mother. By working part-time, she was able to put herself through an honors program in mathematics. After graduation, she worked in the actuarial department of an insurance company until she and her new husband, Daniel, an up-and-coming lawyer, decided to have a family. Because she had missed out on a happy home life, having one now was important to Gloria. But, once more, she was disappointed. At 39, with four teenagers, she was on her own again. Although Daniel did pay some child support, the money wasn't enough to maintain the standard of living the family was used to, so Gloria returned to school for a year to train as a math teacher.

Being a teacher seemed like a good career choice. She would have contact with people, the salary was good and the hours and holidays would give her time to be at home with the children. By all external standards, Gloria was successful. After teaching elementary school for four years, she was promoted to principal, where she stayed for five more years. But when the school administration offered her a promotion to a larger school, Gloria turned it down. She reflects, "I was feeling tired and irritable." Frequent outbursts of tears and anger seemed to have no apparent cause. The laughter seemed to have gone from her life. Feeling bored and trapped, Gloria knew she was no longer growing in her job. "I had no intellectual stimulation. I had mastered the job. Even if I had moved on to the other school, it just would have been more of the same." That fall, she fell ill. Bones aching, she huddled in bed. Friends told her to go to the hospital. But Gloria knew it was only the flu. She also knew that what was truly making her ill was that she really didn't know what to do with the rest of her life. She stayed in bed for 10 days. Finally, she asked for a sabbatical. "I needed time to rethink the direction my career was taking."

Gloria's body was giving her messages, but labeling her feelings was hard. Most life changes are heralded in advance by just such physical cues. At first, you ignore them. Eventually, you cannot. You may feel lousy a lot or you may feel that something is wrong with your relationship or that you never laugh anymore. Everyone's body has some physical equivalent for fear, despair or euphoria — a dull ache in the gut, a feeling of heaviness inside, tears that well up like a flood, a sense of soaring. Sometimes, these feelings are hard to label and to distinguish.

It is easy to project the blame for these feelings onto other people or situations. You may shout with frustration that "No one understands me" or "My wife is impossible to live with!" But regardless of where you first pin the source of your discontent, sooner or later you must reckon with the knowledge that you just don't like what you are becoming. The ultimate target of these negative feelings, whether conscious or unconscious, is yourself. How did you become this trapped, stagnant, joyless person?

Perhaps you've been working five or 10 or more years in your job and it appears to be going well. You've had steady promotions, good raises, praises from superiors and admiration from subordinates. Even your parents are proud of you. Then, one day, you get a queasy feeling that something is — missing. But what? Like the victim of an accident, you anxiously grope around to feel if your arms and legs are still attached. You run the film of your life in reverse, but still you can't figure out what's wrong. Often, no one single event is responsible. Instead, it's been a gradual process. You may have been seriously ill or your marriage may be falling apart or someone close to you may have died. Many of these feelings can be traced back to your job. Most "uneasy feelings" that Questers experienced are precipitated by some negative aspect of their work. Often, the discontent was intensified by some critical life event and self-evaluation began.

These feelings may persist for months or years, depending on your ability to tolerate them or your masochism. Sooner or later though, you must translate your dissatisfaction into some forward-looking project. While it is still much too early to speak of "plans" at this point, you will sense that something needs to be done.

STAGE TWO: DEFINING THE PROBLEM

Once Gloria admitted she had a problem, she was able to move into stage two: defining the problem. A year-long sabbatical allowed her to enroll in a psychology program. Being a psychologist was a "fantasy" goal from way back. "In thinking about my career, I realized that I went into teaching for the wrong reasons. I made a cold-blooded decision because I needed the money and liked the hours. But I was never 100 percent happy in teaching. My subconscious was telling me that I could change and try something that I had wanted to try for a long time." Because Gloria was no longer responsible for the children, taking a risk was okay. Even if she did fail, she would be the only one to suffer.

Gloria had entered the second stage of decision-making. This stage is usually a subtle modulation from Stage One, like a change of key in music. Feelings of uneasiness are translated into vague impulses that you'd like to chuck the job and start on something entirely new. Gloria was aware she couldn't stay in teaching, so she thought of trying her long-time dream, psychology.

At this point in the decision-making process, your goals will be quite fuzzy. They may be wistful, full of yearning without much expectation of gratification, and yet, they may also contain a kernel of hope. That kernel can blossom into a clearer idea of how you would like things to be. The danger now is that you will abort the fantasies as too distracting or unrealistic. Dismissing these fantasies prematurely means ruling out possibilities. Be charitable to your brainchild. Ideas and fantasies need care and nourishment. Listen carefully to your fantasies, you may discover that they reflect your deepest needs.

Fantasy exercises can help to clarify what you would like to do, but are afraid to try. If you haven't already tried one of these exercises, turn to the risk section in Chapter Three. By spelling out your fantasies, you can use them to make the transition from "If only I could" to "By God, I will — start my own business, make my marriage work, quit this job I loathe!"

Gloria did. Her second stage began with the realization that she wanted to get out of teaching and try psychology. By listening to her own fantasy, she was parting with a familiar way of life and taking her first step into the unknown. Setting a tentative goal for the future is an important preliminary step in the decision-making process.

STAGE THREE: IT'S NOT EASY

Gloria's "I will!" was followed by the third stage of the decision-making process, "But can I?", as anxiety asserted itself. Many experience such conflicting emotions before taking a risk.

Gloria, for instance, was afraid because she was leaving the security of a monthly paycheck and a pension. As she stepped into an unknown future, she felt conscious of her 49 years. How would she do? She had no job in sight. But she was also excited about testing herself, about trying something new and challenging, about experiencing adventure and change.

Being anxious about risk-taking is normal. Many feel apprehensive about losing their known world. In Gloria's case, she was trading the horrors of the known for those she couldn't yet imagine. She was giving up a lot.

WHEN ANXIETY IS TOO GREAT

If the prospect of undertaking a change is so great that your stomach is constantly churning, you can't sleep, you have constant headaches or you feel you're developing an ulcer, your body, in its wisdom is telling you to forgo the risk. Don't persist in the face of pervasive anxiety.

Milton, a highly-skilled rehabilitation counselor, was approached by a prospective partner to start up an executive recruitment agency. For weeks before making the move, he went straight to bed immediately after dinner and pulled the sheets over his head. He tried to make light of it by brushing off his exhaustion as the terror anyone might feel at starting a new venture. But, in his personal and professional life, Milton had undertaken many risks before and had never felt this way. Clearly, his physical response was evoked by something else. He later discovered that the hard-sell, aggressive style required for executive recruiting was not for him. His underlying fears turned out to be prophetic. The difference in basic values and counseling styles between the two partners proved to be such a handicap that within five months both had agreed to disband.

Yvonne had a similar experience. She applied to a school of social work. Soon after being accepted, she developed a chronic headache. It disappeared the day she called the school's director to say she wouldn't be attending. Yvonne's body was correctly telling her that she didn't have the temperament for social work. She felt she would need more autonomy and would get too involved in her clients' problems. Today Yvonne is a happy and successful freelance journalist.

The moral seems clear: if your body tells you to "stop", consider rejecting the risk. Doing so may also be a risk — the risk of trusting your deep feelings more than some abstract notion of what ought to be best for you. Lists or inventories may be useful in making risky decisions, but ultimately they won't work unless feelings are also considered. One ulcer can counterbalance a bigger paycheck any day.

WHEN THERE IS NO ANXIETY

Little anxiety and very few negative feelings about an impending risk can be just as debilitating. What's wrong? Well, first of all, the risk may not really be a risk. Perhaps what you are moving to has many virtues and a highly-predictable outcome. Almost no danger is involved. Or, maybe the negative aspects of your current situation are so overwhelming that there seems to be no other choice. If everything about your present job is unbearable, then the decision to change may feel like a compulsion rather than a decision. Without a sense of choice, there is little ambivalence. Or, you may be avoiding, rationalizing or denying the anxiety you actually do feel.

Inner emotional preparation, which weighs losses as well as gains, fears as well as hopes, is a necessary prerequisite for successful risk-taking. When you give up valued connections, anxiety is an appropriate response. The losses of risk-taking can be profound; prepare for them by confronting them.

It is only natural that the prospect of change should toss you back and forth between fear and hope, exhilaration and anxiety, panic and a sense of adventure. These mixed feelings need to surface and be accepted.

STAGE FOUR: REVVING UP

Preparing for risk also takes resourcefulness. Most Questers try to be in charge of change by planning, having realistic and up-to-date information and preparing a contingency plan. To invite change takes courage and hope; to see it through takes skill. Gloria explored psychology by taking three night school courses while she worked. Then, during her sabbatical, she studied full-time. Her contingency plan was to return to teaching, at least for a while.

To make good decisions, you also must control the elements of the risk that are controllable.

SETTING TENTATIVE GOALS

Questers tend to think carefully about what they want to do. They separate their needs and desires from what society dictates or what friends and family desire. Most Questers establish tentative short- and long-term goals. Rather than viewing these goals as a huge, all-encompassing mass (changing a job), they break them down into manageable sub-goals (learning more about their needs, interests and strengths, or reading about the kinds of occupations that fit their personal characteristics). Examined task by task, each step is much more manageable. Breaking down your goal into manageable units makes the formidable possible.

Many Questers set their goals by their career fantasies and desired lifestyles. They are not afraid to daydream a little. They have learned that goals that are too low will just lead to more dissatisfaction. As they gather more information about themselves and their career options, Questers review and revise their goals. These goals are measurable and concrete, but not ironclad. Gloria's tentative long-term goal was to leave teaching. Her fantasy goal was to be a psychologist. She enrolled in a psychology program, but just in case her fantasy didn't work out, she retained the option of returning to teaching. Taking courses in psychology gave her time to explore herself and the field to determine if she was suited to her new career choice. Her commitment to leave teaching and enter psychology was flexible enough to allow her to make changes if her plans didn't jell.

EXPLORING

Seeking relevant, up-to-date information is a basic step in illuminating the dark, unknown world one enters in making a major career change. Many Questers use this information as a guide for at least part of the journey. Two kinds of information can be essential to any occupational shift: knowledge about yourself and knowledge about your career options in the current economy. You will also need to know where you can get this information, what books and directories to consult, the personal contacts you will need and what professional assistance — workshops or counseling — is available.

Gloria learned more about herself and her career options from a vocational psychology course. She learned about the types of jobs in psychology that would be most suitable for her, as well as the probabilities of finding a compatible position. This information also helped reduce some of Gloria's anxiety.

The mechanics of finding information have been thoroughly described in a number of books. These are listed in Suggested Readings.

NETWORKING

Another way Questers keep abreast of information in their fields is through networking. Through professional meetings, workshops and conferences, they develop and maintain contacts with people in occupations of their choice.

EVALUATING OPTIONS

Once Questers have assessed their personal characteristics and identified and explored their career options, they pursue their dreams. Doing so isn't always easy. Although scoring alternatives and calculating probable losses and gains is important, these practices have their limitations. Imperfect information, human impatience and the difficulty of adding to your equation the emotional components of hope and fear, not to mention unconscious projections and fantasies, complicate the process. Still, listing the pros and cons of each choice, taking into consideration your personal characteristics and heeding your inner voice are valuable steps in taking risks.

PREPARING FINANCIALLY

The risks of changing occupations can be reduced if you prepare yourself financially. Melissa's nest egg, for example, enabled her to conduct a full-time job search. Gloria prepared herself financially by taking a sabbatical. That monthly paycheck gave her the opportunity to learn more about herself and the field of psychology, as well as to learn new skills and knowledge. Both women, and Umberto, learned to get along on a considerably lower income so that their savings and money would stretch further. Some Questers' spouses went back to work full-time to supplement or even bring in all the family's income. One Quester, who went into business for himself, reduced his lifestyle dramatically. He says, "It got to the point where I had to reduce my lifestyle substantially. I was living off. . .rice and watered-down tomato soup."

Some Questers who returned to school were able to obtain financial aid packages from the public or private sector. To help finance their studies or business ventures, many Questers borrowed from friends and relatives. Others approached liberal bank managers with well-researched proposals.

Don't use lack of money as an excuse for not making a career change. Like the Questers, as you work towards your career goal, you will find ways of surviving. But for a while, you will have to work hard, think creatively and be willing to forgo some material comforts. Few Questers regret these sacrifices.

SEEKING SUPPORT

Dispelling misinformation, reducing ignorance or having financial resources tend to make Questers feel more secure in their decisions. But they don't live by facts and material needs alone. Questers' job shifts are made easier and their anxieties reduced when they have the support and guidance of others. Whenever you begin any large, new venture, you need to feel that people you are close to care. Many Questers received assistance from mates, family members, friends and colleagues. Others sought help from spiritual advisers or professional counselors. Not only can others provide encouragement and empathy, but they can also help you to see your decision more objectively and to critically analyze it. Gloria received lots of support and encouragement from a friend, Brad. A professor and the director of psychological services for her school division also gave her encouragement to get a Ph.D. Positive feedback from clients and professors gave her a tremendous sense of accomplishment. Hard work, a sense of humor and prayer have also helped many Questers to cope with major changes.

REDUCING THE RISK

One reason why career changes evoke so much anxiety is that they seem irreversible. But this is not necessarily so, particularly if you think hard and creatively. Many Questers tend to build in fail-safe and retreat positions, contingency plans for an alternative course of action if the present one turns out to be a disaster. Just knowing that there are other possibilities reduces the risk. Identify the worst possible disaster that could occur, then decide what you could do about it. Doing so will not only relieve some of your anxiety, but it will also prepare you for that possible outcome. Gloria's "worst possible disaster" would have been to return to teaching. Having that contingency plan reduced her anxieties and negative fantasies.

During your life there will be times when you have to make choices that close off other options. You may have to select a college, accept one position over the other, or even quit a job. Unless you keep two important points in mind, that knowledge can be paralyzing. What you need to remember, first of all, is that most decisions that seem irreversible are not. Secondly, although you almost always give up some options, you gain others. The experience you gain on the job you hate might well put you in a good position to land a job you will love. Plus, there are usually ways of satisfying more than one option. One woman who agonized over whether to enter law or medical school satisfied both interests by entering law school, but specializing in medical malpractice. All it takes is a little innovation.

RESTRUCTURING THE RISK

Another way many Questers have learned to reduce risks is by giving risk a different value or priority in their lives. They thus change its emotional impact. They tend to look at the other side of an issue by asking themselves what they are leaving out or how the pluses balance against the negatives. Changing the priority you assign to it can also make a risk seem less intimidating. Must you really define yourself by your success on a new job, or, if you fail, could you simply look for a more suitable job?

One secret of many Questers' success is the ability to re-define or re-label situations. For example, they may shift their thinking from success versus failure to learning versus stagnating. Most Questers learn from their failures. It is in the process of dealing with failure that you will be transformed into a Quester. A number admit to having failed at a major personal or professional endeavor, but they usually found it a useful experience. Many Questers don't give up after a loss or retire in fear from the fray.

REDUCING THE URGENCY

In times of acute pressure, Questers have learned not to panic. Deadlines can be moved. Gloria didn't make her decision to leave teaching immediately. She took a year's sabbatical to give herself time to think. A time limit, particularly one imposed by someone else, need not be cast in stone. A prospective employer will wait another day or two while you mull over a job decision. In any major life decision, you can learn to allow yourself breathing or incubating time.

A word of caution: Don't continually extend a self-imposed timeline. There's a difference between giving yourself a buffer to reflect on an offer or decision and procrastinating. Once you commit yourself to realistic goals, and set deadlines, put your plan into action.

MAKING PLANS

After Questers do what they can to prepare for their change and manage risk, they make a choice and develop a tentative plan. Their planning is usually preceded by a number of questions they ask themselves about personal characteristics and desired career and life goals.

Many Questers try to make their career choices a reversible process so that they may move in more than one direction at any given moment. If this sounds like hard work, it is.

STAGE FIVE: INCUBATING

When they have done all they can to reduce the risks of career change, Questers tend to let go of the process. They let their de-cisions incubate. By turning away from the muddle of decision-making, they let a deeper part of themselves, their subconscious, have its say. Gloria wasn't consciously thinking about pursuing a Ph.D. in psychology, but she let the suggestions of her professor and school director incubate. Gradually, as she kept working to complete a master's degree, the idea resurfaced. Rather than forcing the decision, she let it rest in her mind.

The incubation period allows the intuition to surface. Some educators advise you to use intuitive and analytical thought in combination. Typically, intuitive insights both precede and follow the exhaustive use of analysis, reason and logic. The failure to resolve problems sometimes is due to the inability to put them into perspective. Being overly concerned with certain facets of a problem may cause you to skip over better solutions. Intuition permits you to delve into the conscious and subconscious storehouse of everything you have ever learned. Tapping this rich reservoir enables you to perceive the many possible solutions inherent in complex problems.

Since intuitive insights are not under the control of the will, it is usually best to wait for a solution to develop on its own. Of course, you can't always predict when it will come. You must tackle problems consciously by compiling as much information as possible and analyzing the data. The intuitive hunch may come as a flash or, as it did for Gloria and Umberto, as the result of many months of serious research. "Sleeping on it" allows the intuitive or incubative process to take over. Many creative people report finding solutions to problems either upon awakening or during a moment of reverie. Almost everyone has had the experience of groping for a name or memory, only to have it swim obligingly to the surface soon after stopping pursuit of it.

Turning away or letting go may seem like procrastination, but it can be distinguished in two ways. First, rather than feeling guilty about it, you consent to it. Second, rather than a shut down, it represents an attentive waiting, a poised readiness. Sometimes, you move ahead best by sitting still. It takes time for seeds to germinate. At some point, particularly before moving into action, it is not only permissible, but desirable, to let go so that your deepest convictions can emerge.

STAGE SIX: GO FOR IT

Questers don't move into action until they have prepared themselves both cognitively and emotionally. But once they have, they get going. This entrance into a new risk usually begins with an exit. In Gloria's case, the action stage began when, after her sabbatical, she was interviewed by the school board about a new principalship. Would she accept it? Gloria decided not to. That first step precipitated her movement toward her goal to attain a Ph.D., then to establish herself in private practice. After taking the first step, she took others by applying to the Ph.D. program, serving an internship and starting a small private practice two days a week while she completed her dissertation.

Letting go and taking the plunge always begins the action stage. Regardless of how well you prepare, acting on any decision always means taking some steps into the unknown. There is always something new to learn about yourself and the situation. But once a commitment to change is made, the rest of the process is always easier. For most Questers, this stage, though risky, always brings a heady sense of relief. Finally, you've done all the dreaming, researching, thinking, worrying and phoning and are ready to quit or to accept the job.

STAGE SEVEN: VIEW FROM THE TOP

Gloria was asked to evaluate the gains and losses she experienced from her career move. "There is no way I could go back," she replied. "It would be like dying. I think it's far better to keep trying new things because you're not going to grow if you sit still." As Gloria says, for every risk she took there has been a positive payoff. "And each time I risked, I learned to do it more effectively. I really feel that there isn't much that I can't do at this point in my life. I feel I've walked a million miles, mostly on my own." Like all of us, Gloria has fallen on her face, but she has learned something from every negative experience.

Would she do anything differently? "Not very much," Gloria replies. She has made errors in her practice and has been something of a workaholic. But her only true regret is that she stayed so long stagnating in a job.

Fortunately, Gloria had few doubts about succeeding: "You have to believe that even though all of the odds are against you, you'll make it." Visualizing herself in the situation she wanted to be in helped Gloria to move forward. And, while she doesn't always feel confident, she has learned to put her doubts on the back burner.

Having succeeded at this risk, Gloria has definite plans for her future. She wants to keep working, learning and growing, though not at the pace she had to set to obtain her Ph.D. and start a practice. Now she wants to reap the benefits of her hard work, to have more time for herself, her partner and her family. Gloria feels her age was a definite benefit.

Gloria's evaluation of her gains echoes that of most Questers who change occupations. The majority feel that they acquire a considerable amount of personal satisfaction and a sense of inner harmony. They attain greater self-awareness and believe that they gain greater control over their personal and professional destinies. Enhanced job satisfaction and involvement, improved relationships with spouses or partners and family members, more leisure time, healthier, more rewarding lifestyles and more meaningful lives are among the other rewards they mention.

The good feelings that result from taking a risk (even if the results don't turn out as hoped) can be incredible. First, there's the gain of seeing yourself as a survivor, as someone who can accomplish something. Mastery, or the sense of competence and achievement that comes from seeing that you can control a difficult situation, is an important gain. When you test yourself by risking, you are forcing yourself to grow by calling on skills, talents and perceptions that have never been used in the same ways before.

The urge to risk reflects the need for achievement. Correctly approached, taking risks can enhance that sense of accomplishment so intimately connected with self-confidence. Many people say that even when things didn't work out, they were nevertheless pleased with themselves for venturing, for asserting themselves, for testing their mettle and for not stagnating.

A second, related, good feeling comes from learning more about yourself, whether you succeed or fail. The lessons you learn from your failures are sometimes the most precious. Risking gives you an opportunity to explore your needs and values, your coping skills, your stretching limits and your bottom line.

If you have tackled a life challenge carefully and still experienced a poor outcome, you will probably be discouraged. Learn from your mistakes. You will have other chances. If you foul up, fix it. Expecting to have a perfect career or perfect life is unrealistic.

The fear, excitement, pleasure and joy of changing jobs rejuvenates most Questers. They tend to learn some pretty important lessons from their career moves. As one says, "Money is far from being the most important thing in life. On the contrary, it can be a trap that becomes a false goal and creates the illusion of security." "Growth is a gain," says another Quester. "If you are just living for the next coffee break or the next vacation or raise or retirement or death, you are not really living. To be open and alive in the present, to experience the present as fully as possible, and to make my own sense of it is what matters to me."

THE IMAGINARY DEFICIT

Most Questers feel like those you have met. They haven't really tallied up any major deficits from their career moves. Some experienced material losses, such as loss of a steady income, retirement benefits, security, seniority, investments and health or insurance benefits. But, in the eyes of many Questers, these losses are minor. Though a number, particularly those who became self-employed, took substantial pay cuts to become established, they retrieved these losses. Most felt planned risk-taking paid off and will practice the same steps again when they take their next risk. Only about 25 percent said they would do something differently. Among this group, most said they would leave a stagnant job sooner, pursue a work problem with a senior company executive, take more time to explore additional options, leave more gracefully or seek the aid of a career counselor.

Making changes is a necessary part of growing. But the responsibility for making the alterations to enhance your personal and professional life rests with you. Sometimes this means taking a step out into the unknown and parting with a familiar way of life. And, if that's the case, muster all the courage you can and think of yourself as a new Quester, because you will become one. Remember, next time it will be even easier.

WHAT'S YOUR DECISION-MAKING STYLE?

How do you go about making risky decisions? Are you a planned risk taker, like most Questers, balancing the intuitive, emotional self with your intellectual, rational self? Or are you impulsive, agonizing, delaying and anxious? Or intuitive, impulsive and careless? Although most people rarely are completely consistent in their decision-making style, most of us can detect some regularity in the way we make important decisions. Think of the important life decisions you have made, for example, about marriage, divorce, major residential moves or career shifts and then answer the following questions. You may not be able to answer some with complete confidence, but give the answer that comes closest to what you believe. This is not a test. It's just a device to help you better understand your own decision-making behavior. For each item, choose one response that best describes how you usually respond to making a big decision.

1. In making a major decision:
    ____ A. I usually plan things. I am thoughtful and organized.
    ____ B. I usually can't make up my find. Frequently, I'll

    put things off until tomorrow.

    ____ C. I tend to do what feels right. I usually make up my mind quickly.

2. In making a major decision:

    ____ A. I think of a number of alternatives, but stop after a reasonable search.

    ____ B. I keep producing and going over possible choices.

    ____ C. I make a quick, overall survey of possibilities, hoping something will hit me.

3. In deciding among alternatives:

    ____ A. I take reasoning and feeling into account.

    ____ B. I try to use reasoning almost entirely.

    ____ C. I almost exclusively listen to my feelings.

4. In thinking about consequences:

    ____ A. I tend to think of both the good and bad outcomes.

    ____ B. I tend to focus on the bad things.

    ____ C. I expect things to work out okay.

5. Before making a decision:

    ____ A. I feel a mixture of anxiety and excitement.

    ____ B. I feel mostly anxiety.

    ____ C. I feel mostly excitement.

6. In making major decisions:

    ____ A. I take a fairly long time.

    ____ B. I take a very long time.

    ____ C. I take a little time.

7. Before taking a major decision in my life:

    ____ A. I think it out carefully, then decide with as few regrets as possible.

    ____ B. I agonize over the alternatives.

    ____ C. I make up my mind quickly and stick to it.

8. Once I make a decision:

    ____ A. After checking it out, I usually rally behind it.

    ____ B. I experience serious doubts and may change my mind.

    ____ C. After launching into action, I usually don't think about it.

9. After I have acted on a decision:

    ____ A. I tend to think about what I have learned from it.

    ____ B. I tend to worry and regret not doing something.

    ____ C. I tend to put it out of my mind.

TOTAL NUMBER OF:

    ____ **A. Responses**

    ____ **B. Responses**

    ____ **C. Responses**

SCORING AND INTERPRETATION

If you had 6 or more A responses, then you, like many Questers, tend to plan your risks, taking both your intuition and reasoning into account. You make decisions fairly slowly and are more concerned with reasonably good outcomes than with fear of failure or the need to make a perfect decision. You usually plan and review, but without worrying a great deal.

If you scored 6 or more B responses, then you tend to be an agonizing, delaying, anxious risk taker. You may make big decisions with great effort, indecision and fear of making mistakes. You may take a great deal of time to ruminate and worry about the decision.

If you scored 6 or more C responses, you are probably an intuitive, impulsive, careless risk taker. You tend to make decisions quickly, with little experience of mixed feelings. You may feel inappropriately optimistic and spend little time in introspection.

Very few people are entirely A, B or C risk takers. Most are mixtures. Because of this, there can be a number of types of risk-taking styles, ranging from cautious to impetuous. The man who is slow to take a career risk may be more impetuous in another area of his life, such as when buying real estate or playing the horses. A woman who operates largely on hunch may, through self-discipline, be able to force herself to spell out the consequences of really major changes before taking action. Some such inconsistencies are both inevitable and healthy. No one is a perfect risk taker any more than he or she is a perfect mate, a perfect manager or a perfect friend. But you can learn to be a more effective risk taker.

You can learn to think ahead, plan your progress and negotiate with life as you move toward your goals. Don't be afraid to try. Even if you fail, you win.

9: *Dare to change*

A career change can take months or even years of exhaustive soul searching. Long before you make the move, you need to know the steps involved in a successful move, how to master the troublesome feelings that accompany taking chances, where possible dangers lie and how to increase your gains while minimizing your losses. You will need to understand yourself and your career options, know how to set career goals, where to find advice and assistance on job search and marketing techniques and, if you plan to be self-employed, how to explore business opportunities and plan for success. Creating a life worth living and finding the courage to risk pursuing your dream aren't always easy. But you, like thousands before, can do it. Here are the steps you should take:

I. **PREPARE**
    1. Recognize that you are feeling out of sorts
    2. Clarify the problem
    3. Understand that you will experience ambivalence
    4. Take charge
    5. Explore your options
        a. Get to know yourself
        b. Investigate career options
    6. Narrow your options and weigh the evidence.
    7. Establish support systems
    8. Lay down safety nets

II. **SEARCH FOR THE JOB**
    9. Plan
    10. Define your job targets
    11. Establish information sources

12. Prepare your resume and choose references
13. Market yourself
14. Look before you leap

OR

III. **GO INTO BUSINESS FOR YOURSELF (ALTERNATE GOAL)**
   16. Explore business opportunities
   17. Plan for success

IV. **MAKE THE DECISION**
   18. Let it rest
   19. Make the commitment

The information and techniques provided here are by no means exhaustive. For more in-depth information and assistance on job search or going into business for yourself, investigate other resources such as the books listed in Suggested Readings.

PART A: PREPARING TO BECOME A QUESTER

The preparation phase is an important step in career change. You will want to sort out your feelings, define your problem, assess your personal characteristics and explore your career options. These are the same steps, dealt with in more detail, that you read about in in Chapter Eight.

FEELING OUT OF SORTS

Your body and mind may be sending you messages about the state of your job satisfaction. These sensations are often only visceral. Putting them into words is hard. Eventually, they may become overwhelming or translate themselves into verbal messages that can no longer be ignored. "I can hardly wait till Friday!" is one message. Counting the minutes till your next holiday is another. In this state, you will be feeling disequilibrium or a loss of balance, the first stage of the decision-making process. Listening to and accepting your feelings is an important part of moving beyond your uneasiness. Admitting that you are unhappy is the first risk in making changes. As you will soon discover, the process of changing isn't nearly as painful as your current state.

Seeking a solution to a problem before it becomes too serious makes good sense. Doing so allows you to use your skills to better advantage and enables you to be prepared if trouble strikes. Defining the problem in terms of a relationship with a desired or ideal state is one way of making better decisions.

CLARIFYING YOUR PROBLEM

Clearly defining the problem is the second step in making decisions. You will need a good, written definition of the problem. You must look at the feelings behind your dissatisfaction and clarify what you would like but are afraid to undertake. Begin by working the following into a written statement of the problem and the desired goal.

DESCRIBING THE SYMPTOMS

First, describe the symptoms. What is it about your situation that is unpleasant? What is your desired goal? The discrepancy between these two is what must be overcome. Unfortunately, while you may not like where you are, sometimes it's hard to decide where you want to be. The *Job Satisfaction Questionnaire* and *Job Involvement Questionnaire* may have helped to identify the sources of your dissatisfaction. Here are some additional questions to consider:

• Why am I in this job? Did I choose it for prestige? To be of service? For security? Power? Money? Independence? Challenge? Personal satisfaction? Other reasons? Do I still have these rewards? What benefits am I actually deriving from my job?

• Am I doing my best work? Am I happy doing this work? Is my work damaging my self-confidence? My health?

• Am I committed to my company? Do I have anything to gain by remaining with the company for the rest of my career? Do I have anything to lose by leaving the company? Does my company really need me? Am I proud of my company? Is there any room in this company for my growth? Where do I want to be next year? In five years? Will my company help me get there?

• Are other factors in my life, not job-related, having a detrimental effect on my performance and attitude? Do I have a satisfying and intimate relationship with a partner or spouse? Do I have a partner? If not, would I like one? Do I have satisfying leisure activities? Do I have enough money and time to pursue these? How is my health? Is it affecting my attitudes toward my work and other life components?

- Is a job change necessary? Why or why not? Can I reach my goals in another way?
- Do I want to change employers, occupational fields, become self-employed or take a career pause? Which of these options do I have? Could I change jobs, yet remain in the same company? How easy or difficult do I feel it would be for me to get another job in the same field? In a different field? Do I want to return to school for upgrading? Retraining?
- Have I realized my career dreams? Have I enjoyed success in my career?

If your responses to the above questions and the questionnaires in Chapter Seven indicate that you are dissatisfied, then you may be ready for a job change. List all the good and bad points about your position. If the bad points can be resolved and you are committed to your company, work at improving the weak spots and look for advancement within. If, however, you are dissatisfied with your job, the bad points can't be resolved and you are not committed to the company, you should move on.

DESCRIBING THE BARRIERS

The next step is to describe the barriers blocking you from changing jobs. Examples could be fear or uncertainty about change or loss of secure income, pension or other benefits; fear that the change will interfere with your relationships; fear that you will lose power, prestige or status; guilt that the change might create family hardships; fear of returning to school for retraining or upgrading; or uncertainty about what to do and where to go for help in beginning your career search.

These fears, which may act as barriers to your progress, are based upon assumptions about emotional, cultural and social values. They may have no real basis. Instead of dwelling on them, talk them over with your partner or spouse, a trusted friend or a reputable counselor. Of course, while you will have to make the final decision yourself, talking out a problem can often lead to a solution.

Growing, which is really just abandoning a comfortable position, usually involves pain. Trying to avoid pain by constructing rigid roles, defenses, viewpoints or excuses only makes the process more difficult. The first and most important risk you can take is to be honest with yourself. Accept that you are afraid. Like all emotions, fear has a purpose; it alerts you to take action to protect yourself from loss. Every risk involves fear. Lack of fear should signal that you either don't care whether you lose what is at stake or that you don't believe you are in danger.

One way to cope with fear is to imagine the worst possible

result of your actions. What is frightening about the change? If the worst happened, what would you do? What are the chances of this happening? How do you know? What can you do to prevent these losses? To minimize the losses? Most times, you can plan to reduce a loss. But if the possible losses are so great that even thinking of them is paralyzing, the risk really is too great. Reconsider your position until you uncover an option with which you feel more comfortable.

SETTING YOUR SIGHTS

The key to avoiding potential potholes is to set career goals before you explore new roads. Goals force you to focus on what you really want. Only then can you exploit opportunity and luck to achieve them. So what do you want to do? Where do you want to go professionally? As you think over your responses, remember to be open and creative. Years from now, as you lie near death, what regrets do you imagine you might have?

Considering what you might do is an important step in increasing your job satisfaction. Explore the whole range of possibilities before you. Fantasize about the ultimate goal, your "star". If you could do anything in the world, what would it be? Concentrate. Dare to admit your fondest fantasy. Identifying this dream or star will help you to set realistic objectives. Once you know what you want, you will be more willing to take the risks necessary to achieve it. So don't set your goals too short of what you could attain.

Money, or lack of it, often influences career goals. Yet, selecting a satisfying career and lifestyle requires a clear understanding of not only your financial resources, but also your needs, values, interests, abilities and desired rewards. To determine these, record your goals.

Recording Your Goals

To narrow down your goals, put them on paper. Concentrate first on what you want to do. Record every idea that develops during this free-thinking phase. Don't be inhibited by seemingly unrealistic objectives, record what's really important to you. A clear goal statement will provide you with a valuable perspective from which to take control of your career. Only after you have completed this free-thinking should you consider the practical aspects of a career change.

To establish concrete objectives, consider short-, medium-, and long-range goals. Long-range goals will take from seven to 10 years to achieve, medium-range goals from three to five years and short-range goals anywhere from one month to two years. Questers usually have several short-range goals.

As you read through this chapter, you may want to revise these goals. Not only should you have several alternatives but you should be aware that career planning is an ongoing process that is constantly subject to review and revision. So, while goals should be concrete and measurable, make sure they aren't ironclad. Consider them as guideposts that can be rebuilt throughout the planning stage. You, like most Questers, must be able to balance tentativeness with commitment. Repeatedly reviewing your desires and needs is one way to do so. Finding the answers is seldom easy but, fortunately, the final decision is never really final. Instead, it is a series of tentative steps, planned and launched under favorable conditions, designed to ensure success.

LETTING IT REST

Once you have done this, take time to reflect on your tentative choices. Whether over a weekend or over a holiday, give the problem an opportunity to incubate. This time will act as a filter to help you decide what is important and give you a sense of what feels right.

EXPERIENCING AMBIVALENCE

The decision to change can provoke mixed feelings. You may be anxious, depressed, guilty, yet excited at the prospect of trying something new. You're not alone. A certain amount of ambivalence is natural. Inner emotional preparation, weighing losses as well as gains, fears as well as hopes, are necessary prerequisites for successful risk-taking. As you let go of old structures, perhaps you will discover that you miss the friendly, familiar babble of the gang at the water cooler. Friends may say you're crazy to change jobs. The fear of failing may seize and shake your convictions. At the same time, you may be exhilarated about the opportunity to test yourself, to enjoy some excitement and adventure.

Ambivalence is the push and pull between the desire to approach and the desire to avoid. One day you may think, "Of course, I can change fields. Lots of people do it. It can't be so difficult." The next day, or even minute, you are convinced that, "There are too many unknowns. I'm better off staying put." Both feelings are valid. Careless risk takers need to think through the difficulties ahead before they take action. Anxious risk takers, on the other hand, need to look for the pluses. Rather than focusing on just one set of possible outcomes, try to keep risk-taking in balance by considering all of the pluses and minuses. Fear balanced by excitement and purpose offers the emotional balance that planned risk-taking requires.

Don't let the moment of panic overwhelm you during the preparation stages of risk-taking. Once in action, you will find the situation less fearful.

TAKING CHARGE

To nurture a career, you must take charge of it. Once you are convinced that a job change is in order, go for it. Don't stick with a dissatisfying position any longer. You need to feel in control of your career in order to take steps to get it moving again. Turn a deaf ear to those cynics who will tell you it is immature to expect your job to be interesting and satisfying. Patience may be a virtue but resignation is not. If you are thinking there must be more to life, start making some of your dreams come true. A useful word of caution, however, is not to change jobs while you are in the midst of other turmoil. Making a career move when you are experiencing the pressures of family or marital problems can be disastrous. Wait until you can concentrate fully on your new job. Here is some additional advice:

- **Avoid guilt.** The sense that you have let everyone down can be the most difficult aspect of quitting a job. Don't worry about what your mentor or colleagues may think.
- **Avoid idealizing your former position.** Why mourn a job you have outgrown or one that is no longer meeting your needs? Traditional and emerging fields offer many exciting options.
- **Listen to yourself.** When you make a career switch, you will have to overcome the obstacles of others' expectations. Don't base your self-respect on what a few co-workers, parents or friends think. Underneath is what you really want. And, because you feel better about yourself, a career move may bring you closer to your family. Moreover, no one else can define what you consider dangerous. What is a matter of course to one person may be agony to another. The intensity of a personal risk is largely in the eyes of the beholder.
- **Don't make excuses.** Be honest. As Mark Twain said, "There are 1,000 good excuses, but no good reasons." If your career has been stagnating, deciding to stay can be just as traumatic as making a move. Too often, the refusal to make a decision turns out to be the wrong decision. While circumstances often force people to take lesser jobs, choosing to remain in a position with no hope

of advancement or satisfaction is not only self-defeating, it also can be enormously risky. True, there must be some balance between reflection and action. But if you are just putting in time, the losses of enthusiasm, self-confidence and enjoyment may be greater than you realize.

EXPLORING YOUR OPTIONS

Now that you've determined your goals, you need to decide if they are workable, achievable and realistic. What do you have to work with? What are your options? How can you plan to achieve them?

To lay the groundwork for your career change, you should acquire information about yourself and about your career options. Being well prepared by acquiring accurate information and effective strategies can be a real anxiety reducer. The quality of your decision will be a reflection of the quality, comprehensiveness, realism and accuracy of the information you have. The most fulfilled and satisfied people know themselves, know the demands of the workplace and know how to get where they desire to be.

GETTING TO KNOW YOURSELF

Getting ahead requires a good understanding of yourself. Use a notebook for the exercises that follow. They will help you to assemble an accurate picture of yourself, your past, your present and your dreams and goals. They will also give you a realistic, thorough analysis of your interests, needs, accomplishments and other personal characteristics. Uncovering a you that you didn't even know existed can be fun and exciting. Since there are no right and wrong answers, here's your chance to be honest about who you really are.

IDENTIFYING YOUR INTERESTS

Interests are simply likes and dislikes, preferences or distastes. You can identify your interests by taking an interest inventory or by analyzing activities you enjoy.

Psychological tests, administered and interpreted by a competent psychologist, can be useful for some. They can help illuminate potential new directions, reveal valuable insights and add a sense of certainty about your plans.

On your own, first, think over your leisure activities, public school and continuing education courses. Note those that you liked and excelled at. Review job accomplishments you are particularly proud of and note why. In a notebook, make two lists. One should contain at least a dozen activities you enjoy — the other lists activities you detest. Next to each item, note why each activity is so appealing or unappealing. Now classify your hidden interests into patterns. The two exercises below will help with this. You may want to do one or both exercises.

Exercise One:

An easy way to classify interests is to arrange them on the basis of work tasks you enjoy. Most work tasks involve working with data, people, things and ideas. Read over the descriptions of the four work tasks and then rank them in order of preference, one representing your highest preference and four your lowest.

Data tasks are *impersonal* tasks that involve working with people indirectly (for example, with files, accounts, business communications) or that involve formulating and/or following schedules, directions, business operating procedures and so on.

Ideas tasks are *intrapersonal* tasks involving insights, theories, and new ways of expressing something, perhaps with words, paint, equations or music.

People tasks are *interpersonal* tasks such as caring for, educating, entertaining, serving, persuading or directing others.

Things tasks are *non-personal* tasks involving machines, tools, living things and materials such as food, wood or metal.

The tasks usually blend together in varying amounts. Moreover, although any occupation will involve some work with data, ideas, people and things, only one or two of the work tasks will typically predominate.

Exercise Two

According to the research of John Holland, a vocational psychologist, people can be categorized as one of six personality types, Realistic, Conventional, Enterprising, Social, Artistic and Investigative. The personality types seek out corresponding occupational environments based on their interests. Since it is unlikely that persons fall solely into one of the major personality types, a coding system has been devised to indicate the person's primary and secondary types. These codes are reflected in three-letter combinations — each letter corresponding to the first letter of one of the six types. For example, a code of ESA would indicate that the person is most like the Enterprising type, next most like the Social type and third most like the Artistic type.

Read over the descriptions of the personality types and then rank them according to which types you believe you are. Then translate your three highest types into a three letter code.

Realistic(R): You enjoy activities that involve the precise, ordered use of objects, tools, machines and animals. Examples are agricultural, electrical, manual, physical or mechanical activities. Characteristic occupations are auto engineer, surveyor, carpenter, typesetter and fish and game warden.

Conventional(C): You enjoy activities that involve the precise, ordered use of data; that is, keeping records, filing materials, or organizing numerical and statistical data. Characteristic occupations are usually in the clerical, computational or business fields, such as chartered accountant, credit manager, office worker, library assistant or data processing clerk.

Enterprising(E): You enjoy activities that involve interaction with other people to reach organizational goals or for economic gain. Leadership, interpersonal and persuasive activities dominate your interests. Characteristic occupations are market analyst, lawyer, personnel recruiter or manager of enterprises such as restaurants or retail outlets.

Social(S): You enjoy activities that involve interaction with others for enjoyment or to inform, train, develop, care or educate. Characteristic occupations are claims adjuster, social worker, teacher, minister, interviewer, therapist or community recreation administrator.

Artistic(A): You enjoy activities that involve the use of physical, verbal or human materials to create art forms and products. Activities and objects related to language, art, music, drama and writing fascinate you. Characteristic occupations are drama coach, dance teacher, musician, writer, interior decorator, photographer or artist.

Investigative(I): You enjoy activities that involve the exploration and examination of physical, biological and cultural objects to understand and control them. Scientific and mathematical activities are usually found here. Characteristic occupations are economist, internist, chemist, psychologist, actuary, dentist, computer operator or engineer.

Summarize Your Interests

To summarize your interests, go back over the exercises listed in your notebook. Look for patterns. What interests keep appearing? Identify your interests into the categories described above (data, people, things, or ideas or Holland's types). List these. Have you found any surprises in your interest profile or is it much as you expected? Relate your interests to occupations you would like to explore. For example, if you like activities that involve working with people (interpersonal tasks) or if you like social activities (Social type, Holland's categories), you may be satisfied in occupations such as social worker, therapist or teacher.

The Work Wheel can help you view your interests with occupational options. The body of the Work Wheel shows the locations of 23 job fields (groups of similar occupations) that encompass all 12,099 occupations recognized by the U. S. Department of Labor in the 4th edition of *Dictionary of Occupational Titles* (DOT). Job field names and locations (A to W on the wheel) suggest differences in the work that is done and the people who do it. Although the jobs in a field differ in their wheel locations, most are near the points shown. A job field's location is based on its primary work tasks — working with data, ideas. people or things. Arrows show that work tasks often heavily involve both people and things (◄●►) or data and ideas (ᎥᎥ). Related Holland types are indicated around the edge of the map.

WORK WHEEL

You can see the relationship between the four work tasks (data, ideas, people, things) and Holland's types, shown on the periphery of the wheel. For example, Enterprising (Business Contact) occupations are located at the upper left. Data work tasks and, to some extent, people work tasks predominate. Investigative (Science) occupations are located at the lower right. Ideas work tasks, and to some extent, things work tasks predominate.

Your interests can be translated into spokes on the wheel. Identify your interests on the wheel and then investigate occupations in the related job fields. If you have an ESC code, for example, you might wish to look into job fields in spokes 1, 2 and 3 (Marketing and Sales, Personal/Customer Service, Records and Communications, Management and Planning, Social and Government Services and Education and Related Services).

This is a very simple diagram which might be a start — a way of beginning to look at occupational alternatives. However, it is important to keep in mind that exploring occupational options is much more complicated than this. A number of other personality and work world factors should be understood and considered when investigating options.

Think about your interests as you go through the rest of the suggested activities in this chapter. Add each like or dislike that comes to mind to the list you have noted here and then modify your interest profile if necessary.

PROBING YOUR NEEDS

Needs form the basis of behavior. Since your behavior is composed of actions designed to fulfill or reduce those needs, understanding them can explain a good deal about your internal conflicts, tensions, anxieties or stresses. Such unpleasant feelings are often the result of unfulfilled needs or, alternatively, a conflict among needs. To be satisfied, you must find outlets that satisfy your needs.

The range of human needs is limited only by the imagination, but some needs contribute more to job satisfaction than do others. As you read through the following list of 22 needs that contribute to job satisfaction, check the ones you consider important. Then complete the questions at the end. You will soon see a pattern in your reasons for wanting to work.

    1. **Achievement:** You like the challenge of mastering a difficult task. Work gives you a feeling of accomplishment.

    2. **Adventure:** You hunger for change, a fast pace and excitement.

    3. **Altruism:** Helping others is important to you.

    4. **Associates:** You value contact with fellow workers.

5. **Autonomy:** It is important for you to have control over your work, to work in your own way as quickly or as slowly as you wish, to be free from constraints imposed by others.

6. **Challenge:** You desire work which has an acceptable level of difficulty, responsibility and complexity and which provides you with opportunities for mastery and achievement.

7. **Competition:** You enjoy activities where you can try to outperform others.

8. **Creativity:** You like inventing new things, designing products or developing ideas.

9. **Economic Returns:** You value work which pays well and enables you to buy the things you want.

10. **Esthetic:** Making beautiful objects and contributing to the beauty of the world are important to you.

11. **Growth:** You enjoy jobs in which you can develop your talents and potential, learn new skills, innovate and get things done without having to follow too-rigid regulations.

12. **Intellectual Stimulation:** The opportunity for independent thinking and to learn how and why things work is valuable to you.

13. **Involvement:** You must be involved in, and identify very closely with, your job.

14. **Management:** You enjoy planning and laying out work for others.

15. **Power:** Decision-making responsibility over finances, people, and other resources in your field is an important plus.

16. **Prestige:** You like work which gives you standing or recognition in the eyes of others and evokes both self-respect and the respect of others.

17. **Religion:** It is important for you to adhere to a set of religious or moral principles.

18. **Security:** You desire work which will provide you with the certainty of having a job even in hard times.

19. **Supervisory Relations:** Working under a supervisor who is fair and with whom you get along is a prime consideration.

20. **Surroundings:** You value work which is carried out under pleasant conditions, not too hot or too cold, too noisy or too dirty.

21. **Variety:** You need work that provides you with an opportunity to do different kinds of tasks.

22. **Way of Life:** You like work that allows you to live the way you choose and to be the person you wish to be.

Summarize Your Needs

Once you have checked off the needs that apply to you, look back over the list and pick the top six needs you most desire from a job. Rank these from one (most desired) to six (less desired). Now go back to your scores on the *Job Satisfaction Questionnaire* and rank order the six job facets which you believe are most important to you. Also rank order the six facets which you feel are least important to you. Did you rate the needs which are most important to you VS? If not, these facets will represent unfulfilled needs that have probably spurred you on to a career change. Again, rank order the six needs you would like most from a job. Also note the six that are least important. Pay attention to your needs because they represent job facets which you consider important.

ASSESSING YOUR ACCOMPLISHMENTS AND ABILITIES

Interests are frequently confused with abilities. While you may enjoy doing those things you do well, the relationship between interests and abilities is not necessarily high. People with high literary interests, for example, are not necessarily capable of producing a novel, poem or play. They simply enjoy reading literature. Prospective employers are interested mainly in what you have accomplished through a lifetime of paid and unpaid experiences. Evaluating your experiences as objectively as possible will add new dimensions to the complex and emerging picture of you. Here's how to do it.

First, look at what you have accomplished in job-related, indirectly job-related, educational, personal or civic endeavors. For example, if you have worked as a controller, your accomplishments could include several things: designed a computerized reporting system used by three subsidiary companies; worked closely with outside consultants to rationalize the use of microcomputers within the company; regulated inventory to reduce short-term interest charges incurred by the company; taught a financial class to graduate students at a local university. Note how much you enjoyed these activities. Use action words to describe them: designed, researched, trained, supervised, directed, wrote, managed, created, negotiated, or prepared. Make the list as long as possible. Ask your spouse, close friend or colleague to help you identify these accomplishments. Be sure not to neglect the accomplishments subordinates made under your direction or supervision. These, too, belong in your list of accomplishments. Think back over your career carefully. What was done better because of you? What would not have been done without you? What do you consider your most important or most satisfying job-related accomplishments?

Also include those educational accomplishments of which you are most proud. Unless you have only recently graduated, do not include high school accomplishments. List college courses and activities, graduate work and continuing education. Include both direct and indirect educational accomplishments; those that related directly to your studies and those, such as extra-curricular activities, performed while attending school.

Personal or civic accomplishment are achievements directly related to hobbies and civic, charitable or religious activities. They should relate to, or demonstrate your competence in, some aspect of work. For example, a major contribution to a fund-raising effort can demonstrate organizational or sales ability.

You may also have an untapped talent that can be turned into a new occupation. Ask friends what dormant talents they suspect you possess. You may even want to take a battery of tests from a psychologist or career counselor that can reveal a wide range of possibilities.

The next step is to analyze each of the accomplishments you have listed. Consider them one by one and then list the skills, knowledge or personal attributes that enabled you to achieve them. Think about your personality as well as the specific skills and abilities you have acquired. These accomplishments might include the ability to program a computer, to use insurance actuarial tables or to interpret psychological tests. Personality traits worth listing might include patience, willingness to work hard, ability to handle people or logical thinking capability. The list could look like this:

Achievement: Increased number of volunteers at local hospital by more than 30 percent.

Skills, knowledge and personality traits required to achieve this: Organizational skills, sales ability, capacity to motivate people, public speaking, hard work, ability to overcome resistance.

Now summarize your accomplishments. As you review the results, select the six accomplishments that are repeated most often and list them in order of frequency.

Finally, list your weaknesses. These often turn out to involve tasks you dislike doing. For instance, you may feel so uncomfortable at meetings that you become inarticulate. Or, you may hate the paperwork that goes with your job so you put if off and get backlogged. Figure out workable strategies to reduce your weaknesses. For instance, to improve your performance at meetings, take a speech course or join Toastmasters. To straighten out your paperwork, set aside 30 minutes each day as catch-up time.

ASSESSING OTHER PERSONAL CHARACTERISTICS

Taking stock of your other personal characteristics is another essential step in the search for self-knowledge. Certain characteristics seem to be essential in almost all kinds of work. Being responsible, efficient, resourceful, flexible, cooperative, objective and sensible are basic to a professional attitude. They are necessary traits for almost any occupation. On the other hand, some personal characteristics are very important only in specific occupations and may actually be undesirable in others. While being a loner may be fine for a scientist spending long hours on research, it is not particularly suitable for a construction worker who has to perform as part of a team.

To discover your other personal characteristics, make a list of about 10 that best describe you. Use adjectives such as: active, assertive, attractive, calm, careful, competent, confident, curious, discreet, democratic, eager, energetic, enthusiastic, helpful, humorous, loyal, mature, obliging, open-minded, precise, sociable, stable, strong-minded, tolerant or warm.

COMPLETING THE PICTURE

Little by little, you've put together a wonderful picture of yourself. Nobody has precisely the same combination of qualities. Look back at how you have evaluated various aspects of yourself. Decide how your interests, needs, accomplishments and other personal characteristics add up. What pattern do they form? Which qualities would you like to use in a job? What would you like to change?

To synthesize this information, you will need to answer these questions: What needs, interests, accomplishments and other personal qualities do you want to use in your work? How would you like to develop these further? What plans should you have to do this?

The next step is looking at career options. You may be surprised to discover just how many there are.

INVESTIGATING CAREER OPTIONS

As you read and worked through the preceding pages, you engaged in focused self-exploration, self-assessment and soul-searching. Up to now, you have given most of your attention to your private world -- what you dream of, need, want, are and could become. Starting there is appropriate but stopping there is inadequate. Now it's time to look at reality. Before you decide to change employers, you will want to check out some alternatives.

ENHANCING YOUR LIFESTYLE

Before considering a career change, determine if other non-job-related aspects of your life are having a detrimental effect on your performance and attitude. Are you missing an enjoyable and intimate relationship with a partner or spouse? Do you have satisfying leisure activities? If not, you may discover that one of the reasons for your dissatisfaction is the gap in other components of your life. Feeling alone and lonely or having an unhappy marriage can cause anyone's attitude and performance to drop. Maybe this is the time to get involved in a community activity or a hobby. Doing so can add new, rewarding dimensions to your life that may indirectly make your job more satisfying.

You may have decided that, at least for a while, you can get what you want by remaining in the same company. As a result, you may want to make some adjustments to your current job or transfer to another type of job. Let's take a look at each of the options.

LIVING WITH YOUR PRESENT JOB

A key way to make job changes is to gain the recognition and support of the political powers who affect it. To do so, you must understand your job's political environment and how to handle it effectively. Office politics need not be vicious or self-serving. By playing along, you are being sensitive to how key people react, people in roles that greatly affect your work. How much power you have is determined by both the formal organization (the organizational chart) and the informal organization (the actual relationships that exist among individuals). Understanding the formal relationships is easy but to figure out the informal relationships that exist in your organization, you must be observant. What roles do people really play? Who is involved in outside activities with whom? The combination of key individuals' information sources, pipelines, seniority, personalities and relationships all decide how much power they have.

As you try to evaluate the politics of your work environment, ask yourself these key questions: What kinds of people are my bosses? What are their backgrounds? What are their goals? How do they live? What are their beliefs? Remember that religious, social and ethnic backgrounds can be terribly important. After you have identified who holds the power and what kind of people they are, you will have to examine whether you can reasonably expect their support.

To discover how your boss feels about you and how you think he or she would rate your performance, score yourself from A to E (A representing very good and E representing very poor) on the following points: How well do I perform my overall job? How well do I know what my boss wants? Do I help him achieve his performance goals? Do I help him to do his job effectively? Am I sensitive to his biases? Do I communicate effectively with him? How loyal do I feel toward him? Is he proud to have me on his team? Do I make a difference in the operation? Do I set priorities well and work toward them? Do I anticipate my boss's needs? Am I well-motivated? How well do I meet deadlines? How well do I communicate? Am I effective in leading and participating in meetings? Are my efforts appreciated? Do I receive credit or recognition for my contribution?

The answers should help you identify your strengths and weaknesses and discover ways to do better work and present a more favorable image. Here are some other things you can do. First, develop a program to overcome the deficiencies that you noted in this performance rating. Second, make sure that you are devoting enough time to highest-priority projects. If not, plan a work schedule that will get those high-priority items off your desk quickly and efficiently. Third, improve your conduct in meetings. Be prepared, contribute ideas and, without compromising your values, try not to take controversial stands that will antagonize the most powerful committee members. Fourth, motivate yourself. Maybe you have become complacent about your job. You have nothing to lose by making an intensive effort to improve your performance; you could have a lot to gain. Most of all, you could considerably improve your management skills. Effective self-improvement can give you tools that will be keys to the rest of your career. These improved skills will come in handy when you do decide to move on.

Having top management on your side can make you considerably more promotable and increase the challenges that come your way. If the physical structure of your company makes this impossible, explore ways to creatively redesign or restructure your job. Faced with similar situations, to get the challenge they crave, some Questers have virtually rewritten their responsibilities. Try to develop your own challenges. Visualize what would happen if another highly-motivated person was promoted to your job. How would he or she tackle it? What challenges would another person find in your job? If someone else in your position could contribute more to the company, your lack of challenge may lie in your attitude or performance. Try to be indispensable. If it's not possible to develop challenges on your current job — and sometimes it isn't — then it's time to consider another job or a transfer.

GETTING ANOTHER TYPE OF JOB IN YOUR COMPANY

Sometimes it's just as desirable to change positions within your company as to seek a new job outside of it. Doing so is far less risky than trying to make the transition to a new occupation and a new company. If you know your skills and goals and can present yourself effectively to the right people, you might be able to move over to a different position right in the same organization. Determine if there might be another position within the company that could satisfy your needs. The next step is to develop a favorable image with the key person there. At an appropriate time, make your interest known. You may have to be patient but if you've made a favorable impression, you could be in luck.

You have the best chance of finding a good job in the company if you anticipate, and keep several steps ahead of, any major changes that may occur. Otherwise, you may find yourself competing with many for very few positions. As companies pare down their work forces, it's even more important to be alert to your organization's plans.

BROADENING YOUR CAREER HORIZONS

If you do decide to stay where you are, expand your thinking about your career. Figure out your options, then pursue them. Researching occupations will not only reduce uncertainty by providing information but will also temper fantasies which can be more idealistic than practical. Explore, in depth, at least 10 occupational options in at least three diverse fields.

GETTING THE FACTS

As you study each occupation, consider the nature of the working conditions, training and education required and how you can acquire these. Examine the pay and fringe benefits, methods of entering, employment outlook, opportunities for advancement, related occupations, and advantages and disadvantages perceived by people in these fields. Compare each to your personal characteristics, aspirations and desired lifestyle. Here are some resources to use in determining your suitability for an occupation:

Printed Material: Directories, pamphlets and books contain invaluable information on occupations. A list of useful printed material available in most public libraries is provided in Suggested Readings.

Rehearsing: Besides just reading about an occupation, why not try it out? Obtain an evening or weekend job, or work as a volunteer or trainee during your next vacation. Consider taking a job on probation while you enjoy a year-long sabbatical. "Shadow" someone who's doing the job already. To get a clearer picture of what the work is really like, spend a day or two at his or her side. Try out jobs related to hobbies or launch an interest you can pursue upon retirement.

Interviews: Another good way to collect information is to talk to people in the occupation in which you are interested. These could be friends, relatives, lovers, contacts you make over the telephone or personnel in professional, trade or business associations. Prepare carefully by including questions related to the guidelines suggested earlier. Follow-up each meeting with a thank-you note. Information interviews are valuable for many reasons. They establish contacts. They can also uncover a prospective employer's needs and lead to a phone call sometime later asking you to fulfill them. A former freelance writer, who learned that poor writing costs companies money, now conducts writing workshops for executives.

Computer Guidance Systems: If you'd like assistance with your career choices but are not willing or able to talk to a counselor or psychologist, try one of the occupational information systems available at some career counseling centers.

CHANGING OCCUPATIONAL FIELD

A change in occupational field will usually require even more exploration. Initially, at least, it will probably also offer lower pay. But even though your success will involve many more unknowns, starting anew needn't mean starting at the bottom. If you have launched a creative assault on the job market, you can usually find new challenges that equal or better the ones your previously enjoyed. Even if you change occupational fields, your past experiences and knowledge will hardly be wasted.

If changing fields is your choice, and it has been successful for a number of Questers, research your options thoroughly. Bear in mind that people in the prospective field may try to dissuade you because you may not have the appropriate background. Before giving up, determine if their warnings are valid.

GOING INTO BUSINESS FOR YOURSELF

Perhaps you have already considered going into business for yourself. The number of self-employed in North America is increasing steadily.

Part of the trend toward self-employment was caused by recessionary dips. As people found themselves unemployed, laid off or unable to find desirable work elsewhere, many carved out their own niches. Business people who planned well, cut corners and knew how to work hard, did very well indeed. Opportunities abound.

When you create a business, you become the employer, controlling your work and lifestyle and choosing where you live and work. Research on job satisfaction indicates that self-employed people are among the happiest workers. Most self-employed Questers are living proof. Questers who went into business for themselves scored very high on the *Job Satisfaction Questionnaire* and the *Job Involvement Questionnaire*.

Like many Questers, people who go into business for themselves usually possess a strong need for autonomy, have a broad range of talents, desire variety and flexibility and are not afraid to take chances. They are able to get along well with others and have the perseverance, self-discipline, energy and stamina to work long hours to carry them over the rough spots. Money is not their primary motive, although, in the long run, many do well financially. If you have dreamed of being your own boss, don't let the fear of losing a steady paycheck stop you. Economic security is a personal possession. Relegating it to others is a mistake. Consider the hundreds of thousands of people who sweated out years of stagnation in boring jobs only to have inflation make a nightmare out of retirement.

GETTING THE EDUCATION YOU NEED

Every occupation, including self-employment, requires some education or training, formal or informal. Investigate the length and type of program required, alternative education or training routes and their suitability. University broadens the mind and teaches much-needed skills, but you may also gain appropriate knowledge from workshops, seminars, night school courses, independent study, correspondence school, on-the-job training or serving an apprenticeship. Before deciding how to go about entering a new field, consult with professionals and company executives to learn how much training, and what kind, is essential.

Don't despair if university or college is the preferred route. Thousands of adults return to school every year to discover that they are very good students. Because they often have clearer goals and more experience than they did when they were young, mature adults earn higher grade point averages than younger students.

If you believe you can't afford a college education, consider that financial aid for adults is available. Corporations will often pay for part or all of your schooling. Up-to-date pamphlets on financial aid are available in most libraries. Colleges that do try to accommodate adults often offer some of the following options:

- **Part-time study.** In addition to evening and summer programs, some schools now offer weekend college. Courses are given from Friday afternoon through Sunday evening several times a month.
- **Experiential learning.** A few colleges and universities will accept some type of credit for work or volunteer experience. Proper documentation (usually in portfolio form with samples) is required to determine the number of credits acceptable. Although it is next to impossible to earn such credit at the graduate level, this can put you several steps ahead in an undergraduate program.
- **Exams for credit.** You can be tested on your knowledge and skills in areas where you already have experience by taking an exam. Although most institutions limit the credit you can earn this way, allowance for up to a year's worth of credit is possible.
- **Credit through contract.** By devising your own curriculum, you may be able to earn a degree outside the classroom. The usual procedure is to draw up a mutually-agreeable learning contract, specifying what will be learned and required to obtain credit.
- **Correspondence courses.** In addition to standard correspond-

ence courses, consider radio or television courses and educational cassettes. Some universities are especially set up for "distance education." Find out about these.

NARROWING YOUR OPTIONS

The key to a successful job search is to aim for a position that meets a high percentage of your needs and values. This requires establishing priorities and evaluating alternatives. As you enhance your self- and occupational knowledge, your priorities will be refined. To narrow your career options even further, complete the following checklist for each occupation you are considering.

Statement	True	False
1. I have the necessary intelligence and skills to do the job.	___	___
2. The job or self-employment opportunity is compatible with my needs, values, interests and other personality characteristics.	___	___
3. I can acquire the necessary knowledge and skills to do a good job.	___	___
4. I know how people in this occupation (or who are self-employed in this field) live on and off the job. I find this an acceptable lifestyle.	___	___
5. I can afford the necessary training required for the job or I can obtain the necessary finances to go into business for myself.	___	___
6. I can imagine staying in this occupation for at least four years.	___	___
7. My spouse (or close friends) believes I can succeed at this job.	___	___
8. My weaknesses or shortcomings will not be a problem (health, vision, hearing, size, strength, personality traits and so forth).	___	___
9. I know where to obtain the necessary training or experience to enter this occupation or to become self-employed.	___	___
10. I have identified all the potential difficulties in preparing for and working in this field.	___	___
11. I know what safeguards I can build in to protect myself from the difficulties or problems identified above.	___	___

Rank the top four occupational options in order of the most True responses. These are your best prospects.

WEIGHING THE EVIDENCE

Career options can be prioritized mathematically to determine the best ones for you. First, make a chart. Draw a series of vertical and horizontal lines so that the paper is composed of squares. On the top of the page, list all the criteria (one in each square) most important in a job. Include needs (income, responsibility, public image, creativity, challenge, achievement, variety and so on), interests, skills and the degree of perceived risk. Relocation possibilities, required study, lifestyle and approval or disapproval of spouse or partner are other considerations to include. Down the left side of the page, list each occupational option. For each option, consider the criteria identified at the top of the page. If an option doesn't satisfy a criterion, place a minus (-) sign in the appropriate column. If the criterion exists, but not as much as desired, record a zero (0). Finally, if the criterion exists to a desired state, record a plus (+) sign. Add up the points for each option and place them in a total column at the far right. The occupation with the most pluses will best meet the greatest number of criteria important to you. Study these numbers to see why this option appears to be superior.

Thinking It Over

What does your intuition tell you about these options? If one option is not an obvious choice, review your criteria, make some changes and listen carefully to your inner voice. If necessary, take some time out to reflect upon your priorities until one option feels right.

ESTABLISHING SUPPORT SYSTEMS

Once you have decided to change jobs, don't try to be a hero and make the change entirely on your own. Be open to support. You'll feel better emotionally, intellectually and even financially, if you have help from a close and supportive family or friends.

A reputable professional career counselor or industrial psychologist can also provide support, help you identify your needs and interests, give you accurate, up-to-date job and labor information, as well as offer objective feedback. But a poor one costs time and money and may weaken your self-confidence, so stick with an accredited professional. Set up a preliminary meeting to determine what service is provided and at what cost. Ask for references. Free or inexpensive counseling is readily available at colleges, continuing education centers, churches and some organizations. You may also consider participating in workshops.

From wherever you seek help, be careful not to be constrained by words like "you should" or "you ought to". While you may tolerate such comments from a partner or relative, be wary if a counselor or therapist lays this trip on you.

In the final analysis, go with your feelings, interests and needs. Even the most talented counselor can't make decisions for you or guarantee that you will find the dream job.

LAYING DOWN SAFETY NETS

Few decisions are iron-clad, but to protect yourself from surprises, build in a fail-safe or retreat position. Constructing a safety net will help reduce anxiety. Review your responses to the questions in the section called "Describing the Barriers", then consider the following: What is frightening about the change? What do you stand to lose? What are the barriers that are preventing you from reaching your goals? What are some steps you could take to overcome them? Who are the people who might help you reach them? What are your chances of success? Why? What are some possible positive and negative outcomes? What are the chances that negative outcomes will occur? How can the odds be reduced? Do the positive outcomes outweigh the negative outcomes? Do you still want to achieve your goal?

By preparing for the negative as well as the positive, you are preparing a backup plan. Realizing that there are no right or wrong moves can also be helpful. Viewing a career mistake as a detour or growth opportunity may allay your uneasiness. After all, experience really is the best teacher.

MANAGING YOUR MONEY
How you manage your financial resources will also be vital to your success. Before changing or quitting jobs or returning to school, determine how long you can live without an income. How much will you need to live on and where will you get it?

If you are employed, financial planning will consist of estimating the expenses involved in a search. More planning is necessary if you are unemployed. You will eliminate a deadline controlled by finances alone if you allow yourself a certain amount of time; for example, six months. A careful review of expenses, financial strengths and potential income may disclose that you can manage for several months without a salary.

Develop a budget that takes into account your net worth, monthly cash flow and total job search expenses. To determine your assets, find out exactly what you can expect in pension funds, severance or other pay-outs from your present employer as well as unemployment benefits. Include income, savings, possible student loans or assistance from relatives. What will you need to survive each month? (Consider housing, food, school, furniture, clothing, dry cleaning, medical insurance, recreation, car and miscellaneous expenses.) Add 15 percent as a cushion. Can you lower your standards for a while? Create a survival budget and prepare for the worst by cutting out unnecessary expenses and saving religiously.

Careful planning and the willingness to live on less temporarily will stretch the amount of time you can go without a full-time job. As a result, you will have more time to find that ideal position.

PART B: SEARCHING FOR THE JOB

Now that you've gained additional insights to yourself and the work world, take a look at the goals and time frames you set earlier. Were they realistic? Sufficiently ambitious? Just right? Are they consistent with the occupational goals you set after exploring career options? If not, you'll need to make some changes.

PLANNING

Planning requires developing a step-by-step method of attack. You will need to devise a well-thought-out campaign to market yourself. It will help if you create an action plan that answers the following four questions: Where do I begin? Whom do I need to see? When do I begin? How do I begin?

Write down your plans. Written plans tend to be more logical and efficient. And the act of recording each step will give you a handy timetable against which to assess your progress. Planning can also give you a greater sense of security and a better chance to control your life. Few people proceed immediately from starting point to goal. Many intermediate steps must be taken along the way. Be as specific as possible about what each step involves before you act on it. You might, for example, decide to go back to school before taking a job. In that case, find out about programs that give credit for experience or by examination. Whatever you finally decide, take time to write each step. This will keep you motivated and moving.

The next step is learning how to market yourself. But first, a word of advice: once you have made up your mind, act. Regardless of prevailing economic conditions, good jobs are always obtainable. So don't use the state of the economy as an excuse.

DEFINING JOB TARGETS

You are now ready to define the targets of your marketing effort. Pursue three or four career options simultaneously. They may be in the same or diverse industries, or have similar or entirely different responsibilities. The intent is to expand your opportunities by selling yourself to several different markets.

When you have substantial experience and wish to remain in one field, concentrate your efforts there. Define second and third targets by considering a different type or size of organization or a new geographic location. Different resumes and letters are required for each target.

All targets must relate to both your immediate and long-range objectives as well as to past accomplishments, needs and interests. Demonstrate your probable future success by matching accomplishments that relate best to a prospective employer's needs. But be careful not to sell yourself as a generalist. Employers want people with specific skills.

Clearly, to succeed, you must define each target as specifically as possible. Decide on the size and type of company, the geographical area, position title and desired job description. Finally, determine which targets are your first, second and third choices.

ESTABLISHING INFORMATION SOURCES

Throughout the search, you will need substantial information about prospective employers. Many extensive business information sources are available in local libraries. Ask a librarian to help you locate these. In addition to trade periodicals and professional association publications, check out the local chamber of commerce directory of industrial and business firms, industrial directories published by government departments and the yellow pages of your telephone directory.

Besides these sources, try networking. Keep abreast of new developments and add to your list of colleagues and acquaintances by joining professional, trade or civic groups and attending professional meetings or workshops. Networking knows no boundaries. Horizontally and vertically it reaches into all ranks of business. A key to its success is the fact that people like to do business with individuals they know. Networkers tend to nurture each other because they can select associates without guesswork.

PREPARING YOUR RESUME

Prepare a resume, using one of the many guides available at libraries and bookstores. Consider your resume a sales tool. Write it in positive language and emphasize your accomplishments. Most of all, phrase it carefully to satisfy the needs of each job target.

CHOOSING REFERENCES

Selecting and cultivating references requires care. You will want to maintain close contact with these people throughout your campaign. Select business or professional people who have known you well in one or more of your most recent positions and will talk positively about your abilities. If possible, choose individuals or jobs that relate closely to the positions (in equal or superior levels of responsibility) to the one you are seeking. Have at least one reference whose position is above or similar to that of the probable caller.

MARKETING YOURSELF

Now that you have done everything possible to make the risk of changing jobs manageable, move into action. Don't just passively answer help wanted advertisements or send out resumes. Take charge. Once you act, worry and confusion will disappear. And, once you make a commitment to a new job, stick with it. Be creative, show initiative and be positive.

ACCENTUATING THE POSITIVE

The fear of rejection can be a major obstacle. This can best be overcome by conducting a thorough search and uncovering several opportunities. Obviously, some will neither want nor need your "product", the talent and experience pool that you represent. Remember, you want only one job and the market is huge.

Starting off the right way is crucial. The impressions you make to possible employers in the first few minutes will make or break the sale. To be successful, you will need to develop a positive image – a neat, appropriate appearance and a self-assured demeanor. Ensure that your written and verbal communications are positive, direct and to the point. Act comfortable with your accomplishments and confident about your future. The key is to stick with it. If you miss one job, tell yourself that a better one exists and you are going to get it.

IDENTIFYING JOB OPPORTUNITIES AND CONTACTING EMPLOYERS

You are now ready to begin making initial contact with the job market. Throughout your campaign, the objective is to secure the maximum number of interviews with potentially-interested employers. You need to make many contacts — as many as your information and time will permit.

The Confirming Letter

Every telephone or meeting contact requires a confirming letter. A polite, pleasant, unexpected reminder that you appreciate the assistance and consideration will encourage the recipient to remember you.

MAKING PERSONAL CONTACTS

Personal contacts are business or professional people who are in a position to help you. They may be close friends, customers or associates. The best ones will be in the field you hope to enter. You will want to request a meeting with them to discuss your career search and to leave a resume. Follow up with a letter thanking them for their offer to assist.

ANSWERING HELP WANTED ADVERTISEMENTS

Help wanted advertisements are a good source of potential job opportunities, but because of the extent of their use and the volume of replies to them, you must respond to many advertisements to generate any responses. Answer all enticing prospects, even those which are a month or more old, until you accept a new position. Your written application should be accomplishment-oriented, responding directly to the qualifications stated in the advertisement. Outline your accomplishments in the opening sentence, then go on to explain the reason for writing, referring to the advertisement and further illuminating your abilities. In the final paragraph, request an interview. If the company name is known, state that you will phone within 10 days. This will ensure that your letter is reviewed and allow you to gather useful information about the job, plan your approach and assess your chances. Calling will also demonstrate your interest and assertiveness. Begin by introducing yourself and explaining that you want to ensure the letter was received. Ask how many candidates will be interviewed and how and when they will be chosen. Again, request an interview.

THE MAIL CAMPAIGN

One of the most effective methods of finding job opportunities is a massive, direct mail marketing campaign. This direct contact with executives in a large number of firms may uncover opportunities that are not, and never will be, advertised. The resulting interviews may convince a company to create a new position just to get you into the organization. When a well-qualified candidate appears, most companies would prefer hiring him or her to the expense and time involved in searching for and interviewing applicants. Your job is to find these companies.

The most important task in a campaign of this nature is to have your letter read by interested personnel who also have the authority to hire. Be sure to match the organization to your job target as closely as possible. Include as many companies as you can but don't neglect medium-sized or smaller organizations. That new position could be anywhere.

The recipient of your letter should be the individual to whom you would report if given the job. The next best choice is the person to whom that individual reports. Organize and word each letter to respond to the recipient's probable interests. Begin with the single accomplishment most indicative of your competence in that job. The second sentence and paragraph will be a bridge between your opening statement and the remainder, indicating why you are writing. Show how you might respond to one of the reader's needs or how you could help to solve a problem he or she might have. Introduce a listing of your accomplishments, itemizing four or five that best relate to the target. Organize the following (third) paragraph to outline biographical information. Then use the final paragraph to request an interview and indicate whether you expect to be contacted by the company or whether you plan to phone. For particularly interesting companies, you will want to take the initiative. Say so.

Most responses will be polite refusals. Don't be discouraged by the volume of rejections. They are normal. Some letters will be positive, either suggesting you call for an interview or asking for additional information. Again, respond promptly and positively. Sooner or later, you'll get an acceptance letter.

IDENTIFYING SPECIFIC COMPANIES

Much of what follows in the next three paragraphs is suitable only for very bold people who are stimulated by difficult challenges. Others may find these suggestions inconsistent with their nature.

Of all the organizations you target, one or two will be highly-desirable prospective employers. Make these separate targets. First, identify why you want to work for these organizations, then gather more information to develop your case for employment.

To pursue an individual organization or opportunity, you will need two types of information. The first is a general, but complete, history and description of the firm, including the department, division or subsidiary of interest. The second type is information required to develop a thorough, convincing case for your employment. Gather as much information as possible. When this is complete, develop a case for your employment. Concentrate on the contribution you can make. Demonstrate how hiring you will contribute to the company's performance or success. Finally, try to show from past accomplishments how you are the best suited person to fulfill this need. Summarize your case in a concise, written report.

The next step is to contact the person who has direct responsibility for the functions you intend to perform. You will want to induce this person to hire you. Even though the objective may be clear, the purpose of this meeting is to exchange information. Concentrate on the organization's needs, how to answer them and the expected results. The intent is to stimulate your contact's curiosity. Bring a list of questions, be alert and sensitive to the other person's responses and write a follow-up letter. Thank your contact for his or her interest, then in subsequent interviews, continue to expand the case that you are the best candidate to produce the projected results. Gradually become more assertive until you receive a job offer or at an appropriate time, can request employment and initiate negotiations yourself. Continue to pursue your interest until you have reached a successful conclusion or investigated every possible approach. Only then give up the search.

EXTENDING YOUR NETWORK

Uncertainty about your future career focus is perfectly all right. Too much enduring discomfort about the uncertainty may be unnecessary, however. Many competent career counselors are available.

What other job search avenues should be explored? Try executive recruiting firms, college placement offices, trade and professional associations, accounting firms and chambers of commerce. Executive recruiters, who take on employee searches at a company's expense, are only too glad to steal qualified people from competitors or to hear from you. Although most are looking for specialized talent, all have high-level contacts with many organizations. If you are conducting a national search for a position at the level of district manager, general manager or higher with a company employing more than 500 people, register with executive recruiters. See your phone book or consult the American Management Association for guidance. For a campaign covering a large geographic area, investigate the placement office at your alma mater. For a local campaign, register with all nearby universities and colleges. Trade and professional associations may also provide placement services. Investigate them all.

BEING EFFECTIVE IN INTERVIEWS

Now that a wide audience of potential employers is aware of you, expect interested ones to begin phoning. The calls will be of three types: a simple request for an interview, a request for additional information or a conversation that can range from several questions to a nearly-complete employment interview. Whatever the purpose, be sure to get the caller's complete and correct name and title. Be prepared to discuss your background and experience, explain the contribution you expect to make and why you are making a change. By concentrating on the most important aspects of the job and relating your accomplishments to the problems requiring immediate attention, you will be stimulating the caller's interest and preparing for the subsequent interview. If, by the end of the conversation, the caller has not suggested an interview, you should do so. If the caller does not wish to set up an interview until a later date, indicate that you will follow up the conversation with another call to arrange for an interview time.

The Initial Interview

The initial interview usually determines if you receive a job offer. Whether with one person or a selection board, this may be the only opportunity to sell yourself to the prospective employer. It may also be your only opportunity to gather sufficient information about the job, the organization and the people to properly evaluate an offer. The key is preparation. Research the company. Prepare questions to ask and review those that will be asked of you. Then plan how to manage and structure the interview to your own advantage.

The first objective of any interview is to convince an employer that you can make a contribution and are the best candidate for the position. And, because both you and the organization are selling and evaluating, you will want to use the interview to gather enough information about the company and its members to evaluate the job in relation to your own abilities, other personal characteristics and objectives. Regardless of what might be appropriate once you are on the job, you will also want to attend an interview wearing conservative attire. Practice good posture. Look the interviewer in the eye as you negotiate the choppy waters of interviewing etiquette. And, remember to take along a note pad, copies of your resume, a written list of questions and an outline of the information you have gathered about the organization, including any correspondence. Once in the interview, guide the questions and discussion in a manner that satisfies your objectives. Be alert and sensitive to the reactions and feelings of the interviewer. Avoid persisting with questions he or she cannot answer or seems to find disconcerting. If you feel unsure, practice first with a friend.

Most questions you will be asked will concern the relationship among your personal characteristics, accomplishments and the prospective position. You will be asked to describe yourself, your background, likes and dislikes and motivation. Typical questions could be: What are some of your most significant accomplishments? What do you think is the main force behind your success? Were there any unusual difficulties you had to overcome? What did you particularly like about the last job you had? What did you like least? How did you go about making important decisions? What types of decisions are easiest for you to make? What kinds of decisions are most difficult? How do you think your subordinates would describe you as a delegator? What pattern of organization do you follow? Why do you think you are an effective supervisor? Describe one or two innovations you are particularly proud of? What are your main assets, strengths and limitations? What are your hopes for the future? Why do you want to work for this company? How can you make a contribution? If you consider a question too personal, say so. Otherwise, try to be as open as possible.

The questions you ask are often more important than your answers to the ones asked of you. By asking the right questions, you demonstrate what you know and the contributions you can make. Your questions can also guide the discussion into areas where you can comment on accomplishments. Finally, by asking questions, you will get the information you need to evaluate the company and the job. Sample questions are: What is the first problem that needs the attention of the person you hire? How has this position been performed in the past? Why is it vacant now? What is the scope of the authority I have? How would you define your management philosophy? Sprinkle these questions throughout the interview. Intersperse them among the interviewer's. But be sure they relate to the company and the job. Be positive and direct. You have sold yourself and now must take the time to evaluate this and other opportunities.

LOOKING BEFORE YOU LEAP

Before you accept any position, get the facts. Going blindly into a job can prove disastrous. Ask tough questions. They could enhance your position as a good executive and thoughtful employee. Find out what happened to the last person in the job? Why did he or she leave? Why hasn't the company found a candidate from within? As important as the questions are the interviewer's reactions. A defensive, hostile or evasive response may be a signal that there is a real problem.

Follow up by meeting prospective peers and top brass. Ask them about their jobs, the company and its problems. Find out how they spend their time. Discover if there may be problems in working with the immediate supervisor or subordinates. People chemistry is a crucial element in any job. If you don't like the people, the duties will be irrelevant. Try to determine the nuances of the decision-making process, the pecking order, the philosophy of the top brass and whether night or weekend work is expected. If you don't understand how an organization works, you'll be frustrated. For example, do your bosses go by the book or are they entrepreneurs who believe rules are made to be broken? How do they feel about professional women? Many questions need to be asked before the big picture falls into place.

Most important of all is to "know thyself". Many factors are involved in job happiness. If the job requires a move across the country or from suburb to city center, to a new industry or a different-sized company, make sure you can adapt. Inquire about salary increases, stock options, company benefits, pension plans, vacations, club memberships, opportunities for promotion and relocation expenses. Then, once you and the potential employer have reached agreement on all aspects of the offer, get it confirmed in writing.

Depending on how far along you are in your job search campaign, the time during which you can appropriately consider an offer will vary from a few days to a month. In most cases, you should limit this time to three weeks. Your objective is to gain only sufficient time to expedite and evaluate additional offers. You can do this by immediately advising other prospective employers of your deadline. Do this only if you are definitely interested in the first offer. If the other organization is not ready to make a decision, you may be turned down prematurely.

ASSESSING THE OPTIONS

Each job offer needs to be thoroughly evaluated, both individually and in comparison to others. Never accept an offer on the spot. Making a commitment is the single most difficult act in risking. It is the moment when you declare your intentions. Even if you have received only one offer, evaluate it carefully. You have three options: to accept, to delay and re-contact other prospective employers, to reject it and return to your job search campaign with new and expanded effort.

BEWARE OF PITFALLS

Certain traps need to be avoided when you make such important decisions. Any one or combination of these hazards can wreck your career or at least put it in a holding pattern. Be wary of:

   • **Taking a job you don't enjoy because you want to be**

employed
  - Working for someone you don't respect and admire
  - Producing or selling goods or services you don't believe in
  - Failing to follow a course of continuous education
  - Failing to be loyal to your organization
  - Relying on long experience with one company for security
  - Refusing to consider out-of-town openings when you change jobs
  - Accepting a promotion to a job you don't fancy just for money or prestige
  - Failing to take a cut in salary when it could further your career goals
  - Getting too much unsaleable experience; sticking to a specialized job without considering if there is a job demand in the area
  - Resigning in a snit
  - Rushing into a job without evaluating it clearly
  - Taking a job that has poor chemistry
  - Staying in a job or taking a job because of security

WEIGHING THE FIT

Once you've collected the required information to make a reasonably objective informed decision, the struggle isn't over. You may still find it difficult to assess one job against another. One way to reach a decision is to make a weighted assessment. To do so, along one side of a piece of paper, write out the factors that are important to you. Assign each a number from one to ten. These numbers should reflect the importance of each factor in your job. Low numbers reflect a relatively unimportant consideration while high numbers are factors that are vital to your job. You will want to weigh your needs, values, interests, abilities and aspirations. Consider, for example, responsibilities and authority, the supervisor, peers and subordinates, company size and style, opportunity to use your talents, location, salary and equity potential, work hours, commuting and traveling time, security, challenge, growth potential, recognition, spouse's preference and overall preference.

Once you have completed the above task, give each company a rating for each factor. To get a total, multiply this number by the weighting you gave each factor considered important to you (needs, values, interests, abilities and aspirations). For example, if you feel that salary is very important, give it a weighting of nine. If one company meets the salary you want, give that company a 10 for salary. Multiply the two (nine times 10) for a total of 90. If another organization offers $2,000 less than the salary you want, rate that company a five, then multiply it by nine for a total of 45. Once you have calculated the amount for each factor, add up the figures and see which company scores highest.

PART C: MAKING THE DECISION

How can you tell whether a decision is right? You have just completed weighing the evidence to determine which job options are best for you. These responses should have clarified your feelings about job alternatives or self-employment. But this may not be enough. In really big decisions, time and continuous re-examination are needed. There is no easy way.

LETTING IT REST

Finally, it all comes down to intuition. The right decision will feel right. Intuition is the surfacing of knowledge already stored in the subconscious. This filtering process can help you decide what is important and comfortable. Intuition, although often overlooked, is a significant aspect of taking risks. By combining your intuition with objective analysis, you use a more holistic approach to solving problems. Intuition can make you more open to opportunities. Intuition is more tangible and quantifiable than the mystical event many people consider it to be. If your intuition is sending you alarm signals, buy time. Extend your deadline. A prospective employer will usually wait two or three days while you mull over a job decision. Give yourself time for reflection so you can better understand what is happening in your life.

MAKING THE COMMITMENT

If your intellectual and emotional preparation are sound, if you have done whatever you can to manage the risk and protect against disaster, and if the decision still feels right, get going. No matter how elaborate the preparation, the next stage always demands a leap into the unknown. In addition to situational unknowns, you will have to face unknowns deep within yourself. All rational planning leads, if only momentarily, to an act of faith. This moment of free fall may disrupt your sense of orientation. But because it usually brings with it a heady sense of relief, this minute may also feel like the least risky step in the whole process. After you have done all the dreaming and thinking and worrying and planning, you are ready to re-establish yourself at last. One study, in fact, showed that skydivers feel less afraid when they are actually about to hurl themselves into space than when they are on the ground deciding whether or not to go up for a jump. You will probably discover the same applies to you.

A dream begins to become reality only at the moment of action. A race doesn't begin until one leaves the starting blocks. From that point on, competence, commitment and determination will decide your future. Decide now that you will succeed and become a Quester. If you want to, choose to, and do take the right steps, you will become one. Don't give in to thoughts of failure. Setbacks are just an opportunity to learn. They are but detours on the road to your goals.

CONFIRMING YOUR ACCEPTANCE

After you have accepted an offer and established a starting date, confirm this acceptance in writing. Also write to each of the other firms that made offers. Thank them for their consideration and advise them that you have accepted another position. This polite follow-up will leave you in good stead with them should a desirable position become available in the future.

If you have decided to go into business for yourself, you will have much more to do. You must go through various steps such as writing a proposal, obtaining financing, deciding on your business type and location, finding a lawyer and an accountant, purchasing equipment and supplies, determining marketing techniques and hiring personnel needed to get a business on its feet. Take your time. You'll want to start it off right.

RESIGNING

Before moving to a new position or starting a business, it will, of course, be necessary to resign from your current job. The starting date of your new job or business should permit sufficient time for an orderly completion or transfer of unfinished tasks. Maintain good relations with your former employer and avoid harming the morale of colleagues. You may require their help in the future.

EVALUATING YOUR DECISION

When you've worked hard at making a decision, it's not only satisfying but necessary to evaluate it. Doing so can help you learn to become more effective in making future decisions. Ask yourself the following questions:

- Do I feel good about making the move? Do I attain the job satisfiers that are most important to me? Are my needs being met?

Am I using my skills and abilities? Is my level of job satisfaction, as measured by the *Job Satisfaction Questionnaire*, any higher?

- What other gains did I derive from the move?
- What did I lose?
- What contributed to my success? To my failure?
- If I were to do it all over again, what would I do differently? Could I have achieved the same results with less work?
- Who was most helpful? How can I strengthen that relationship? Who let me down? Does he or she know?
- What pleasant surprises did I encounter from my move that I didn't anticipate?
- How do I feel about the degree of success or failure I have achieved? If my efforts were only partially successful or a complete disaster, can I think of any way this can be turned to my advantage? What did I learn from the experience? Would I do the same thing over again?
- How do I feel about myself as a consequence of taking the risk?

Even when things don't work out as hoped, many people are pleased with themselves for venturing forth and testing their mettle. When you take on a big challenge, you are bound to feel more purposeful and courageous. Next time around, you will be a more successful risk taker. The more you understand and prepare for risks, the easier it will be to overcome your anxiety.

Evaluation is a continuing process. Assess yourself, your needs, goals and job satisfaction periodically to determine if your developing personality fits your position and lifestyle. When you feel your job or some other component of your life needs modifying, make the necessary changes to bring them into harmony with your personality. Nothing remains static. To continue to grow and develop, you must constantly modify who you are. Why wait for a crisis to clear your vision? Don't miss out on the joys of living. Achieve the well-being that comes from living your life to the fullest each and every day.

If, after three, six or 12 months, you find you are not reaching your goals, don't hesitate to seek help. Many people have difficulty translating ideas into action but, with the help of a competent professional, they can accomplish this. Do what you must to complete the task. Accept the possibility that you may have made an error. Mistakes do happen. Learn from them. Next time you will emerge stronger.

KEEP GOING

As you grow and develop your potential, the rewards will be

enormous. Along with the satisfaction that results from using the full range of your abilities comes independence, self-confidence, maturity, purpose, greater flexibility and the power to effect change. You will become stronger and wiser, but don't stop here. Most important risks merely open the door to greater risks. If you take the right chances, those that encourage growth and fulfillment, you will find that you will want to take additional risks. Each time you gamble, risking becomes a little easier.

There really is no substitute for risk as a way to grow. Knowing you have honestly faced the painful struggle and accepted the trade-offs and losses involved, yet proceeding in spite of them, is extremely gratifying. To have a satisfying life, you will need to risk again and again until you have created the best possible life for yourself, a life where you feel comfortable being yourself, without apology or pretense. A life where you can have choices in an uncertain job market.

> *Life is a challenge, meet it.*
> *Life is an opportunity, take it.*
> *Life is an adventure, dare it.*

Suggested readings

The books in this list are only examples. Your local library or bookstore should have other useful references on related topics.

Accredited Institutions of Higher Education. (See latest edition). Washington, D.C.: American Council on Education.

Accredited Post Secondary Institutions and Programs. (See latest edition). Washington, D.C.: U. S. Government Printing Office.

Alexander, Joe. (1984). *Dare to Change: How to Program Yourself for Success.* New York: New American Library.

American Universities and Colleges. (See latest edition), Washington, D.C.: American Council on Education.

Aslanian, C. B., & Schmeltzer, H. B. (1980). *Adult Access to Education and New Careers: A Handbook for Action.* Princeton, NJ: College Entrance Examination Board.

Assagioli, Robert. (1973). *The Act of Will.* New York: Viking.

Atchley, R. C. (1983). *Aging: Continuity and Change.* Belmont, CA: Wadsworth.

Ball, J. S. & Krickus, M. A. (Eds.) (1982). *Families and Work: Traditions and Transitions.* Washington, D.C.: American Association of University Women.

Basow, S. A. (1980). *Sex-Role Stereotypes: Traditions and Alternatives.* Monterey, CA: Brooks/Cole.

Bear, John. (1984). *Bear's Guide to Money for College.* Berkeley, CA: Ten Speed.

Bear, John. (1982). *How to Get the Degree You Want: Bear's Guide to Non-Traditional College Degrees.* Berkeley, CA: Ten Speed.

Beck, A.T. (1970). *Depression: Causes and Treatment.* Philadelphia, PA: University of Pensylvania Press.

Berman, P.L.A. (1986). *The Courage of Conviction*. New York: Ballantine.

Berne, Eric. (1972). *What Do You Say After You Say Hello?* New York: Grove.

Boll, C.R. (1978). *Executive Jobs Unlimited*. New York: Macmillan.

Bolles, R. N. (1978). *The Three Boxes of Life*. Berkeley, CA: Ten Speed.

Bolles, R. N. (1986). *What Color Is Your Parachute?: A Practical Manual for Job-Hunters and Career Changers*. Berkeley, CA: Ten Speed.

Bolles, R. N., & Crystal, J. C. (1974). *Where Do I Go From Here With My Life?* Berkeley, CA: Ten Speed.

Bregelson, J. I. (1982). *Job Resumes: How to Write Them, How to Present Them, Preparing for Interviews*. New York: Grosset & Dunlop.

Brim, O.G., & Kagan, J. (Eds.) *Constancy and Change in Human Development*. Cambridge, MA: Harvard University Press.

Brown, Barbara. (1980). *Supermind: The Ultimate Energy*. New York: Harper & Row.

Burns, D.D. (1985). *Intimate Connections*. New York: New American Library.

Burns, D.D. (1981). *Feeling Good*. New York: New American Library.

Buscaglio, Leo. (1982). *Living, Learning and Loving*. New York: Fawcett, Columbine.

Buskirk, R. H. (1977). *Your Career: How to Plan It — Manage It — Change It*. New York: New American Library.

Canadian Classification and Dictionary of Occupations. (See latest edition). Ottawa, ON: Information Canada.

Career Thresholds. (A training package of how people find jobs). Monograph 16, Washington, D.C.: U. S. Government Printing Office.

Catalog of Federal Domestic Assistance. (See latest edition). Washington, D.C.: U. S. Government Printing Office.

The Catalyst Staff. (1981). *Marketing Yourself: The Catalyst Guide to Successful Resumes and Interviews*. New York: Bantam.

Cohen, W.A. (1978). *The Executive's Guide to Finding A Superior Job*. New York: AMACOM.

The College Bluebook. (See latest edition). New York: Macmillan.

College and University Programs in Canada. (See latest edition). Ottawa, ON: Information Canada.

Coudert, Jo. (1965). *Advice From A Failure*. New York: Stein & Day.

Cowle, Jerry. (1979). *How to Survive Getting Fired and Win*. Chicago, IL: Follett.

Directory of Canadian Universities. (See latest edition). Ottawa, ON:

Association of Universities and Colleges of Canada.

Dictionary of Occupational Titles. (See latest edition). Washington, D.C.: U. S. Government Printing Office.

Directory of Post Secondary Schools with Occupational Programs, Public and Private. (See latest edition). Washington, D.C.: U. S. Government Printing Office.

Dunnette, M.D. (Ed.) (1983). *Handbook of Industrial and Organizational Psychology*. New York: Wiley.

Education Directory: Higher Education. (See latest edition). Washington, D.C.: U. S. Government Printing Office.

Edwards, Betty. (1979). *Drawing on the Right Side of the Brain: A Course in Enhancing Creativity and Self-Confidence*. New York: J. P. Tarcher.

Ellis, Albert., & Knaus, W. J. (1977). *Overcoming Procrastination*. New York: The New American Library.

Erikson, E. H. (1963). *Childhood and Society*. New York: Norton.

Erikson, E. H. (1968). *Identity: Youth and Crisis*. New York: Norton.

Evans, Christopher. (1980). *Understanding Yourself*. New York: New American Library.

Frankl, Viktor. (1977). *Man's Search for Meaning*. New York: Pocket Books.

Germann, Richard & Arnold, Peter. (1982). *Bernard Haldane Associates' Job and Career Building*. Berkeley, CA: Ten Speed.

Goldstein, Jerome. (1982). *In Business For Yourself: A Guide To Starting Your Own Business and Running It Your Way*. New York: Scribner.

Goodman, J. S., Uhle, S., & Walworth, S.S. (1979). *Directions for Change: A Career Development Workbook*. Rochester, MI: Oakland University Continuum Center.

Gould, R.L. (1978). *Transformations: Growth and Change in Adult Life*. New York: Simon & Shuster.

Goulding, M.C., & Goulding, R.L. (1979). *Changing Lives Through Redecision Therapy*. New York: Brunner/Mazel.

Gray, D.A. (1985). *Start and Run a Profitable Consulting Business*. Vancouver, BC: International Self-Counsel Press.

Greenberg, G.S. (1983). *Comprehensive Stress Management*. Dubuque, IO: William C. Brown.

Greene, G.G. (1975). *How to Start and Manage Your Own Business*. New York: McGraw-Hill.

Grieff, B.S. & Hunter, P.K. (1981). *Trade Offs: Executive, Family, and Organizational Life*. New York: New American Library.

Gross, Ronald. (1982). *The Independent Scholar's Handbook: How to Turn Your Interest in Any Subject Into Expertise*. Reading, MA: Addison-Wesley.

Gross, Ronald. (1982). *Invitation to Lifelong Learning*. New York: Cambridge.

Grossman, Richard. (1978). *Choosing and Changing: A Guide to Self-Reliance*. New York: Dutton.

Guide for Occupational Exploration. (See latest edition). Washington, D.C.: U. S. Government Printing Office.

Haldane, Bernard. (1976). *Job Power Now*. Washington, D.C.: Acropolis.

Haldane, Bernard. (1982). *Career Satisfaction and Success: How to Know and Manage Your Strengths*. New York: AMACOM.

Half, Robert. (1983). *The Robert Half Way to Get Hired in Today's Job Market*. New York: Bantam.

Hanson, P. G. (1985). *The Joy of Stress*. Islington, ON: Hanson Stress Management.

Harris, T. A. (1969). *I'm OK — You're OK*. New York: Harper & Row.

Hill, Napoleon, & Stone, W.C. (1960). *Success Through a Positive Mental Attitude*. Englewood Cliffs, NJ: Prentice-Hall.

Holland, J.L. (1985). *Making Vocational Choices: A Theory of Vocational Personalities and Work Environment*. Englewood Cliffs, NJ: Prentice-Hall.

Holtz, Herman. (1984). *Beyond the Resume: How to Land the Job You Want*. New York: McGraw-Hill.

Hopke, W.E. (Ed.) (1984). *The Encyclopedia of Careers*. Chicago, IL: J. G. Ferguson.

Hooper, D. (1980). *You Are What You Think*. Danville, CA: Hooper.

Knudsen, Ruth. (Ed.) *Women and Success*. New York: Morrow.

House, J. S. (1981). *Work Stress and Social Support*. Reading, MA: Addison-Wesley.

Irish, R.K. (1975). *If Things Don't Improve Soon, I'm Going to Ask You to Fire Me: The Management Book for Everyone Who Works*. New York: Doubleday.

Jackson, Tom. (1978). *Gorilla Tactics in the Job Market*. New York: Bantam.

James, J. D. (1977). *Starting a Successful Business in Canada*. Vancouver, BC: International Self-Counsel Press.

James, Muriel, & Jongeward, Dorothy. (1978). *Born To Win*. New York: New American Library

Janis, I.L., & Mann, Leon. (1977). *Decision-Making: A Psychological Analysis of Conflict, Choice and Commitment*. New York: Free Press.

Jongeward, Dorothy, & Scott, Dru. (1976). *Women as Winners*. Reading, MA: Addison-Wesley.

Kelley, R. E. (1981). *Consulting: The Complete Guide to a Profitable Career*. New York: Charles Scribner's Sons.

Kerr, C., & Rosow, J. M. (Eds.) (1978). *Work in America: The Decade Ahead*. New York: Van Nostrand Reinhold.

Laken, Alan. (1973). *How to Get Control of Your Time and Your Life*. New York: Peter H. Wyden.

Lalonde, Geoffrey. (1980). *4 Minutes to the Job You Want*. New York: McGraw-Hill.

Leefeldt, Christine. (1979). *The Art of Friendship: Getting Close*. New York: Pantheon.

Leonard, Linda. (1982). *The Wounded Woman*. Athens, OH: Swallow.

Levinson, D.J., Darrow, C.N., Klein, E.B., Levinson, M.H., & McKee, Braxton. (1978). *Seasons of a Man's Life*. New York: Knopf.

Levinson, J.C. (1979). *Earning Money Without a Job: The Economics of Freedom*. New York: Holt, Rinehart & Winston.

Lewis, William, & Schuman, Nancy. (1985). *Back to Work: A Career Guide for the Returnee*. Woodbury, NY: Barron's Educational Series.

Loans Available in Canadian Universities and Colleges. (See latest edition). Port Credit, ON: National Student & Information Centre.

Long, Charles. (1981). *How to Survive Without a Salary*. New York: Sterling.

Lull, C.S. (1984). *How to Land a Better Job*. Lincolnwood, IL: VGM Career Horizons.

Lowenthal, M.F., Thurner, M., & Chcriboga, D. (1975). *Four Stages of Life: A Comparative Study of Men and Women Facing Transitions*. San Francisco, CA: Jossey-Bass.

Marris, Peter. (1975). *Loss and Change*. New York: Anchor.

Maslow, A.H. (1954). *Motivation and Personality*. New York: Harper & Row.

Mayer, N. (1978). *The Male Mid-Life Crisis: Fresh Start After 40*. New York: New American Library.

McLean, A.A. (1978). *Work Stress*. Reading, MA: Addison-Wesley.

McLeish, John. (1983). *The Challenge of Aging*. Vancouver, BC; Douglas & McIntyre.

Medley, H.A. (1984). *The Neglected Art of Being Interviewed*. Berkeley, CA: Ten Speed.

Mencke, Reed & Hummel, R.L. (1984). *Career Planning for the Eighties*. Monterey, CA: Brooks/Cole.

Miller, Donald. (1977). *Personal Vitality*. Reading, MA: Addison-Wesley.

Million Dollar Directory. (See latest edition). New York: Dunn & Bradstreet.

Naisbitt, John. (1984). *Megatrends*. New York: Warner.

Occupational Outlook Handbook. (See latest edition). Washington,

D.C.: U. S. Government Printing Office.

Offer, D.O., & Sabshin, M. (1984). *Normality and Life Cycle: A Critical Integration*. New York: Basic.

Ohles, J. F. (1982). *Private Colleges and Universities*. Westport, CO: Greenwood Press.

Osherson, S.P. (1980). *Holding On or Letting Go: Men and Career Change at Midlife*. New York: Free Press.

O'Toole, James, Scheiber, J.L., & Wood, L.C. (Eds.) (1981). *Working: Changes and Choices*. New York: Human Sciences Press.

Peale, N.V. (1952). *The Power of Positive Thinking*. Englewood Cliffs, NJ: Prentice-Hall.

Perlmutter, Deborah. (1984). *How to Write a Winning Resume*. Lincolnwood, IL: VGM Career Horizons.

Potter, B.A. (1980). *Beating Job Burnout*. San Francisco, CA: Harbor.

Robbins, P. (1980). *Successful Mid-Life Career Change*. New York: AMACOM.

Rogers, Carl. (1951). *On Becoming a Person*. Boston, MA; Houghton Mifflin.

Rothschild, Helene, & Seff, M.K. (1985). *Free to Fly — Dare to be a Success*. Saratoga, CA: R&E Publishers.

Rubin, T.I. (1985). *Overcoming Indecisiveness — The Eight Stages of Effective Decision-making*. New York: Avon.

Rust, H.L. (1979). *Jobsearch: The Complete Manual for Jobseekers*. New York: AMACOM.

Sargent, Alice. (1981). *The Androgynous Manager*. New York: AMACOM.

Satir, Virginia. (1972). *Peoplemaking*. Palo Alto, CA: Science & Behavior Books.

Sauerwine, A.H. (1978). *Career Strategies: Planning for Personal Achievement*. New York: AMACOM.

Schiffman, M. (1967). *Self-Therapy: Techniques for Personal Growth*. Menlo Park, CA: Self-published.

Schrank, L.W. (1985). *Life Plan*. Lincolnwood, IL: VGM Career Horizons.

Schwartz, Lester, & Brechner, Irv. (1983). *Career Finder: Pathways to Over 1500 Careers*. New York: Ballantine.

Selye, Hans. (1956). *The Stress of Life*. New York: McGraw-Hill.

Selye, H. (1974). *Stress Without Distress*. Philadelphia, PA: Lippencott.

Shaevitz, M.H., & Shaevitz, M.H. (1980). *Making It Together as a Two-Career Couple*. Boston, MA: Houghton Mifflin.

Shain, Merle. (1978). *When Lovers Are Friends*. New York: Bantam.

Sheehy, Gail. (1976). *Passages: Predictable Crises of Adult Life*. New York: Dutton.

Shenson, Howard. (1979). *How to Establish and Operate Your Own*

Consulting Practice. New York: Prentice-Hall.

Small, S.T. (Ed.) (1982). *Directory of Franchising Organizations*. New York: Pilot Books.

Solomon, K., & Levy, N.B. (Eds.) (1982). *Men in Transition: Theory and Therapy*. New York: Plenum.

Stevens, Barry. (1970). *Don't Push the River (It Flows by Itself)*. Lafayette, CA: Real People Press.

Tec, Leon. (1978). *The Fear of Success*. New York: The New American Library.

Toffler, Allan. (1970). *Future Shock*. New York: Random House.

Toffler, Allan. (1980). *The Third Wave*. New York: Morrow.

Vaillant, G.E. (1977). *Adaptation to Life*. Boston, MA: Little, Brown.

Veninga, R.L., & Spradley, J.P. (1981). *The Work-Stress Connection: How to Cope With Job Burnout*. Boston, MA: Little, Brown.

Viscott, D.S. (1977). *Risking: How to Take Chances and Win*. New York: Simon & Schuster.

Voydanoff, P. (Ed.) (1984). *Work and Family: Changing Roles of Men and Women*. Palo Alto, CA: Mayfield.

Waitley, Denis. (1985). *The Joy of Working*. New York: Dodd.

Weinstein, Bob. (1982). *Resumes for Hard Times*. New York: Simon & Schuster.

Wells, John. (1986). *Coping in the '80s*. Chicago, IL: Thomas More.

Wheeler, D.D., & Janis, I.L.A. (1980). *A Practical Guide for Making Decisions*. New York: Free Press.

Wheelis, Allan. (1975). *On Not Knowing How to Live*. New York: Harper & Row.

Wheelis, Allan. (1973). *How People Change*. New York: Harper & Row.

White, Earl. (1981). *Nourishing Self-Esteem*. Capitol, CA: Whitenwife.

Wigdor, B.T. (1986). *Planning Your Retirement*. Toronto, ON: Grosvenor.

Wilkenson, W.R. (1983). *Executive Musical Chairs*. San Mateo, CA: Warrington.

Wood, J.R., & Orrin, G. (1981). *Your Hidden Assets: The Key to Getting Executive Jobs*. Homewood, IL: Dow Jones-Irwin.

World of Learning (1986). Lond, ENG: Europa Publications.

Yankelovich, Daniel. (1981). *New Rules: Searching for Self-Fulfillment in a World Turned Upside Down*. New York: Random House.

About the Author

Carole Kanchier has a broad range of knowledge and experience related to counseling, career development, adult development and vocational and industrial psychology. She earned a Ph.D. in Educational Psychology and currently teaches counseling, vocational psychology and adult learning and development at the University of Alberta, Alberta, Canada. Dr. Kanchier also works as a consulting psychologist and educator for business, industry, government and school divisions. Previous work experience includes high school teacher, counselor, guidance department head, publicist, recreation director and dancer/ choreographer. The author of numerous articles based on her research and experience in career development, Dr. Kanchier has also served on a number of professional committees (academic and industrial), has designed several career-related programs, and is often invited to speak at professional conferences and conduct workshops on topics related to adult and career development.